Prentice Hall LITERATURE

All-in-One
Workbook

The British Tradition

PEARSON

Upper Saddle River, New Jersey
Boston, Massachusetts
Chandler, Arizona
Glenview, Illinois

ISBN-13: 978-0-13-366818-6
ISBN-10: 0-13-366818-5

8 9 10 11 V039 16 15 14 13

CONTENTS

All-In-one-Workbook
iii

The Tragedy of Macbeth, *Act II,* by William Shakespeare

The Tragedy of Macbeth, *Act III,* by William Shakespeare

The Tragedy of Macbeth, *Act IV,* by William Shakespeare

The Tragedy of Macbeth, *Act V,* by William Shakespeare

Oedipus the King by Sophocles
from **Faust** by Johann Wolfgang von Goethe

UNIT 3 A Turbulent Time

Works of John Donne

"On My First Son," "Still to Be Neat," and "Song to Celia" by Ben Johnson

"To His Coy Mistress" by Andrew Marvell
"To the Virgins, To Make Much of Time" by Robert Herrick
"Song" by Sir John Suckling

Poetry of John Milton

from Paradise Lost by John Milton
Canto XXXIV *from* The Inferno by Dante

from The Pilgrim's Progress by John Bunyan

"My Last Duchess," "Life in a Love," and "Porphyria's Lover"
   by Robert Browning
Sonnet 43 by Elizabeth Barrett Browning

from **Hard Times by Charles Dickens**

from **Hard Times by Charles Dickens**
"An Upheaval" by Anton Chekhov

from **Jane Eyre by Charlotte Brontë**

Contemporary Commentary: James Berry Introduces

"Dover Beach" by Matthew Arnold
"Recessional" and "The Widow at Windsor" by Rudyard Kipling

"Preludes," "Journey of the Magi," and "The Hollow Men" by T. S. Eliot

"In Memory of W.B. Yeats" and **"Musée des Beaux Arts"** by W. H. Auden
"Carrick Revisited" by Louis MacNiece
"Not Palaces" by Stephen Spender

"The Lady in the Looking Glass: A Reflection," *from* **Mrs. Dalloway,** *from* **A Room of One's Own: "Shakespeare's Sister"** by Virginia Woolf

"The Lady in the Looking Glass: A Reflection," *from* **Mrs. Dalloway,** *from* **A Room of One's Own: "Shakespeare's Sister"** by Virginia Woolf
from **Pedro Paramo** by Juan Rulfo
from **The Nine Guardians** by Rosario Castellanos

"The Lagoon" by Joseph Conrad
"Araby" by James Joyce

"The Rocking-Horse Winner" by D. H. Lawrence
"A Shocking Accident" by Graham Greene

"The Soldier" by Rupert Brooke
"Wirers" by Siegfried Sassoon
"Anthem for Doomed Youth" by Wilfred Owen

Wartime Speech by Winston Churchill

"The Demon Lover" by Elizabeth Bowen

"Vergissmeinnicht" by Keith Douglas
"For Gweno" by Alun Lewis
"Naming of Parts" by Henry Reed

"Shooting an Elephant" by George Orwell
"No Witchcraft for Sale" by Doris Lessing

All-In-one-Workbook
xvi

"In the Kitchen" by Penelope Shuttle
"Prayer" by Carol Ann Duffy

Contemporary Commentary: Anita Desai Introduces "A Devoted Son"
Contemporary Commentary: Anita Desai Listening and Viewing

"A Devoted Son" by Anita Desai

"Next Term, We'll Mash You" by Penelope Lively

from **We'll Never Conquer Space** by Arthur C. Clarke

from **Songbook** by Nick Hornby

Essential Question Workshop

Standardized Test Practice

Answer Sheets

Name _____ Date _____

Unit 1 Introduction
Names and Terms to Know

A. DIRECTIONS: *Write a brief sentence explaining each of the following names and terms. You will find all of the information you need in the Unit Introduction in your textbook.*

1. "Angle land": _____

2. Alfred the Great: _____

3. Magna Carta: _____

4. Bede: _____

5. William the Conqueror _____

6. Henry VII: _____

B. DIRECTIONS: *Use the hints below to help you answer each question.*

1. How did the coming of Christianity change life in England?

   [Hints: When did Christianity arrive? What was English society like before it arrived? What new elements did Christianity bring to England?]

   _____

   _____

2. How did the Norman Conquest change England?

   [Hints: What language did the Normans bring to England? What new social structure did they bring?]

   _____

   _____

3. What difficulties did the English struggle with during the 1300s and 1400s?

   [Hints: What did the Black Death do to the population? What wars afflicted the country? What did Henry VII do?]

   _____

   _____

   _____

Unit 1 Introduction

Essential Question 1: What is the relationship between place and literature?

A. DIRECTIONS: *Answer the questions about the first Essential Question in the Introduction about the relationship between place and literature. All the information you need is in the Unit 1 Introduction in your textbook.*

I. *Responding to an Island Environment*

    a. The early English regarded the sea as _____

    _____

    b. Christian monks changed "The Seafarer" and "The Wanderer" by _____

    _____

    c. In *Beowulf* the "sea-road" led to _____

    d. The mead-hall setting represented _____

    _____

II. *Making a Nation of an Island*

    a. Bede portrayed England as _____

    _____

    b. Chaucer's *Canterbury Tales* helped draw together a national identity by _____

    _____

B. DIRECTIONS: *Complete the following sentence stems based on the Essential Question Vocabulary words.*

  1. A magazine article about our state's *geography* would pay a lot of attention to _____

    _____

  2. An *invasion* usually involves force, because _____

    _____

  3. Someone who is forced into *exile* is forbidden to _____

    _____

Name _____ Date _____

Unit 1 Introduction

Essential Question 2: How does literature shape or reflect society?

A. DIRECTIONS: *On the lines provided, answer the questions about the second Essential Question in the Introduction about writers and society. All the information you need is in the Unit 1 Introduction in your textbook.*

I. *Capturing a Vanishing Tribal World*

    a. *Beowulf* showed that to become a leader, _____

    _____

    b. What world was passing away in *Beowulf*? _____

    _____

II. *Chaucer and Society*

    a. What social types did *The Canterbury Tales* represent? _____

    _____

    b. What were some of the problems in the Catholic Church during Chaucer's time?

    _____

    c. Chaucer portrayed his society without _____

    d. What was a source of political turbulence in the medieval period? _____

    _____

    e. Chaucer reflect the rising middle class by _____

    _____

    f. In dealing with social change, writers do not act like sociologists; rather they show

    _____

B. DIRECTIONS: *Complete the sentence stems based on the Essential Question Vocabulary words.*

    1. One way to settle *controversy* is to _____

    2. A *tribe* is like an extended family because _____

    3. In my family, I often end up in the *role* of the _____

Unit 1 Introduction

Essential Question 3: What is the relationship of the writer to tradition?

A. DIRECTIONS: *On the lines provided, answer the questions about the third Essential Question in the Introduction about the relationship between the writer and tradition. All the information you need is in the Unit 1 Introduction in your textbook.*

I. *Writers and Tradition*

    a. "Tradition" means _____

    b. What did *Sir Gawain and the Green Knight* express through the use of old legends?

    _____

    c. In *Morte D'Arthur* Sir Thomas Malory reworked the story of Arthur in order to

    _____

    d. What are three possible ways in which different tellers changed the story of *Beowulf*?

    _____

    _____

II. *Chaucer's Handling of Tradition*

    a. Chaucer modeled the structure of *The Canterbury Tales* on the earlier _____

    _____

    b. How did Chaucer depart from this model? _____

    _____

    c. Describe the new poetic rhythm that Chaucer developed. _____

    _____

    d. *Beowulf, The Canterbury Tales,* and the medieval retellings of the King Arthur stories show how traditions reach both _____

B. DIRECTIONS: *Complete the sentence stems based on the Essential Question Vocabulary words.*

    1. Ernesto loved the *traditional* Thanksgiving dinner, especially _____

    2. Part of Alice's *inheritance* from her grandfather included _____

    3. My little brother's resistance to going to bed took on a new *form*, and he began to _____

    _____

Name _____ Date _____

Unit 1 Introduction
Following-Through Activities

A. CHECK YOUR COMPREHENSION: *Use this chart to complete the Check Your Comprehension activity in the Unit 1 Introduction. In the middle column, list two key concepts for each Essential Question. In the right column, list a work for each concept.*

Essential Question	Key Concept	Work (Author)
Place and Literature	1. Exile to a foreign land 2. _____	1. "Seafarer" (unknown) 2. _____
Literature and Society	1._____ 2. _____	1. _____ 2. _____
Writer and Tradition	1. _____ 2. _____	1. _____ 2. _____

B. EXTEND YOUR LEARNING: *Use this graphic organizer to help plan your research for the Extend Your Learning activity.*

Language Family: _____	
Word	**Etymology : Ango-Saxon or Norman?**
1.	
2.	
3.	
4.	
5.	
6.	
7.	
8.	
9.	
10.	

"The Seafarer," translated by Burton Raffel
"The Wanderer," translated by Charles W. Kennedy
"The Wife's Lament," translated by Ann Stanford

Literary Analysis: Anglo-Saxon Lyrics/Elegy

Anglo-Saxon lyrics were recited or chanted aloud to an audience by wandering poets. In order to make the poems easier to listen to and to memorize, they were developed with strong rhythms. Each line has a certain number of beats, or accented syllables—almost always four. Many lines have a **caesura,** or pause, in the middle, after the second beat. Anglo-Saxon poetry also contained **kennings,** two-word metaphorical names for familiar things. Note these examples of rhythm, caesura, and kennings in these lines:

Rhythm: No hárps ríng in his héart, nó rewárds,

Caesura: No pássion for wómen, [pause] no wórldly pléasures,

Kenning: Nóthing, only the oceán's heáve;

An **elegy** is a lyric poem mourning the loss of someone or something. Each of these Anglo-Saxon poems provides an example of an elegy.

1. Mark the syllables that have a strong accented beat (´) in these lines from "The Seafarer."

    But there isn't a man on earth so proud,

    So born to greatness, so bold with his youth,

    Grown so brave, or so graced by God,

    That he feels no fear as the sails unfurl,

2. In the lines in passage 1, how many caesuras are there? Write the word that appears before each caesura.

    _____

3. Mark each syllable that has a strong accented beat (´) in these lines from "The Seafarer."

    Those powers have vanished, those pleasures are dead.

    The weakest survives and the world continues,

    Kept spinning by toil. All glory is tarnished.

4. Underline the kenning in these lines from "The Wife's Lament."

    First my lord went out away from his people

    over the wave-tumult. I grieved each dawn

    wondered where my lord my first on earth might be.

5. Why do these poems qualify as elegies? What kind of loss does each poem lament?

    _____

    _____

    _____

    _____

Name _____ Date _____

"**The Seafarer,**" translated by Burton Raffel
"**The Wanderer,**" translated by Charles W. Kennedy
"**The Wife's Lament,**" translated by Ann Stanford

Reading Strategy: Understand the Historical Context

Recognizing the **historical context** and the characteristics of the period in which a work was written helps you notice relevant details and ideas. For example, if you know that Anglo-Saxon culture was male-dominated, you may be able to understand the poet's line: "My lord commanded me to move my dwelling here."

DIRECTIONS: *Use your understanding of Anglo-Saxon historical context to help you understand the following excerpts. In the right column, record how your comprehension is affected by what you know.*

Excerpt	How Historical Context Aids Understanding
1. **"The Seafarer":** "This tale is true, and mine. It tells/How the sea took me, swept me back/And forth in sorrow and fear and pain,/Showed me suffering in a hundred ships. . . ."	1.
2. **"The Wanderer":** "'So have I also, often in wretchedness/Fettered my feelings, far from my kin,/Homeless and hapless, since days of old,/When the dark earth covered my dear lord's face,/And I sailed away with sorrowful heart,/Over wintry seas, seeking a gold-lord. . . .'"	2.
3. **"The Wife's Lament":** "I must far and near/bear the anger of my beloved./The man sent me out to live in the woods/under an oak tree in this den in the earth./Ancient this earth hall./I am all longing."	3.

"The Seafarer," translated by Burton Raffel
"The Wanderer," translated by Charles W. Kennedy
"The Wife's Lament," translated by Ann Stanford

Vocabulary Builder

Word List

admonish   compassionate   fervent   rancor   rapture   sentinel

A. DIRECTIONS: *On the line, write the letter of the definition for each word in the left column.*

___ 1. fervent   A. ill-will

___ 2. compassionate   B. advise; caution

___ 3. sentinel   C. expression of joy

___ 4. admonish   D. someone who guards

___ 5. rancor   E. having great feeling

___ 6. rapture   F. sympathizing; pitying

B. WORD STUDY: *The Anglo-Saxon suffix -ness means "the state of being or quality of." Answer each of the following questions, changing the underlined word to a word with the suffix -ness.*

1. Why did she think the cake was too <u>sweet</u>? _____

    _____

2. How did the <u>bright</u> light affect you? _____

    _____

3. Did you think Ryan was <u>eager</u> enough to convince Mrs. Malone that he should be in the band? _____

    _____

4. What do you think the teacher thought when Alan was so <u>helpful</u> on Thursday?

    _____

Name _____ Date _____

"The Seafarer," translated by Burton Raffel
"The Wanderer," translated by Charles W. Kennedy
"The Wife's Lament," translated by Ann Stanford

Integrated Language Skills: Support for Writing

Use the chart below to organize information for your editorial about the loss of someone or something from your community or school.

Topic	
How the loss made you feel	
Why others should regret the loss	

On a separate page, write a draft editorial that addresses your topic of loss, your feelings about it, and your opinion about why others should regret the loss. Use examples and details to support your opinions.

Name _____ Date _____

Contemporary Commentary
Burton Raffel Introduces *Beowulf*

DIRECTIONS: *Use the space provided to answer the questions.*

1. According to Burton Raffel, who or what drives the plot of *Beowulf?*

   _____

   _____

2. What are two magical qualities that the hero Beowulf possesses?

   _____

   _____

3. What are three ways that Beowulf's name tells us that he is no mere human being?

   _____

   _____

   _____

4. According to Raffel, how does the author of *Beowulf* create suspense at the start of the poem?

   _____

   _____

   _____

   _____

5. Why does Grendel's mother enter the narrative?

   _____

6. According to Raffel, how does the fire-breathing dragon contrast with a good king like Beowulf?

   _____

   _____

7. What arguments does Raffel use to support his claim that *Beowulf* is "very much an Old Testament poem"? Do you find these arguments persuasive? Why or why not?

   _____

   _____

   _____

   _____

   _____

   _____

Burton Raffel
Listening and Viewing

Segment 1: Meet Burton Raffel
- What does Burton Raffel attempt to do to a poem that he translates?
- When discussing translation, Raffel quotes Ezra Pound: "You don't translate what a man says; you translate what a man means." Do you agree or disagree with Pound? Explain.

_____

_____

_____

_____

Segment 2: Burton Raffel on Beowulf
- Why is *Beowulf* a culturally significant poem that we still read today?

_____

_____

_____

_____

Segment 3: The Writing Process
- What are the steps that Burton Raffel goes through while translating a text into English?
- Why do you think it is important to follow such a rigorous method when translating?

_____

_____

_____

_____

Segment 4: The Rewards of Writing
- According to Burton Raffel, why are translations important to society?
- What do you think you could learn from translated literature?

_____

_____

_____

_____

from **Beowulf,** translated by Burton Raffel
Literary Analysis: The Epic/The Legendary Hero

The **epic** *Beowulf* is a long narrative poem that recounts the exploits of the legendary warrior Beowulf. Like other **legendary heros,** Beowulf represents good and earns glory by struggling against the forces of evil represented by several monstrous creatures. He represents the values of his nation, culture, and religion. *Beowulf* is a typical epic poem in its serious tone and elevated language, which portrays characters, action, and setting in terms larger and grander than life. The use of **kennings,** two-word metaphorical names for familiar things, is also a particular characteristic of Anglo-Saxon poetry.

DIRECTIONS: *Read each passage from* Beowulf. *Then list the characteristics of epic poetry and legendary hero represented in it.*

1. So mankind's enemy continued his crimes, / Killing as often as he could, coming / Alone, bloodthirsty and horrible. Though he lived / In Herot, when the night hid him, he never / Dared to touch king Hrothgar's glorious / Throne, protected by God—God, / Whose love Grendel could not know. . . .

   _____

   _____

   _____

2. "Hail Hrothgar! / Higlac is my cousin and my king; the days / Of my youth have been filled with glory. Now Grendel's / Name has echoed in our land: sailors / Have brought us stories of Herot, the best / Of all mead-halls, deserted and useless when the moon / Hangs in skies the sun had lit, / Light and life fleeing together. / My people have said, the wisest, most knowing / And best of them, that my duty was to go to the Danes' / Great king. They have seen my strength for themselves, / Have watched me rise from the darkness of war. . . ."

   _____

   _____

   _____

   _____

3. "Grant me, then, / Lord and protector of this noble place, / A single request! I have come so far, / O shelterer of warriors and your people's loved friend, / That this one favor you should not refuse me— / That I, alone and with the help of my men, / May purge all evil from this hall."

   _____

   _____

   _____

   _____

   _____

Name _____   Date _____

from **Beowulf,** translated by Burton Raffel
Reading Strategy: Paraphrase

Long sentences and difficult language can make a piece of writing hard to follow. When you encounter such passages, it is important to determine the main ideas. In order to do so, you can **paraphrase** the passage, or restate the main ideas in your own words. Paraphrasing will help you make sure you understand the main point of the passage. Look at this example:

Passage from *Beowulf*

"I've never known fear, as a youth I fought
In endless battles. I am old, now,
But I will fight again, seek fame still,
If the dragon hiding in his tower dares
To face me."

Paraphrased

I have been fearless throughout life
and will continue to fight if
the dragon dares to face me.

DIRECTIONS: *Use this graphic organizer to help you paraphrase difficult passages in* Beowulf. *Each time you come across a difficult passage, write it in the column labeled "Passage from* Beowulf." *Then, write any difficult words from that passage in the appropriate column. Define each difficult word, either by using the words surrounding it to piece together its meaning or by looking it up in the dictionary. Next, determine the key ideas in the passage, and jot these down in the appropriate column. Finally, use the key ideas, along with your understanding of the difficult words, to paraphrase the passage. One passage has already been paraphrased for you.*

Passage from *Beowulf*	Difficult Words	Key Ideas	Paraphrase
No one waited for reparation from his plundering claws: That shadow of death hunted in the darkness, . . .	reparation (making up for wrong or injury) plundering (taking by force, theft, or fraud)	No one expected to be repaid for what Grendel took in his claws. Grendel was a shadow of death hunting in the darkness.	No one expected to be repaid for what Grendel took. He hunted in the darkness.

from **Beowulf,** translated by Burton Raffel
Vocabulary Builder

Word List

loathsome   massive   purge   reparation   solace   writhing

A. DIRECTIONS: *For each underlined word, substitute a word or phrase with the same meaning. Write it in the blank following the sentence.*

1. Only a hero of Beowulf's strength could hope to lift the <u>massive</u> sword in Grendel's battle hall.

   _____

2. The third monster, most <u>loathsome</u> of all, had eight eyes on stalks and was covered with slime.

   _____

3. Most epic heroes strive to <u>purge</u> the world of wicked beings.

   _____

4. Snakes can move rapidly with their <u>writhing</u> form of locomotion.

   _____

5. The badly defeated warrior found <u>solace</u> in the affection of his family.

   _____

6. The captured bandits were ordered to give gold to their victims as <u>reparation</u>.

   _____

B. WORD STUDY: *The root -sol- comes from the Latin* solari, *meaning "to comfort." Explain how the root -sol- influences the meaning of the underlined word in each sentence.*

1. Before Beowulf arrived, Hrothgar and his Danes were <u>disconsolate</u> over the deeds of Grendel.

   _____

2. He <u>consoled</u> his little daughter for the loss of her goldfish by promising to buy her a new one.

   _____

3. The Geats grieved <u>inconsolably</u> when the dragon killed their once mighty king, Beowulf.

   _____

4. Although she won the <u>consolation</u> tournament, Allison was disappointed in her performance.

   _____

Name _____ Date _____

from **Beowulf,** translated by Burton Raffel

Grammar and Style: Coordinating Conjunctions

A **coordinating conjunction** links two of the same grammatical sentence parts. For example, a coordinating conjunction may link two subjects, two predicates, or two independent clauses. There are seven coordinating conjunctions: *and, but, or, nor, yet, so,* and *for*. Look at these uses of coordinating conjunctions from *Beowulf*.

Passage	Conjunction and Use
. . . The Almighty drove Those demons out, and their exile was bitter, . . .	The coordinating conjunction **and** connects two independent clauses.
. . . [T]heir ears could not hear His praise nor know His glory. . . .	The coordinating conjunction **nor** connects two predicates.

The coordinating conjunctions *yet, so,* and *for* also serve other functions in sentences. To identify them as coordinating conjunctions, make sure they are used to connect two of the same kinds of sentence parts.

Example	Use
Beowulf was brave, yet he was also smart.	*Yet* is used as a coordinating conjunction to connect two independent clauses.
I have not read *Beowulf* yet.	*Yet* is used as an adverb to modify *have read*.
Beowulf volunteers to fight Grendel, for he sees it as his destiny.	*For* is used as a coordinating conjunction to connect two independent clauses.
I bought a copy of *Beowulf* for two dollars.	*For* is used as a preposition in the phrase *for two dollars*.

A. PRACTICE: *Underline each coordinating conjunction in these lines from* Beowulf. *Tell what sentence parts it connects.*

1. The high hall rang, its roof boards swayed,/And Danes shook with terror.

   _____

2. . . . [T]hey could hack at Grendel/From every side, trying to open
   A path for his evil soul, but their points/Could not hurt him. . . .

   _____

3. . . . [T]he sharpest and hardest iron/Could not scratch at his skin, for that sin-stained demon
   Had bewitched all men's weapons. . . .

   _____

B. Writing Application: *Write a sentence for each of the coordinating conjunctions* for, so, *and* yet. *Make sure you use each as a coordinating conjunction.*

1. _____
2. _____
3. _____

from **Beowulf,** translated by Burton Raffel
Integrated Language Skills: Support for Writing

Use the chart below to organize your ideas for creating your job application. Think about the qualifications for the job. Also, consider the characteristics Beowulf possesses that fit the job.

Job Description	
Qualifications Required	
Beowulf's Characteristics	

On a separate page, draft a job application as Beowulf's. Highlight qualifications that are required for the job of battling Grendel. Keep in mind that your audience is a king.

Name _____ Date _____

from **A History of the English Church and People** by Bede
Literary Analysis: Historical Writing

A **historical writing** is a factual narrative or record of past events, gathered through observation and outside, or secondary, sources. In the excerpts from *The History of the English Church and People*, the author does not reveal his sources, but most probably used his own observations, documents in court or monastic libraries, and stories he heard from others (many probably handed down orally for generations).

DIRECTIONS: *On the lines following each quotation, write what source or sources the author might have used to gather information. Comment on the probable accuracy of the quotation.*

1. "The original inhabitants of the island were the Britons, from whom it takes its name, and who, according to tradition, crossed into Britain from Armorica. . . ."

   _____

   _____

   _____

2. ". . . it is said that some Picts from Scythia put to sea in a few long ships and were driven by storms around the coasts of Britain, arriving at length on the north coast of Ireland. Here they found the nation of the Scots, from whom they asked permission to settle, but their request was refused."

   _____

   _____

   _____

3. In agreeing to allow the Picts to take Scottish wives, the Scots said that ". . . they (Picts) should choose a king from the female (Scottish) royal line rather than the male."

   _____

   _____

   _____

4. "In fact, almost everything in this isle enjoys immunity to poison, and I have heard that folk suffering from snakebite have drunk water in which scrapings from the leaves of books from Ireland had been steeped, and that this remedy checked the spreading poison and reduced the swelling."

   _____

   _____

   _____

Name _____ Date _____

from **A History of the English Church and People** by Bede
Reading Strategy: Analyze the Clarity of Meaning

Authors of nonfiction write to achieve a purpose, whether it be to persuade, to entertain, or to inform. As a reader, your job is to **analyze the clarity of meaning** achieved by the author. To evaluate the author's work, you must look at the way he or she uses various elements of nonfiction.

A. DIRECTIONS: *Reread the excerpt from* A History of the English Church and People. *Answer the following questions to analyze the clarity of meaning and evaluate the author's purpose.*

1. How does Bede organize his information about Britain? _____

   _____

2. Bede combines factual information and narrative/descriptive detail. How does this technique affect the clarity of Bede's discourse? _____

   _____

3. Give an example of hierarchical structure in the excerpt. Why do you think Bede uses this technique? _____

   _____

B. DIRECTIONS: *Use a graphic organizer like the one here as you read the excerpt from* A History of the English Church and People. *Record elements that strike you as you read. Explain how these elements contribute to or distract from Bede's purpose.*

Purpose:		
Nonfiction Element	**Example**	**Contribution**
Repetition of Main Ideas		
Syntax		
Word Choice		

from **A History of the English Church and People** by Bede
Vocabulary Builder

Word List

cultivated   immunity   innumerable   migrated   promontories

A. DIRECTIONS: *Write the word from the Word List that best completes each sentence.*

1. _____ people lined up to shake the king's hand.
2. Some plants provide _____ against particular diseases.
3. Lookouts were posted at all the _____.
4. The farmer _____ the land to ensure a high yield of crops.
5. Many people _____ south during the winter to avoid the cold.

B. DIRECTIONS: *Put a check mark in the blank next to the synonym for the underlined word or phrase in the sentence.*

___ 1. According to Bede there were <u>a vast number of</u> wonderful things in Ireland.
    A. hallowed
    B. ravaged
    C. innumerable
    D. stranded

___ 2. Many people <u>moved</u> to other countries during World War II.
    A. promontories
    B. cultivated
    C. migrated
    D. immunity

___ 3. The lighthouses were perched along the <u>cliffs above the ocean</u>.
    A. promontories
    B. furlongs
    C. cockles
    D. barricades

___ 4. The doctor showed his <u>resistance</u> to the disease by remaining healthy through the epidemic.
    A. promontories
    B. innumerable
    C. migrated
    D. immunity

from A History of the English Church and People by Bede
Integrated Language Skills: Support for Writing

Use the web below to organize your information about the history of Britain and your ideas for development based on Bede's report in *A History of the English Church and People.* Consider the country's population, resources, and geography as you gather ideas for your business memo.

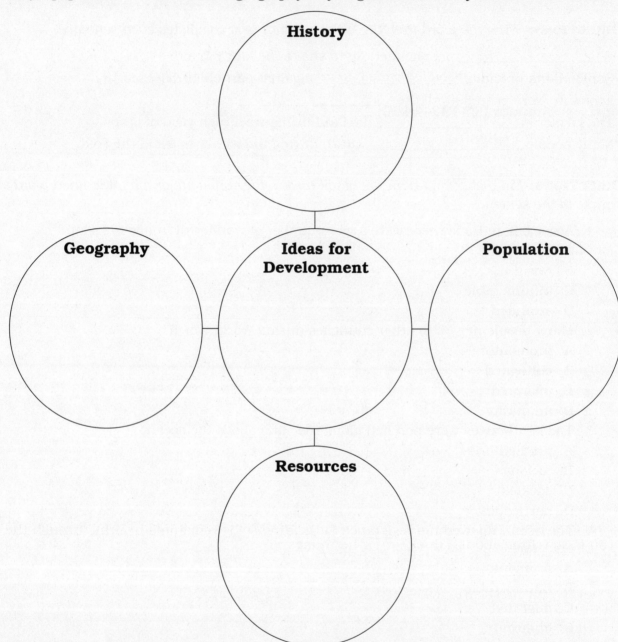

Use a separate page to draft a business memo that clearly and succinctly states your proposal for Britain's development. Be sure to use the proper memo format for your draft.

The Prologue *from* The Canterbury Tales by Geoffrey Chaucer
Geoffrey Chaucer: Biography

Possibly the greatest impact Chaucer made with his writing career was in writing in the English language. At the time, literacy was mostly for the upper classes, who deemed Latin the language of text. Even though he chose to write in English, he was also familiar with Latin, French, and Italian. Much that we know about his life is circumstantial or conjecture because of a lack of records. A very learned man and talented poet, Chaucer set the stage for English literature to come.

A. DIRECTIONS: *Use the following outline to take notes on Geoffrey Chaucer's life.*

I. Geoffrey Chaucer (1343?–1400)

   A. The Poet's Beginnings

   1. _____

   2. _____

   3. _____

   B. The Poet Matures

   1. _____

   2. _____

   3. _____

   C. *The Canterbury Tales*

   1. _____

   2. _____

   D. The Father of English Poetry

   1. _____

   2. _____

B. DIRECTIONS: *Answer the following questions as if you were Geoffrey Chaucer. Make inferences from your prior knowledge of the author.*

1. Your first major work was written as an elegy for John Gaunt's wife. What challenges did you face writing about a duchess for her husband?

   _____

2. What is your most memorable experience as a young man?

   _____

3. How did that experience affect your writing?

   _____

4. What inspired you to write *The Canterbury Tales*?

   _____

   _____

The Prologue *from* The Canterbury Tales by Geoffrey Chaucer
Literary Analysis: Characterization

Characterization is the writer's act of creating and developing the personality traits of a character. Chaucer uses both **direct characterization**—that is, stating facts about a personality directly—and **indirect characterization**—that is, revealing personality through details of appearance, thoughts, speech, and/or actions—to develop the vivid personalities of the pilgrims in *The Canterbury Tales*.

DIRECTIONS: *Read the following passages from the Prologue. In each passage, circle any direct statements about the character's personality. Underline statements about the character's appearance, speech, and/or behavior that reveal his or her personality indirectly. Then, on the lines that follow, summarize what the passage conveys about the character's personality.*

1. There was also a Nun, a Prioress, / Her way of smiling very simple and coy. / Her greatest oath was only "By St. Loy!" / And she was known as Madam Eglantyne. / And well she sang a service, with a fine / Intoning through her nose, as was most seemly, / And she spoke daintily in French, extremely, / After the school of Stratford-atte-Bowe; / French in the Paris style she did not know. / At meat her manners were well taught withal / No morsel from her lips did she let fall, / Nor dipped her fingers in the sauce too deep; / But she could carry a morsel up and keep / The smallest drop from falling on her breast.

   _____

   _____

2. A Sergeant at the Law who paid his calls, / Wary and wise, for clients at St. Paul's / There also was, of noted excellence. / Discreet he was, a man to reverence, / Or so he seemed, his sayings were so wise.

   _____

   _____

3. A worthy woman from beside Bath city / Was with us, somewhat deaf, which was a pity. / In making cloth she showed so great a bent / She bettered those of Ypres and of Ghent. / In all the parish not a dame dared stir / Towards the altar steps in front of her. / And if indeed they did, so wrath was she / As to be quite put out of charity. / Her kerchiefs were of finely woven ground; / I dared have sworn they weighed a good ten pound, / The ones she wore on Sunday on her head. / Her hose were of the finest scarlet red / And gartered tight; her shoes were soft and new.

   _____

   _____

4. The Miller was a chap of sixteen stone, / A great stout fellow big in brawn and bone. / He did well out of them, for he could go / And win the ram at any wrestling show. / Broad, knotty and short-shouldered, he would boast / He could heave any door off hinge and post, / Or take a run and break it with his head.

   _____

   _____

Name _____ Date _____

The Prologue *from* The Canterbury Tales by Geoffrey Chaucer
Literary Analysis: Social Commentary

Social commentary is writing that offers insight into society, its values, and its customs. The writer of social commentary often expresses his or her opinion about society through his or her portrayals of characters and descriptions of events. Chaucer's characters each represent a different segment of society, such as a wife, a knight, a merchant, and a nun, to name a select few. Through his observations and through the words he has his characters say, Chaucer provides a commentary on his society.

A. *Read each passage from Chaucer's* Prologue. *Provide an analysis of each passage. Identify the characters, the details, and the opinions Chaucer directly and indirectly expresses through his writing.*

Passage	Analysis
There was a *Knight*, a most distinguished man, Who from the day on which he first began To ride abroad had followed chivalry, Truth, honor, generousness, and courtesy.	
There also was a *Nun*, a Prioress, Her way of smiling very simple and coy. . . At meat her manners were well taught withal; No morsel from her lips did she let fall, Nor dipped her fingers in the sauce too deep; But she could carry a morsel up and keep The smallest drop from falling on her breast.	
This estimable Merchant so had set His wits to work, none knew he was in debt, He was so stately in negotiation, Loan, bargain and commercial obligation.	

Name _____ Date _____

The Prologue *from* The Canterbury Tales by Geoffrey Chaucer
Reading Strategy: Analyze Difficult Sentences

When you encounter long or involved sentences that seem too difficult to understand, asking yourself *who, what, when, where, why,* and *how* questions can help you figure out their meaning.

DIRECTIONS: *Read the following sentences from the* Prologue. *Then, answer the* who, what, when, where, why, *and/or* how *questions following them to decode their meaning.*

He knew the taverns well in every town / And every innkeeper and barmaid too / Better than lepers, beggars and that crew, / For in so eminent a man as he / It was not fitting with the dignity / Of his position, dealing with a scum / of wretched lepers; nothing good can come / Of dealings with the slum-and-gutter dwellers, / But only with the rich and victual-sellers.

1. What and whom did he know well? _____

2. Whom didn't he know as well? Why? _____

_____

If, when he fought, the enemy vessel sank, / He sent his prisoners home; they walked the plank.

3. What did he do? _____

4. How did he do this? _____

They had a Cook with them who stood alone / For boiling chicken with a marrow-bone, / Sharp flavoring-powder and a spice for savor.

5. Who "stood alone"? _____

6. For what did he stand alone? _____

A Doctor too emerged as we proceeded; No one alive could talk as well as he did / On points of medicine and of surgery, / For, being grounded in astronomy, / He watched his patient's favorable star / And, by his Natural Magic, knew what are / The lucky hours and planetary degrees / For making charms and magic effigies.

7. Whom is this about? _____

8. What can he do? _____

9. How does he treat his patients? _____

_____

But best of all he sang an Offertory, / For well he knew that when that song was sung / He'd have to preach and tune his honey-tongue / And (well he could) win silver from the crowd, / That's why he sang so merrily and loud.

10. What does he do best? _____

11. What does he know he'll have to do when he's done singing? _____

_____

12. Why does he sing so merrily and loud? _____

The Prologue *from* The Canterbury Tales by Geoffrey Chaucer
Vocabulary Builder

Word List

absolution   commission   garnished   prevarication   sanguine   solicitous

A. DIRECTIONS: *Write the word from the Word List that best completes each of the following sentences.*

1. The Franklin is probably most _____ when he is dining, since eating well gives him tremendous pleasure.

2. The Friar believes that _____ should come at a price so that people experience painful consequences for their sinful actions.

3. The Knight's son's garments are _____ with embroidery.

4. The innkeeper is a _____ host, doing all he can to make sure his guests are comfortable and happy.

5. A Pardoner given to _____ ought to be afraid of excommunication.

6. The Friar claims to have a _____ from the Pope to hear confessions.

B. WORD STUDY: *Change each verb into a noun with the suffix -tion. Then, fill in each blank in the sentences with the appropriate noun.*

contribute _____   navigate _____

recreate _____   decorate _____

1. The Knight has in his possession fine horses but wears clothes lacking _____.

2. The Monk prefers hunting for _____ to poring over books and tilling the soil.

3. The Friar gives absolution and an easy penance to those who accompany their confessions with a large financial _____.

4. When it comes to getting a boat from one destination to another, apparently none can compare with the Skipper at _____.

The Prologue *from* The Canterbury Tales by Geoffrey Chaucer
Integrated Language Skills: Support for Writing

Use the chart to organize your ideas to include on your homepage as the host of the Canterbury Blog.

Background Information	
Possible Links	
Advertisements	
Artwork	
Topics of Discussion	
Other	

Use the chart to help you form ideas about the possible posting the characters might make to the blog.

Character	Character's Qualities	Possible Blog Ideas

On a separate page, draw a design of your homepage for the Canterbury Blog incorporating the ideas you listed in the first chart. Then, write several blog entries in character based on your observations of Chaucer's descriptions.

Name _____ Date _____

"The Pardoner's Tale" *from* The Canterbury Tales by Geoffrey Chaucer
Literary Analysis: Allegory/Archetypal Narrative Elements

An **allegory** is a narrative that has both a literal meaning and a deeper, symbolic meaning. On the literal level, it tells a story. On the symbolic level, many or all of its characters, events, settings, and objects symbolize, or represent, abstract ideas and work to teach a moral message. Allegory uses **archetypal narrative elements,** particular basic storytelling patterns, to express common morals and ideas. Such elements include tests of characters' moral fiber, mysterious guides, groups of three, and just endings that reward good and punish evil.

A. DIRECTIONS: *Answer these questions about "The Pardoner's Tale."*

1. What vices do the rioters seem to represent? _____

2. What might the old man represent? _____

3. Which character has a name indicating the abstract idea he represents? _____

4. What might the gold florins represent? _____

5. Consider the events near the end of the tale. What might the revelers' actions toward one another represent? _____

6. What is the moral message that the Pardoner's allegory attempts to teach? _____
_____

B. DIRECTIONS: *On the lines below or on a separate sheet, write your ideas for a modern allegory illustrating the same message as "The Pardoner's Tale" or another moral message. Be sure to include archetypal narrative elements.*

_____

_____

_____

_____

_____

_____

_____

_____

_____

_____

"The Pardoner's Tale" *from* **The Canterbury Tales** by Geoffrey Chaucer
Reading Strategy: Reread for Clarification

Rereading can often help clarify characters' identities and relationships, the sequence or cause of events, unfamiliar language, and other puzzling information. Often, earlier passages provide the key to understanding the puzzling information. Study this example:

Passage
They made their bargain, swore with appetite,
These three, to live and die for one another
As brother-born might swear to his born brother.

Puzzling Detail
What bargain did the three men make?

Reread Earlier Passage
Hold up your hands, like me, and we'll be brothers
In this affair, and each defend the others,
And we will kill this traitor Death, I say!

Clarification
They made a bargain to kill Death.

DIRECTIONS: *For each item below, reread earlier passages of "The Pardoner's Tale" to clarify the possibly puzzling information about which the question asks. On the lines provided, write the details that clarify the information.*

1. In line 102, the publican tells the rioters, "Be on your guard with such an adversary." What adversary is he talking about?

   _____

2. In lines 174–175, one rioter tells the old man, "I heard you mention, just a moment gone, / A certain traitor Death. . . ." What did the old man say earlier about Death?

   _____

3. In line 213, one of the rioters says that they must bring the gold back at night. What reason did he give earlier for doing this?

   _____

4. In lines 260–262, the Pardoner tells us that the youngest rioter "Kept turning over, rolling up and down / Within his heart the beauty of those bright / New florins. . . ." Does the rioter have any florins with him? If not, what does this passage mean?

   _____

5. In lines 304–305, the Pardoner tells us, "Exactly in the way they'd planned his death/They fell on him and slew him. . . ." What was the plan?

   _____

"The Pardoner's Tale" *from* **The Canterbury Tales** by Geoffrey Chaucer
Vocabulary Builder

Word List

apothecary   deftly   hoary   pallor   sauntered   tarry

A. DIRECTIONS: *Read each series of words. Write the word from the Word List that best fits with the other words in the series.*

1. linger, hang behind _____
2. pharmacist, medical person _____
3. ambled, meandered _____
4. paleness, white skin, deathly hue _____
5. ancient, gray, white _____
6. skillfully, cleverly, nimbly _____

B. WORD STUDY: *In each sentence, underline the word that contains the prefix apo-. Then, use your knowledge of the prefix to define the word you underlined.*

1. After insulting the group of businessmen, the engineer apologized.

   _____

2. The apothegm the gambler used when he lost was: "You win some, you lose some."

   _____

3. The minister read the apocryphal writings before the New Testament.

   _____

All-in-One Workbook
29

"The Pardoner's Tale" *from* **The Canterbury Tales** by Geoffrey Chaucer

Integrated Language Skills: Support for Writing

Use the following outline to help you organize your sermon on greed. Remember that you are addressing a contemporary audience and should use present-day examples to support your main ideas. Continue the outline on a separate sheet if necessary.

I. Main Argument: _____

_____

   A. Supporting Idea: _____

_____

      1. Detail or Example: _____

_____

      2. Detail or Example: _____

_____

   B. Supporting Idea: _____
      1. Detail or Example: _____

_____

      2. Detail or Example: _____

_____

On a separate sheet, write a draft of your sermon on greed. Follow the ideas as you organized them in your outline. Be sure to clearly support your argument with your ideas and examples.

Name _____ Date _____

"The Wife of Bath's Tale" *from* The Canterbury Tales by Geoffrey Chaucer
Literary Analysis: Frame Story/Setting

A **frame story** is a story in which one or more other stories unfolds. The frame story usually introduces a set of characters in a particular situation that prompts one or more of these characters to tell a **story-within-the-story.** Chaucer begins The *Canterbury Tales* with a Prologue that provides a frame story. In the frame story, Chaucer introduces the characters who will tell their own stories. The **setting** of the frame story provides the characters with the opportunity to tell their stories. Each of the characters who tells his or her own story then provides an additional setting—the time and place where the character's story takes place. As the narrator's voice changes between stories, so does the setting.

A. DIRECTIONS: *On the lines provided, answer these questions about the frame story of* The Canterbury Tales *and its relationship to "The Wife of Bath's Tale."*

1. What is the main frame story of *The Canterbury Tales*?

   _____

2. What setting does Chaucer supply in the frame story to explain his story collection?

   _____

3. How does the frame and its setting make reading the different stories more interesting?

   _____

   _____

4. In addition to the main story about the knight, what other story does the Wife of Bath tell in part in "The Wife of Bath's Tale"? What settings does she describe?

   _____

   _____

5. Consider the characterization of the Wife of Bath in the general Prologue to *The Canterbury Tales.* How does the story she tells suit her personality and background?

   _____

   _____

B. DIRECTIONS: *What setting would you use in a frame story that would bring together a group of contemporary storytellers? Jot down your ideas for a modern frame story on the lines below.*

_____

_____

_____

_____

_____

"The Wife of Bath's Tale" *from* **The Canterbury Tales** by Geoffrey Chaucer
Reading Strategy: Use Context Clues

You can often figure out the meaning of an unfamiliar word if you examine its **context,** or surroundings, for clues to its meaning. The following list shows common types of context clues and examples in which they appear. In the examples, the possibly unfamiliar words are underlined, and the context clues are in italics.

- **Synonym or Definition:** a word or words that mean the same as the unfamiliar word

    She dined in a bistro, *a small French restaurant.*

- **Antonym or Contrast:** a word or words that mean the opposite of the unfamiliar word or tell you what the unfamiliar word is not

    The race will *begin* at 6 o'clock and terminate three hours later.

- **Explanation:** words that give more information about an unfamiliar word

    Ocelots are *like leopards, only smaller.*

- **Example:** a word or words that illustrate the unfamiliar word, or a word or words that tell what the unfamiliar word illustrates

    Rodents include *rats, mice, and squirrels.*

- **Sentence Role:** hints about the word's meaning based on its use in a sentence. For example, in this sentence, you can tell that a *bistro* is a noun and that it is not abstract, since it can be entered.

    Example: The couple entered the bistro.

DIRECTIONS: *Answer these questions about words in "The Wife of Bath's Tale."*

1. What synonym in line 72 helps you know the meaning of *jollity?* _____

2. What two examples in lines 78–80 help clarify the meaning of *flattery?* _____

    _____

3. In lines 82–84, what does the contrast suggest that *reprove* means? _____

    _____

4. What nearby synonym helps clarify the meaning of *maim* in line 278? _____

5. From the explanation in lines 303–304, what do you think *churl* means? _____

    _____

Name _____ Date _____

"The Wife of Bath's Tale" *from* **The Canterbury Tales** by Geoffrey Chaucer
Vocabulary Builder

Word List

bequeath   contemptuous   esteemed   implored   prowess   rebuke   relates

A. DIRECTIONS: *Use your knowledge of the words in the Word List to decide whether each statement below is true or false. Then, on the line before the statement, write* T *if it is true and* F *if it is false.*

____ 1. Someone who skates with *prowess* often falls flat on her face.

____ 2. A smile is a *contemptuous* expression.

____ 3. A storyteller *relates* a story.

____ 4. People sometimes *bequeath* property to their heirs.

____ 5. Most people enjoy having someone *rebuke* them.

____ 6. If someone *implored* you to leave, they would not want you to move.

____ 7. People often stand up when an *esteemed* figure enters the room.

B. WORD STUDY: *The italicized words in these lines from "The Wife of Bath's Tale" each can have more than one meaning. Use the context to determine which of the two possible meanings applies to the lines from the selection, and circle that meaning. Then, on the line provided, write a sentence illustrating the other meaning of the word.*

1. Ovid *relates* that under his long hair / The unhappy Midas grew a splendid pair / Of ass's ears.

   Possible Meanings: shows a connection   narrates

   _____

2. He begged her not to tell a living creature / That he possessed so horrible a *feature*.

   Possible Meanings: any part of the face   a special newspaper or magazine story

   _____

3. There wasn't a living creature to be seen / Save on old woman sitting on the *green*.

   Possible Meanings: a color blending yellow and blue   an expanse of grass or plants

   _____

4. It was such torture that his wife looked *foul*.

   Possible Meanings: disgusting   hit out of bounds

   _____

"The Wife of Bath's Tale" *from* **The Canterbury Tales** by Geoffrey Chaucer
Integrated Language Skills: Support for Writing

Use the chart to organize the information for your response to criticism. Paraphrase the critic's interpretation, explain your reaction to the critic's interpretation, and provide support for your reaction, using details and examples from the text. Record any new ideas that you develop from your work.

Critic's Interpretation:		
My Reaction:		
Supporting Detail:	**Supporting Detail:**	**Supporting Detail:**
New Ideas About Original Text:		

On a separate page, draft your response to criticism. Make sure that you clearly state your opinion of the critic's interpretation, include supporting details for your opinion, and provide additional insight into the original text.

Name _____ Date _____

"The Wife of Bath's Tale" *from* The Canterbury Tales by Geoffrey Chaucer
Grammar and Style: Correlative Conjunctions

Correlative conjunctions are paired conjunctions that connect two words or groups of words of equal significance.

Correlative Conjunctions				
either . . . or	neither . . . nor	both . . . and	whether . . . or	not only . . . but also

EXAMPLES

We will **either** read "The Wife of Bath's Tale" **or** "The Pardoner's Tale."
Neither Jamal **nor** Freida will be in class today.
The class wants to read **both** Chaucer **and** Bede.
We will decide **whether** we should go out **or** stay home.
The story provides **not only** entertainment **but also** social commentary.

Be careful not to confuse *either* and *neither* when they are used alone. In such a case, the word is used as either an adjective or a pronoun.

EXAMPLES

Neither of us could make it to the show. (pronoun)   **Neither** one will fit. (adjective)
Either works for this job. (pronoun)   **Either** shirt will be fine. (adjective)

DIRECTIONS: *Use correlative conjunctions to combine the sentence pairs.*

1. The knight would die. The knight would go on a quest.

   _____

   _____

2. The knight did not want to die. He did not want to marry an old woman.

   _____

   _____

3. The knight had to decide to marry the old woman. He had to decide to die.

   _____

   _____

4. The knight got to live. The knight had a beautiful wife.

   _____

   _____

Name _____ Date _____

from **The Canterbury Tales** by Geoffrey Chaucer
from the **Decameron** by Boccaccio
Literary Analysis: Comparing Frame Stories

A **frame story** story is a story in which one or more other stories unfolds. The frame story usually introduces a set of characters in a particular situation that prompts one or more of these characters to tell a story within a story. Many writers of frame stories use the technique to bring together tales from a variety of sources. Frame stories can make fantastic stories easier for readers to accept because the frame is realistic. They can make the act of storytelling seem more natural while capturing the quality of the oral tradition.

When you compare frame stories, you have to look at a variety of levels of comparison. You need to examine the actual frames of the works and make comparisons between elements of the two. Then you need to look at the stories within the frame to make comparisons.

DIRECTIONS: *Use the following chart to organize your ideas for comparing the frames of* The Canterbury Tales *and the* Decameron.

The Canterbury Tales	*Decameron*
Main frame story:	Main frame story:
Premise for storytelling:	Premise for storytelling:
Effect of premise:	Effect of premise:

from **The Canterbury Tales** by Geoffrey Chaucer
from the **Decameron** by Boccaccio
Vocabulary Builder

Word List

courtly   deference   despondent   frugally   impertinence   affably

A. DIRECTIONS: *Write the word from the Word List that best completes each sentence.*

1. The child was reprimanded for his _____ when he shouted back at his mother.

2. The page was expected to show _____ to the king.

3. Luis's grandmother spent her money _____, as she feared the steady depletion of her retirement fund.

4. The Arthurian legend of the knight and a queen was a _____ romance.

5. The young girl looked _____ when her glass menagerie fell to the floor and shattered into a thousand pieces.

6. As I complained of this season's long, bitter winter, my friend responded _____ that the approaching summer would seem all the more sweet.

B. DIRECTIONS: *On each line, write the letter of the word or phrase that is most nearly opposite in meaning to the Word List word.*

___ 1. affably
   A. calmly
   B. regularly
   C. wittily
   D. nastily

___ 2. frugally
   A. weakly
   B. wastefully
   C. shrewdly
   D. loudly

___ 3. despondent
   A. inattentive
   B. frustrated
   C. relaxed
   D. joyful

___ 4. impertinence
   A. freedom
   B. patience
   C. respect
   D. affection

___ 5. deference
   A. disrespect
   B. closeness
   C. eagerness
   D. vigor

from **The Canterbury Tales** by Geoffrey Chaucer
from **The Decameron** by Boccaccio
Integrated Language Skills: Support for Writing to Compare Literary Works

Use the following chart to organize your ideas for writing a comparison of themes.

Boccaccio—"Federigo's Falcon"	Chaucer—"The Wife of Bath's Tale"
Plot Summary:	Plot Summary:
Main Characters:	Main Characters:
Characters' Actions and Beliefs:	Characters' Actions and Beliefs:
Theme:	Theme:

Consider these questions as you prepare your essay:

What is the theme of each story?
How does each author present this theme?

On a separate page, use information from your chart and answers to your questions to help you organize ideas as you draft your essay. Make sure you clearly state each theme and your major points of comparison.

from **Sir Gawain and the Green Knight,** translated by Marie Borroff
from **Morte d'Arthur** by Sir Thomas Malory

Literary Analysis: Medieval Romance

Medieval romances were the popular adventure stories of the Middle Ages. Originally cast in verse, they were later sometimes told in prose. In England, the best known of the medieval romances are based on the legends of King Arthur and his knights. **Legends** are anonymous traditional stories about the past. They may be based in fact but are always embellished with descriptions of heroic figures and memorable deeds, quests and conquests, or tests of strength and character.

DIRECTIONS: *Following is a series of characteristics of medieval romances, which are often based on legends. On the lines below each characteristic, cite at least two details from* Sir Gawain and the Green Knight *and* Morte d'Arthur *that illustrate the characteristic.*

1. Medieval romances convey a sense of the supernatural.

   Sir Gawain and the Green Knight: _____

   _____

   Morte d'Arthur: _____

   _____

   _____

2. Medieval romances give a glamorous portrayal of castle life.

   Sir Gawain and the Green Knight: _____

   _____

   Morte d'Arthur: _____

   _____

3. Chivalric ideals—bravery, honor, courtesy, fairness to enemies, respect for women—guide the characters.

   Sir Gawain and the Green Knight: _____

   _____

   Morte d'Arthur: _____

   _____

4. Medieval romances are imbued with adventure.

   Sir Gawain and the Green Knight: _____

   _____

   Morte d'Arthur: _____

   _____

   _____

from **Sir Gawain and the Green Knight,** translated by Marie Borroff
from **Morte d'Arthur** by Sir Thomas Malory

Reading Strategy: Main Idea

The **main idea** of a passage is its key point or message. When you read a passage, you need to make sure you understand the point the author is making. To do so, you need to determine which information is the most important. **Summarizing** is one way to check your understanding of what you have read. A summary briefly states the main idea and key details in your own words. A summary is always much shorter than the original, but it must reflect the original accurately. Look at this example from *Morte d'Arthur.*

Passage	Main Idea and Key Events	Summary
King Arthur smote Sir Mordred under the shield, with a thrust of his spear, throughout the body more than a fathom. And when Sir Mordred felt that he had his death's wound, he thrust himself with the might that he had up to the burr of King Arthur's spear, and right so he smote his father King Arthur with his sword holden in both his hands, upon the side of the head, that the sword pierced the helmet and the casing of the brain.	King Arthur speared Sir Mordred. Sir Mordred felt that he was dying from the wound, but he forced himself to hit King Arthur in the head.	Sir Mordred and King Arthur fought a terrible battle. Sir Mordred was killed and King Arthur was wounded in the head.

DIRECTIONS: *Use this graphic organizer to summarize this excerpt.*

Passage	Main Idea and Key Events	Summary
. . . Sir Lucan departed, for he was grievously wounded in many places. And so as he walked he saw and harkened by the moonlight how that pillagers and robbers were come into the field to pill and to rob many a full noble knight of brooches and bracelets and of many a good ring and many a rich jewel. And who that were not dead all out there they slew them for their harness and their riches. When Sir Lucan understood this work, he came to the King as soon as he might and told him all what he had heard and seen.		

from **Sir Gawain and the Green Knight,** translated by Marie Borroff
from **Morte d'Arthur** by Sir Thomas Malory
Vocabulary Builder

Word List

    adjure   adroitly   entreated   interred   largesse   peril

A. DIRECTIONS: *Each excerpt below is from one of the poems. Choose the word from the Word List that best matches the meaning of the italicized word or phrase.*

1. First I ask and *appeal* to you, how you are called
That you tell me true. . . . _____

2. Sir Mordred did his devoir that day and put himself in great *danger.* _____

3. . . . Withdrew the ax *skillfully* before it did damage. _____

4. . . . and there they *pleaded with* Sir Mordred . . . _____

5. . . . contrary both to *noble spirit* and loyalty belonging to the knights . . .
_____

6. "What man is there here *buried* that you pray so fast for?" _____

B. WORD STUDY: *The word root -droit- means "right." In the following sentences, decide whether the italicized word is used properly. If it is, write "correct." If it is not, rewrite the sentence using the correct form of a word with the root -droit-.*

1. Because of his *adroitness* with a football, Charley was unable to make the football team.

_____

2. Amber was very *adroit* at gymnastics, so she knew she would never go to the Olympics.

_____

3. Marla is no longer *maladroit* in her movements now that she takes ballet lessons.

_____

4. Tad prides himself on his *maladroitness,* having never broken a leg in all his years as a skier.

_____

from **Sir Gawain and the Green Knight,** translated by Marie Borroff
from **Morte d'Arthur** by Sir Thomas Malory
Integrated Language Skills: Support for Writing

Use the graphic organizers below to help you think of ideas. Choose an event or a situation that Sir Gawain would react to that could become an interior monologue.

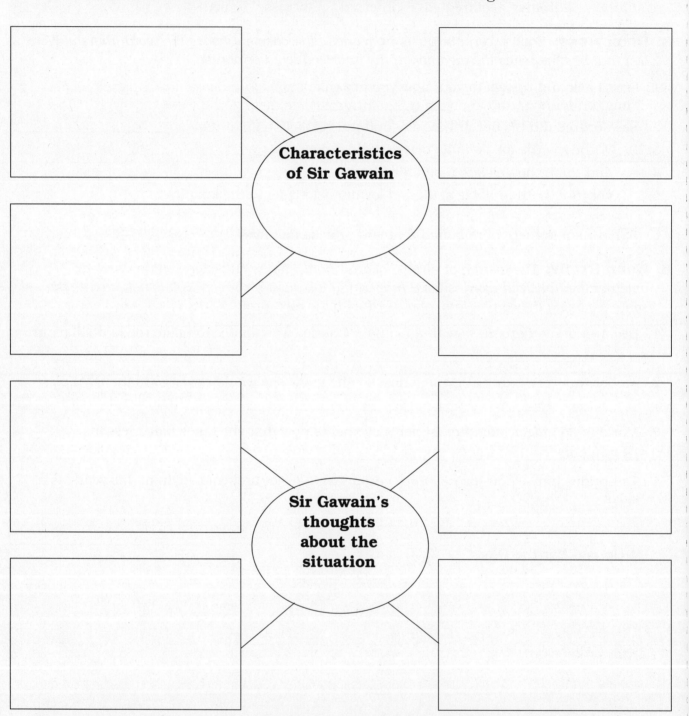

Use a separate page to draft Sir Gawain's interior monologue. Write in the first person as though you are Gawain, talking to himself.

Letters of Margaret Paston
"Twa Corbies" Anonymous
"Lord Randall" Anonymous
"Get Up and Bar the Door" Anonymous
"Barbara Allan" Anonymous

Primary Sources: Letters and Ballads

Primary sources, such as **letters** and **ballads,** often require an understanding of historical context and of language used in a different era. For this reason, scholars provide text aids to help clarify the works. Introductory and side notes give details about time and place. Footnotes may explain unfamiliar words or dialect, or regional language spoken by a group of people. Analyzing, evaluating, and applying this information will help you achieve a deeper understanding of primary sources.

DIRECTIONS: *Use the following chart to analyze and evaluate text features to clarify your reading of the letters and ballads.*

Letter/Ballad	Text Feature	How It Clarifies or Explains the Work
Letters of Margaret Paston		
"Twa Corbies"		
"Lord Randall"		
"Get Up and Bar the Door"		
"Barbara Allen"		

Letters of Margaret Paston
"Twa Corbies" Anonymous
"Lord Randall" Anonymous
"Get Up and Bar the Door" Anonymous
"Barbara Allan" Anonymous
Vocabulary Builder

Word List

alderman   assault   asunder   certify   ransacked   remnant   succor

A. DIRECTIONS: *On each line, write the word from the Word List that has the same meaning as the italicized word or phrase in the sentence.*

1. Two thieves broke into a house and *pillaged* every room in search of valuables.
   _____

2. The *official* voted against a proposal to raise parking meter rates in her district.
   _____

3. The only *remainder* of the delicious meal was a spoonful of mashed potatoes.
   _____

4. The pirates planned to *violently attack* the trade ship and steal any cargo on board.
   _____

5. Nurse Florence Nightingale offered *aid* to wounded soldiers during the Crimean War.
   _____

6. The explosives expert recommended using dynamite to blow the boulder *into pieces*.
   _____

7. Only an anthropologist will be able to *verify* whether the artifact is authentic.
   _____

B. WORD STUDY: *Many words in the English language have Anglo-Saxon roots. Look up each of these words and identify their language of origin.*

1. **ransack:** _____

   _____

2. **Tuesday:** _____

   _____

3. **before:** _____

   _____

Name _____ Date _____

Essential Questions Workshop—Unit 1

In their poems, epics, and nonfiction works, the writers in Unit One express ideas that relate to the three Essential Questions framing this book. Review the literature in the unit. Then, for each Essential Question, choose an author and at least one passage from his or her writing that expresses an idea related to the question. Use this chart to complete your work.

Essential Question	Author/Selection	Literary Passage
What is the relationship between place and literature?		
How does literature shape or reflect society?		
What is the relationship of the writer to tradition?		

Name _____ Date _____

Names and Terms to Know

A. DIRECTIONS: *Write a brief sentence explaining each of the following names and terms. You will find all of the information you need in the Unit Introduction in your textbook.*

1. Copernicus: _____

2. Henry VIII: _____

   _____

3. armada: _____

   _____

4. Elizabeth I: _____

   _____

5. James I: _____

6. Martin Luther: _____

B. DIRECTIONS: *Use the hints below to help you answer each question.*

1. What role did the Italian Renaissance play in the coming of the English Renaissance?
   [Hints: What does "Renaissance" mean? What happened during the Italian Renaissance? What happened during the English Renaissance?]

   _____

   _____

   _____

2. How did the Protestant Reformation influence English society?
   [Hints: What happened in Europe during the Protestant Reformation? How did England become a Protestant nation?]

   _____

   _____

   _____

3. Why was Queen Elizabeth's reign a golden age in England?
   [Hints:What happened to England as a nation during Elizabeth's reign? What happened in English literature?]

   _____

   _____

   _____

Unit 2 Introduction

Essential Question 1: What is the relationship between place and literature?

A. DIRECTIONS: *Answer the questions about the first Essential Question in the Introduction about the relationship between place and literature. All the information you need is in the Unit 2 Introduction in your textbook.*

1. *A Real Place as Launching Pad for the Imagination*

   a. Elizabethans came to the theater to be _____

   b. William Shakespeare wrote his play *Macbeth* in order to _____
   _____

2. *Drama and the Expansion of London*

   a. Why were plays staged outside of London's city limits? _____
   _____

   b. Why did writers come to London? _____
   _____

3. *Pastoral Dreams*

   a. What did Greek and Roman pastoral poems do?
   _____

   b. English poets wrote pastorals in order to
   _____

   c. Give an example of one English pastoral and its author. _____

4. *Change in the Meaning of "England"*

   a. What two events launched England on the world stage? _____
   _____

   b. By the early 1600s, English writing was being read by _____

B. DIRECTIONS: *Complete each sentence stem based on the Essential Question Vocabulary words.*

   1. In *kingdoms*, the length of the monarch's reign _____

   2. A *pastoral* landscape is _____

   3. Nations that set out to *colonize* other lands _____

Unit 2 Introduction

Essential Question 2: How does literature shape or reflect society?

A. DIRECTIONS: *On the lines provided, answer the questions about the second Essential Question in the Introduction about the writer and society. All the information you need is in the Unit 2 Introduction in your textbook.*

1. *Belief as an Issue*

   a. During this time the religious affiliation of England changed _____ times.

   b. How were religious and political loyalties tied together during the time of the Tudors? _____

   c. Why was Sir Thomas More executed? _____

   d. What was Mary Tudor's policy regarding religion? _____

2. *Writers' Response to Problems of Belief*

   a. What was the " King James Bible" intended to accomplish? _____ _____

   b. What scientific issues were also in dispute at this time? _____ _____

   c. What is a major theme in Shakespeare's play *Macbeth*? _____

   d. How did Columbus, Luther, Galileo, and Copernicus affect people's beliefs? _____ _____ _____

B. DIRECTIONS: *Complete the sentence stems based on the Essential Question Vocabulary words.*

1. *Beliefs* are different from facts in that _____

2. Someone who has divided *loyalties* might find it difficult to _____

3. An *illusion* is ultimately disappointing because _____

Unit 2 Introduction

Essential Question 3: What is the relationship of the writer to tradition?

A. DIRECTIONS: *On the lines provided, answer the questions about the third Essential Question in the Introduction about the relationship between the writer and tradition. All the information you need is in the Unit 2 Introduction in your textbook.*

1. *Rediscovering the Classics*

   a. Both the Renaissance and the Reformation involved going back to _____
   _____

   b. How did the views of the ancient Greek and Roman classic writers differ from the views of traditional Christians? _____
   _____

   c. What is Humanism? _____

2. *Something Old Becoming Something New*

   a. Give three examples of classic works that were translated into English during the Renaissance. _____
   _____

   b. What is blank verse, and who contributed to its development? _____
   _____

   c. Elizabethan drama has its origins in _____

   d. English variations of the sonnet were created by _____
   _____

3. *Religion and Literary Tradition*

   a. What was the "breeches" Bible? _____

   b. Describe how the "King James Bible" came into being. _____
   _____

B. DIRECTIONS: *Complete the sentence stems based on the Essential Question Vocabulary words.*

1. By definition, a *renaissance* would follow a period of _____

2. Reading the *classics* helps us to connect our own time to _____

3. If something is in need of a *reformation*, it must be _____

Unit 2 Introduction
Following-Through Activities

A. CHECK YOUR COMPREHENSION: *Use this chart to complete the Check Your Comprehension activity in the Unit 2 Introduction. In the middle column, list two key concepts for each Essential Question. In the right column, list a key author for each concept. (One set of answers is given for the question about the writer and tradition.)*

Essential Question	Key Concept	Work (Author)
Place and Literature	1. _____ 2. _____	1. _____ 2. _____
Literature and Society	1. _____ 2. _____	1. _____ 2. _____
Writer and Tradition	1. Use of comic relief with tragedy 2. _____	1. William Shakespeare 2. _____

B. EXTEND YOUR LEARNING: *Use this graphic organizer to help plan your brochure for the Extend Your Learning activity.*

Back cover (image + text) _____ _____	Front cover (image + text) _____ _____

Page 1 —history of Globe —Image of old Globe:	Page 2 —continued history _____ _____

Page 3 _____ _____ _____ _____	Page 4 _____ _____ _____ _____

Page 5 _____ _____ _____ _____	Page 6 _____ _____ _____ _____

Sonnets 1, 35, and 75 by Edmund Spenser
Sonnets 31 and 39 by Sir Philip Sidney
Literary Analysis: The Sonnet

The **sonnet,** a lyric poem of fourteen lines, originated in Italy. The Italian, or **Petrarchan,** sonnet is divided into two parts. The first eight lines form the *octave* and the next six lines the *sestet.* While the Italian sonnet had a fairly strict rhyme scheme, English poets took many liberties with the sonnet form. Sir Philip Sidney used an *abab abab* rhyme scheme in addition to the Italian *abba abba* rhyme scheme for the octave. In the sestet, Sidney's rhyme schemes were *cdcdee, cddcee,* or *ccdeed.* The **Spenserian** sonnet, named for Edmund Spenser, uses the *abab, bcbc, cdcd, ee* rhyme scheme.

Recognizing the Sonnet Form

A. DIRECTIONS: *In this sonnet by Spenser, bracket and label the stanzas and rhyme schemes.*

Lyke as a ship that through the ocean wyde,
By conduct of some star doth make her way,
Whenas a storme hath dimd her trusty guyde,
Out of her course doth wander far astray.
[5] So I whose star, that wont with her bright ray,
Me to direct, with cloudes is overcast,
Doe wander now in darknesse and dismay,
Through hidden perils round about me plast.
Yet hope I well, that when this storme is past
[10] My Helice the lodestar of my lyfe
Will shine again, and looke on me at last,
With lovely light to cleare my cloudy grief.
Till then I wander carefull comfortlesse,
In secret sorrow and sad pensivenesse.

Sonnet Sequence

B. DIRECTIONS: *A **sonnet sequence** is a group of sonnets linked by subject matter or theme, and following certain conventions. Compare two of the sonnets from the sonnet sequence* Astrophel and Stella *by Sir Philip Sidney by answering the following questions about Sonnets 31 and 39.*

1. To what inanimate object is each sonnet addressed?
   A. Sonnet 31 is addressed to the _____.
   B. Sonnet 39 is addressed to _____.
2. The speaker in each sonnet desires something from the one addressed.
   A. In Sonnet 31, he wants _____.
   B. In Sonnet 39, he wants _____.
3. Both poems are lyric and reflect the speaker's feelings.
   A. In Sonnet 31, he feels _____ about the way women treat men.
   B. In Sonnet 39, he feels a _____ for peace.

Name _____   Date _____

Sonnets 1, 35, and 75 by Edmund Spenser
Sonnets 31 and 39 by Sir Philip Sidney

Reading Strategy: Paraphrase

Poetic language often uses condensed imagery to convey the poet's ideas. **Paraphrasing,** or restating passages in your own words, can help you understand and explore a poem's meaning. When paraphrasing poetry, look for the main ideas within the imagery. Think about what the images might be representing and how those images convey a bigger theme.

Spenser, Sonnet 1, lines 1–3:	"Happy ye leaves when as those lily hands, / which hold my life in their dead doing might, / Shall handle you and hold in love's soft bands, . . . "
Paraphrase:	The pages of a book are happy when held in the beautiful, soft hands of my beloved, hands that also hold me in their power.

DIRECTIONS: *In the chart below, paraphrase one of Spenser's sonnets and one of Sidney's sonnets.*

Try these tips as you paraphrase a sonnet:

- Break down the sonnet into parts (octaves, quatrains, sestets, or couplets).
- Paraphrase parts, not every line.
- Focus on complete thoughts.

Sonnet	Paraphrase

Sonnets 1, 35, and 75 by Edmund Spenser
Sonnets 31 and 39 by Sir Philip Sidney
Vocabulary Builder

Word List

balm   deign   devise   languished   wan

A. DIRECTIONS: *Match each word in the left column with its definition in the right column. Write the letter of the definition on the line next to the word it defines.*

___ 1. balm   A. weak
___ 2. wan   B. lower oneself
___ 3. deign   C. grew weak
___ 4. devise   D. something that heals
___ 5. languished   E. plan

B. WORD STUDY: *Fill in the blanks in the following sentences with the appropriate form of the word* languished: languish *(verb),* languid *(adjective), or* languor *(noun).*

1. Maria's _____ caused her mother to worry.

2. The _____ breeze offered little relief from the sweltering heat.

3. Jamie's severe depression causes him to grow more _____ daily.

4. Keats continued to _____ from the effects of tuberculosis.

5. As I watched the dreamy _____ of the slow-moving river, I could feel my eyelids grow heavy.

Sonnets 1, 35, and 75 by Edmund Spenser
Sonnets 31 and 39 by Sir Philip Sidney
Grammar and Style: Subordinating Conjunctions

A **subordinating conjunction** connects two ideas by placing one below the other in importance. Subordinating conjunctions introduce subordinate (dependent) clauses. These conjunctions might appear between the ideas they connect, or they might appear at the beginning of a sentence.

Common Subordinating Conjunctions

after	although	because	before
how	if	than	though
unless	until	where	while

Examples:

<u>Although</u> sonnets all have fourteen lines, some follow a different rhyme scheme.
Spenserian and Petrarchan sonnets are different <u>because</u> they vary in technique.

A. PRACTICE: *Complete each sentence with one of the subordinating conjunctions listed above.*

1. _____ I read Spenser's sonnets, I had to look at the footnotes to understand the language.

2. The sonnets were less difficult to understand _____ I expected them to be.

3. _____ Spenser was agonized by his love, he still couldn't quite thinking about her.

4. _____ I read the sonnets by Spenser and Sidney, I had a new appreciation for their writing.

5. Spenser and Sidney are considered literary greats _____ they made such significant contributions to English literature.

B. Writing Application: *Choose one of the sonnets or another work of literature to write about. Construct three sentences about that work of literature using a subordinating conjunction in each. An example has been completed for you.*

Example:

<u>In Sonnet 35, Spenser says that nothing in the world seems important because the idea of his love overshadows it all.</u>

1. _____

    _____

2. _____

    _____

3. _____

    _____

Name _____ Date _____

Support for Writing

Use the graphic organizer to help you plan and organize information for your manual for a sonnet. Place a checkmark by the sections you want to include in your manual. Then, take notes on the information you want to include.

	Section	Information to Include
	Preface	
	Table of Contents	
	Overview	
	In-Depth Descriptions of Each Part	
	Step-by-Step Instructions	
	Frequently Asked Questions	
	Where to Find Help	
	Glossary	
	Diagrams	

"The Passionate Shepherd to His Love" by Christopher Marlowe
"The Nymph's Reply to the Shepherd" by Sir Walter Raleigh
Literary Analysis: Pastoral and Universal Theme

A **pastoral** is a poem or another work that celebrates the pleasures of a simple life in the country. The term comes from the Latin word *pastor,* which means "shepherd." Pastoral poems generally display some or all of these features:

- The speaker is a shepherd, or herder of sheep.
- The shepherd describes the simple joys of country living.
- The shepherd usually addresses or describes a shepherdess whom he loves.
- The shepherd uses much more sophisticated vocabulary and imagery than would be expected from the simple rural fellow he pretends to be.
- The picture of rural life is highly idealized, ignoring the hardships of living close to the land, and instead, making such an existence seem carefree.
- The actual audience for the poem is an educated urban reader or member of court seeking to escape the complexities of his or her life by reading about what he or she imagines to be the free and untroubled existence of ordinary country folk.

Pastoral poems often express **universal themes,** which express ideas and emotions that transcend time and place. Many universal themes express ideas about love—such as its connection to youth or nature—that we can relate to today, hundreds of years after the poems were written.

A. DIRECTIONS: *On the lines provided, answer these questions about "The Passionate Shepherd to His Love."*

1. Who is the speaker in Marlowe's poem, and whom does he address?

   _____

2. What basic request does the speaker make of the person he addresses?

   _____

3. How would you describe the portrait the speaker paints of country living?

   _____

4. Identify two instances in which the speaker exaggerates the joys of country life.

   _____

   _____

5. Cite two examples of sophisticated language and imagery in Marlowe's poem.

   _____

   _____

B. DIRECTIONS: *On the lines below, identify a universal theme expressed by these two poems.*

_____

_____

_____

"The Passionate Shepherd to His Love" by Christopher Marlowe
"The Nymph's Reply to the Shepherd" by Sir Walter Raleigh
Reading Strategy: Analyze Similar Themes

To **analyze similar themes** in two poems, compare and contrast the poems' patterns of organization and repetition. That is, look at the thoughts expressed in each stanza of the poems and at the words that each poem repeats.

If you identify such similarities and differences, you will be able to tell if the two poets basically agree or disagree in their presentation of a shared theme. For example, imagine two poems about winter. They both include such words as *winter, snow, bare trees*, and *icicles*. In one poem, each stanza describes the visual beauty of these elements. In the other poem, each stanza focuses on the starkness and coldness of these elements. Analyzing the poems' presentation of a similar theme, we could say they sharply differ in their views of winter, one making it seem beautiful and the other, forbidding.

DIRECTIONS: *Complete the chart shown here to help you analyze the theme of pastoral life as presented in "The Passionate Shepherd to His Love" and "The Nymph's Reply to the Shepherd." (Some responses are filled in for you.) Then write a statement explaining the views the two poems present on the pleasures of pastoral life.*

	"The Passionate Shepherd"	**"The Nymph's Reply"**
Stanza 1	Repetition: *live, love, pleasures* Detail: **Live with me as my love and enjoy the pleasures of nature with me.**	Repetition: *live, love, pleasures* Detail: **If your description of these pleasures were true, I would be your love.**
Stanza 2	Repetition: Detail:	Repetition: Detail:
Stanza 3	Repetition: Detail:	Repetition: Detail:
Stanza 4	Repetition: Detail:	Repetition: Detail:
Stanza 5	Repetition: Detail:	Repetition: Detail:
Stanza 6	Repetition: Detail:	Repetition: Detail:

How does each poet come to view the pastoral theme? _____

_____

_____

"The Passionate Shepherd to His Love" by Christopher Marlowe
"The Nymph's Reply to the Shepherd" by Sir Walter Raleigh

Vocabulary Builder

Word List

gall   madrigals   melodious   reckoning   wither

A. DIRECTIONS: *For each item below, write* T *if the statement is true. Write* F *if it is false.*

____ 1. Elizabethan women wore *madrigals* in their hair.

____ 2. A screeching voice is very *melodious.*

____ 3. A person filled with *gall* is often mean.

____ 4. At the end of a meal, a waiter or waitress brings the *reckoning.*

____ 5. Illness might cause someone's skin to *wither.*

B. WORD STUDY: *Based on what you have learned about the origin and meaning of the word* gall, *circle the letter of the best answer to each item below.*

1. Which of these might fill a person with *gall?*
   A. unfair treatment   B. a new pet   C. a loud noise   D. true love

2. Which of these words most likely has the same origin as *gall?*
   A. *choler,* meaning "easily angered"
   B. *bile,* meaning "inclination to anger"
   C. *gallant,* meaning "brave"
   D. *galley,* meaning "a large ship"

3. Which sentence uses the word *gall* to mean "bitterness"?
   A. Stefania had the *gall* to show up an hour late for our meeting.
   B. A loose saddle can *gall* a horses back.
   C. The ancient Greek doctor said the man's humors were unbalanced: he had too much *gall.*
   D. Fern's lack of loyalty as a friend filled me with *gall.*

All-in-One Workbook
58

Name _____ Date _____

"The Passionate Shepherd to His Love" by Christopher Marlowe
"The Nymph's Reply to the Shepherd" by Sir Walter Raleigh

Support for Writing

Use the chart below to take notes for your **comparison-and-contrast essay.** Review the poems, writing notes and citing examples that show how the speakers' views are alike and different.

	"The Passionate Shepherd to His Love"	"The Nymph's Reply to the Shepherd"
Love		
Nature		
Time		
Material World		

Sonnets 29, 106, 116, and 130 by William Shakespeare
Literary Analysis: Shakespearean Sonnet

Read the following sonnet by Michael Drayton (1563–1631). First indicate the rhyme scheme by writing the appropriate letters on the lines at the right. Then answer the questions that follow the poem.

Calling to mind since first my love began _____

Th'incertain times oft varying in their course. _____

How things still unexpectedly have run, _____

As please the Fates, by their resistless force, _____

[5]   Lastly, mine eyes amazedly have seen _____

Essex great fall, Tyrone his peace to gain. _____

The quiet end of that long-living Queen, _____

This King's fair entrance, and our peace with Spain, _____

We and the Dutch at length ourselves to sever. _____

[10]   Thus the world doth, and evermore shall reel, _____

Yet to my goddess am I constant ever, _____

Howe'er blind Fortune turn her giddy wheel. _____

Though heaven and earth prove both to me untrue, _____

Yet am I still inviolate to you. _____

Lines 7–10 refer to the failure of the Earl of Essex (Robert Devereux) to conquer the Earl of Tyrone (Hugh O'Neill), to the death of Elizabeth I, who was succeeded by James I, and to other historical events.

1. According to the rhyme scheme, is Drayton's sonnet an example of Shakespearean form or of Petrarchan form? _____

2. What is the premise stated in the poem? _____
_____

3. What is the conclusion stated in the poem? _____
_____

4. In what way is Drayton's philosophy similar to Shakespeare's? _____
_____

Sonnets 29, 106, 116, and 130 by William Shakespeare
Reading Strategy: Explain Impact of Text Structures

Readers analyze and **explain the impact of text structures on clarity of meaning** in literature by looking at how the form of a work expresses and influences what is being said. The form of the sonnet—its three quatrains and ending couplet— molds its contents. An idea, situation, or problem is usually presented in the first eight or twelve lines. This means that thoughts must be shaped to fit three quatrains, while the final couplet provides a succinct conclusion in a burst of rhyme. For example, Sonnet 130 examines the features of the speaker's beloved one by one, each time making a case against overstating her worth. The descriptions are beautifully suited to the concise format of the quatrain as each line builds on the last, leading to the surprising conclusion in the couplet.

DIRECTIONS: *Use this graphic organizer to help you understand the impact of text structures on clarity of meaning in Shakespeare's sonnets. As you read each sonnet, use the middle column to summarize in a sentence or two what the initial idea, situation, or problem is. Then, in the last column, briefly describe what you think the concluding couplet is saying.*

Sonnet	Idea, Situation, or Problem	Conclusion
Sonnet 29		
Sonnet 106		
Sonnet 116		
Sonnet 130		

Sonnets 29, 106, 116, and 130 by William Shakespeare
Vocabulary Builder

Using the Root -*chron*-

A. DIRECTIONS: *The root -chron- comes from the Greek word* khronos, *meaning "time." Complete the following paragraph using the -chron- based words provided.*

synchronize	chronic	chronologer
synchronicity	chronicle	chronology

Mr. Khronos has suffered from anxiety all his life. Some say he's a _____ worrier. His problem is that he's always watching the clock. He has to—it's his job. As a _____ of geological history, he measures time in terms of fixed periods and events. When not at work, Mr. Khronos collects clocks and keeps a _____ of his purchases. Once, a friend bought him a Felix the Cat clock at the very same moment he was picking one out for himself at another store. Talk about _____! Not surprisingly, he has managed to _____ all the timepieces in his house to Greenwich Mean Time. At some time in the future, someone will probably write the _____ of the life and times of Mr. Khronos.

Using the Word List

alters   chronicle   impediments   prefiguring   scope   sullen

B. DIRECTIONS: *Write the word from the Word List that best matches each situation that follows.*

1. She was imagining her future life as his wife. _____

2. The father of the bride did all he could to stop the wedding. _____

3. The groom oversaw the extent of the crisis. _____

4. He kept a careful account of the key events in their relationship. _____

5. Her mother's wedding dress fit the bride nearly perfectly, but some pieces of old lace needed replacing. _____

6. After her father put a stop to the wedding, she fell silent for weeks. _____

Name _____ Date _____

Sonnets 29, 106, 116, and 130 by William Shakespeare
Support for Writing

Use the graphic organizer to structure the information you have gathered about imagery. Fill in each section of the organizer to plan the basic outline of your essay.

Thesis		
Image / Emotions / Ideas	**Image / Emotions / Ideas**	**Image / Emotions / Ideas**

Relationships Among Images / Emotions / Ideas

Conclusion

On your own paper, begin your draft using the information and organization as a basis for your analysis of your chosen sonnet's imagery.

Elizabeth's Speech Before Her Troops by Queen Elizabeth I
Examination of Don Luis de Córdoba
Primary Sources: Speech and Eyewitness Account

A. DIRECTIONS: *Answer the following questions about speeches and eyewitness accounts.*

1. What purpose does a speech often serve? How does this purpose affect word choice?

   _____

   _____

2. What purpose does an eyewitness account serve? What elements can affect the authenticity of the account?

   _____

   _____

B. DIRECTIONS: *Use the following flowchart to organize the events and information from the* Examination of Don Luis de Córdoba.

Examination of Don Luis de Córdoba Eyewitness account of the defeat of the Spanish Armada

↓

↓

↓

Elizabeth's Speech Before Her Troops by Queen Elizabeth I
Examination of Don Luis de Córdoba
Vocabulary Builder

Word List

concord   galleons   obedience   realms   stead   treachery   tyrants   valor

A. DIRECTIONS: *Complete each sentence with an appropriate word from the Word List.*

1. The king requested the knight escort the queen in his _____,
   for he trusted him like a brother.

2. Noble monarchs, who live to serve their people, know nothing of _____.

3. _____ expect total and utter submission from their subjects.

4. The Spanish Armada consisted of many _____.

5. The knight proved his _____ when he risked his life to save the queen.

B. WORD STUDY: *The word* concord *comes from the Latin* concordia, *meaning "agreement." This word includes the Latin root* cord, *which means "heart." Use the following words that share the root* cord *to complete the sentences.*

concord   cordial   accord   discord

1. The warring factions finally agreed on the proposed peace _____.

2. The _____ hostess stood at the door and welcomed us to her home.

3. The _____ between mother and son stemmed from an argument about
   his curfew.

4. The company's plan to increase bonuses brought about _____ between
   the management and employees.

Name _____   Date _____

from The King James Bible
Literary Analysis: Psalm, Sermon, Parable, Metaphor and Analogy

Psalms, sermons, and parables are literary forms found in the Bible. A **psalm** is a lyric poem or a sacred song praising God. A psalm usually contains **metaphors** that imply comparison by speaking of one thing as if it were another. Many psalms were originally written to be sung. A **sermon** is a speech with a moral or religious message, usually spoken by one person to a group. Sermons often use **analogies** to compare abstract relationships to familiar ones in order to help people better understand. A **parable** is a short story that conveys a moral or religious lesson. Parables have simple plots and often contain dialogue.

DIRECTIONS: *Read each passage and answer the questions that follow.*

1. And he arose, and came to his father. But when he was yet a great way off, his father saw him, and had compassion, and ran, and fell on his neck, and kissed him.

   And the son said unto him. Father, I have sinned against heaven, and in thy sight, and am no more worthy to be called thy son.

   But the father said to his servants, Bring forth the best robe, and put it on him; and put a ring on his hand, and shoes on his feet.

   What elements in this passage are characteristic of parables? _____

   _____

2. Behold the fowls of the air: for they sow not, neither do they reap, nor gather into barns; yet your heavenly Father feedeth them. Are ye not much better than they?

   A. What is the religious message in the passage? _____

   _____

   B. Is this a psalm, sermon, or parable? _____

   _____

   C. What analogy is made in this passage? _____

   _____

3. He maketh me to lie down in green pastures; he leadeth me beside the still waters.
   He restoreth my soul: he leadeth me in the paths of righteousness for his name's sake.

   A. What metaphors are used in this passage? _____

   _____

   B. To whom does *He* refer? _____

   _____

   C. What elements in this passage are characteristic of psalms? _____

   _____

from The King James Bible

Reading Strategy: Infer Meaning and Determine Main Idea

Some passages from the Bible include difficult language and images that require you to **make inferences,** or draw conclusions, about the meaning of the passage. You can **infer meaning** by using the following strategy. First, ask yourself what you already know about the words or images in the passage. Second, look for context clues that help you understand the meaning. Look at this example from Psalm 23 showing how you can infer meaning.

Biblical Passage	What I Know	Context Clues
Thou preparest a table before me in the presence of mine enemies; thou anointest my head with oil; my cup runneth over.	I know that he's speaking to God and that he is using metaphors.	The psalm begins with the phrase "The shepherd," which means God is taking care of him; anointing with oil is probably a sign of honor; a cup that runs over must refer to having more than enough.

From these clues, the reader can infer that God is protecting the poet from his enemies, honoring him, and providing him with all that he needs.

DIRECTIONS: *Use this chart to help you infer the meaning of difficult passages in* The King James Bible. *Each time you come across a difficult passage, write it in the column labeled Biblical Passage. In the next column, write what you know about the words or ideas in the passage. Then write clues to the meaning that you find in the context. Finally, combining what you know together with the context clues, write what you think is the main idea of the passage.*

Biblical Passage	What I Know	Context Clues	Meaning

from The King James Bible
Vocabulary Builder

Using the Root *-stat-*

A. DIRECTIONS: *Combine the word root -stat-, which means "to stand," with each prefix or suffix listed below to make a word. Then use that word in a sentence.*

1. Suffix *-ic* Word: _____

   Sentence: _____

2. Prefix *thermo-* Word: _____

   Sentence: _____

3. Suffix *-ion* Word: _____

   Sentence: _____

4. Suffix *-us* Word: _____

   Sentence: _____

Using the Word List

entreated   prodigal   righteousness   stature   transgressed

B. DIRECTIONS: *The questions below consist of a related pair of words in CAPITAL LETTERS followed by four lettered pairs of words. Choose the pair that best expresses a relationship similar to that in the pair in capital letters.*

____ 1. RIGHTEOUSNESS : INJUSTICE ::
   A. pleasure : pain
   B. accurate : correct
   C. anger : emotion
   D. rule : control

____ 2. TRANSGRESS : DISOBEY ::
   A. break : rule
   B. shade : tree
   C. argue : quarrel
   D. hope : future

____ 3. ENTREAT : FORGIVENESS ::
   A. ask : favor
   B. answer : deny
   C. work : achieve
   D. deny : admit

____ 4. PRODIGAL : FORTUNE ::
   A. careful : careless
   B. glass : windows
   C. height : mountain
   D. wasteful : possessions

____ 5. STATURE : MAN ::
   A. archer : skill
   B. inches : feet
   C. agility : dancer
   D. speaker : listener

Name _____ Date _____

Support for Writing

A parable is organized like a story. It is built around a problem that one or more characters try to solve. Various events occur as the characters try to solve the problem. Eventually, a solution is found, and the parable comes to an end. In the process of telling the plot, a moral is taught. Use the lines below to organize your ideas for a parable that supports a moral in which you believe.

Who are the characters, and what do readers need to know about them?

_____

_____

_____

What is the problem that sets events in motion?

_____

_____

What happens as the characters try to solve the problem?

1. _____

2. _____

3. _____

4. _____

5. _____

How is the problem solved?

_____

_____

_____

_____

The Moral:

_____

_____

_____

Contemporary Commentary

Frank Kermode Introduces *Macbeth* by William Shakespeare

DIRECTIONS: *Use the space provided to answer the questions.*

1. Identify two liberties that Shakespeare takes with history in *Macbeth*.

   _____

   _____

   _____

2. According to Kermode, why did Shakespeare portray Banquo in a favorable light?

   _____

   _____

3. In the passage shown from Act I and discussed by Frank Kermode, what conflict does Macbeth experience?

   _____

   _____

4. What are three reasons that Macbeth should *not* kill King Duncan?

   _____

   _____

   _____

5. Why is Macbeth's soliloquy so famous, according to Kermode? Do you agree or disagree with Kermode here? Briefly explain your answer.

   _____

   _____

   _____

   _____

   _____

6. What factor does Kermode single out in order to explain the extraordinary range and flexibility of Shakespeare's language in *Macbeth*?

   _____

   _____

7. How does *Macbeth* comply with native ethical traditions, according to Kermode?

   _____

   _____

All-in-One Workbook

Contemporary Commentary
Frank Kermode Listening and Viewing

Segment 1: Meet Frank Kermode
- What is the job of a literary critic?
- Why do you think literary criticism is important to society?

_____

_____

_____

_____

Segment 2: Frank Kermode Introduces Shakespeare
- Why do you think Shakespeare has become a cultural icon?
- What do sports and theater have in common, according to Frank Kermode?

_____

_____

_____

_____

Segment 3: The Writing Process
- When Frank Kermode writes, what does he assume about his audience?
- How do you think this shapes his writing?

_____

_____

_____

_____

Segment 4: The Rewards of Writing
- According to Frank Kermode, why is it important to learn how to read well?
- Why do you think it is important to learn to read difficult texts, such as the works of Shakespeare?

_____

_____

_____

_____

Macbeth
William Shakespeare: Biography

William Shakespeare's influence ranges far and wide from his lifetime even until today. His works have influenced major artists, writers, and all speakers of the English language. Some of the biggest names in modern literature call upon Shakespearean tradition, including James Joyce, T.S. Eliot, and Virginia Woolf. Contemporary authors, such as Jane Smiley in *One Thousand Acres,* call upon Shakespeare (*King Lear* in Smiley's case). His theatrical works have been inspirations for other playwrights and moviemakers. Some movies are direct remakes, sharing the same titles as the plays. Others call upon the famous plots, such as *West Side Story's* retelling of *Romeo and Juliet.*

A. DIRECTIONS: *Use the following chart to organize your notes on Shakespeare's life and influence.*

William Shakespeare (1564—1616)				
Early Years	**Marriage and Family**	**Acting/Writing Career**	**Literary Works**	**Influence**

Name _____ Date _____

The Tragedy of Macbeth, Act I, by William Shakespeare
Literary Analysis: Elizabethan Drama

In the years before Elizabeth I came to power in England, troupes of actors traveled the English countryside performing religious plays. They performed wherever they could: in the courtyards of inns, in town squares, and in open areas on the outskirts of villages. Many of the plays they presented were based on biblical stories.

During the Elizabethan period, the style of English drama changed radically. Permanent theaters were built, giving actors not only an artistic home, but also the luxury of perfecting certain aspects of presentation. Plays began to veer away from religious themes. Instead, audiences found themselves watching plays about familiar problems and events. Playwrights used poetic language and rich imagery to tell a wide variety of stories—from dramas about tragic figures to comedies about hapless lovers. This kind of theater, with its nonreligious entertainment value, became very popular. Audiences loved watching plays about characters with motivations and feelings they could understand.

DIRECTIONS: *Answer the following questions about Act I of* The Tragedy of Macbeth.

1. What might the three witches represent to an audience used to watching plays with religious themes?

   _____

2. In what ways might the content of the following speech be said to echo the religious sentiments of Shakespeare's audience?

   . . . But I have spoke
   With one that saw him die, who did report
   That very frankly he confessed his treasons,
   Implored your Highness' pardon and set forth
   A deep repentance . . .

   _____

   _____

3. In the following speech, what is Lady Macbeth saying about her husband's character? How might such sentiments about Macbeth win an audience's sympathy?

   Glamis thou art, and Cawdor, and shalt be
   What thou art promised. Yet do I fear thy nature;
   It is too full o' the milk of human kindness
   To catch the nearest way. Thou wouldst be great,
   Art not without ambition, but without
   The illness should attend it. . . .

   _____

   _____

Name _____ Date _____

The Tragedy of Macbeth, *Act I,* by William Shakespeare
Literary Analysis: Soliloquy

The term *soliloquy* comes from the Latin *solus,* which means "alone." When a character delivers a soliloquy, he or she is usually alone on stage. A **soliloquy** is a long speech made by a character in a play. In a soliloquy, a character mulls over thoughts and feelings, expressing them aloud to the audience. In essence, a soliloquy amounts to a character thinking aloud. Characters can reveal their true thoughts, feelings, fears, and motivations to the audience without other characters gaining this information. Soliloquies provide important information to the audience.

DIRECTIONS: *Reread Lady Macbeth's soliloquy at the beginning of Act I, scene v. Answer the following questions about the soliloquy.*

1. What does Lady Macbeth share in the first part of her soliloquy? What purpose does this serve?

   _____

   _____

   _____

   _____

   _____

2. What do readers learn about Lady Macbeth's opinion of her husband from the second part of her soliloquy?

   _____

   _____

   _____

   _____

3. What is Lady Macbeth's fear? What is her plan?

   _____

   _____

4. Based on the thoughts, feelings, fears, and motivations she shares, how would you assess Lady Macbeth's character?

   _____

   _____

   _____

   _____

The Tragedy of Macbeth, Act I, by William Shakespeare
Reading Strategy: Analyze Information from Text Features

Playwrights use stage directions to help readers, actors, and directors understand how a play should look when it is staged. Stage directions can give readers hints about mood, setting, movement, and characters' intentions. Look at these opening stage directions.

An open place.
[*Thunder and lightning. Enter* THREE WITCHES.]

With very few words William Shakespeare has told you a great deal about the play.

1. Where does the scene take place?
   In "An open place," a place where there are no trees, hills, or houses.

2. What is going on at this place?
   "Thunder and lightning." The weather is bad, and the mood is a little frightening.

3. Who is in the scene?
   "Three witches enter." Right away, the reader can tell that something strange is about to happen.

DIRECTIONS: *Stage directions can guide the reader to a better understanding of a play's action. Use a graphic organizer like this one to help you pick up hints from the stage directions.*

Act/Scene	Characters	Setting	Specific Action
Act I, Scene i	Three witches	An open place	Thunder and lightning. Three witches enter.

Notes in the margin of *The Tragedy of Macbeth* and other plays provide another useful tool. To get more from what you read, see if you can figure out an annotated term or expression before you look at the margin note. Usually the context of the play provides clues. Look at these lines from *The Tragedy of Macbeth:*

MALCOLM. . . . He died
As one that had been studied[3] in his death,
To throw away the dearest thing he owed[4]
As 'twere a careless[5] trifle.

The lines may seem confusing, but if you look at the context, you will find hints about the meaning. The context makes it clear that Malcolm is praising the Thane of Cawdor for the noble way in which he died. According to Malcolm, the Thane's death turned out to be his greatest achievement. Knowing this, when you read "He died / As one that had been studied in his death," you might be able to guess that *studied* means "prepared for" or "rehearsed." Then, to check your interpretation, look at the margin note.

All-in-One Workbook
75

The Tragedy of Macbeth, Act I, by William Shakespeare
Vocabulary Builder

Word List
imperial   sovereign   surmise   treasons   valor

A. DIRECTIONS: *Fill in each blank with the word from the Word List that best completes the sentence.*

1. Macbeth's _____ in battle was unsurpassed.

2. "Acts of betrayal against the king are _____!" cried the general.

3. Macbeth's plans were faulty because they were based on a _____.

4. King Duncan is the _____ ruler of Scotland.

5. Macbeth's _____ virtues have impressed the king.

B. WORD STUDY: The Tragedy of Macbeth *is a play about the misuse of political and personal power. There are many words in the English language that have political associations. Here are a few such words you will find in Shakespeare's play:* thane, earl, lord, king, traitor. *Think of other words that might apply to political situations and relationships in the United States. For example, in the United States there are no lords or kings but there is a president. On the lines below, write as many words having to do with American political relationships as you can think of.*

_____   _____   _____

_____   _____   _____

_____   _____   _____

_____   _____   _____

Name _____ Date _____

The Tragedy of Macbeth, *Act I,* by William Shakespeare
Support for Writing

Use the idea web to record and organize ideas for your speaker introduction.

Facts About Duncan

Character Traits of Duncan

Introducing King Duncan

Anecdote

Insights

On a separate sheet, write your speaker introduction using the notes you took as a guide.

The Tragedy of Macbeth, Act II, by William Shakespeare
Literary Analysis: Blank Verse, Prose, and Comic Relief

Blank verse consists of lines of poetry written in iambic pentameter. Each line contains five poetic feet of stressed and unstressed syllables. The form is flexible and versatile and can produce the effect of smooth, natural speech in a way that other metrical patterns cannot. For this reason, Shakespeare relied primarily on blank verse throughout his plays. However, Shakespeare occasionally used prose, especially for the speech of characters from lower stations in life. He often uses these characters, and their break from "lofty" language, as a source of comic relief. He also employed occasional rhymes when it seemed appropriate to a particular character: The witches in *The Tragedy of MacBeth*, for example, often speak in rhymes. Finally, like most dramatists of the English Renaissance, Shakespeare often used one or more rhymed lines of dialogue to signal that a scene had ended or that new players must make their entrances, in this way alerting offstage players or other members of the company.

A. DIRECTIONS: *Following is a series of passages from* The Tragedy of Macbeth. *On the line below each passage, identify it as "rhyme" or "blank verse." Then scan the lines that are in blank verse by marking the stressed and unstressed syllables.*

1. **SECOND WITCH.** When the hurlyburly's done.
   When the battle's lost and won.

   _____

2. **ROSS.** I'll see it done.
   KING. What he hath lost, noble Macbeth hath won.

   _____

3. **ROSS.** The King hath happily received, Macbeth,
   The news of thy success. And when he reads
   Thy personal venture in the rebel's fight,
   His wonders and his praises do contend
   Which should be thine or his.

   _____

B. DIRECTIONS: *Read the following excerpt from the Porter's speech in Act II, scene iii. Paraphrase the lines and explain how the use of prose and its content provide comic relief following the intense scene with Macbeth and Lady Macbeth.*

PORTER. Here's a knocking indeed! If a man were porter of hell gate, he should have old turning the key. [*Knock.*] Knock, knock, knock! Who's there, i' th' name of Beelzebub? . . . Faith, here's an equivocator, that could swear in both the scales against either scale; who committed treason enough for God's sake, yet could not equivocate heaven.

   _____

   _____

   _____

The Tragedy of Macbeth, Act II, by William Shakespeare
Reading Strategy: Patterns of Organization

Some readers see that a text is written in verse and automatically assume they will have a difficult time understanding it. Verse texts can indeed seem more complicated than prose. However, there are many tools a reader can use to break verse down into manageable and understandable ideas. A good strategy is to read verse passages for the ideas that they present rather than simply as individual lines of poetry. Look at the way the author uses **patterns of organization** to present ideas. The main ways that Shakespeare organizes his text are the meter, the line breaks, the punctuation of sentences, and the occasional use of rhyme. To clarify the meaning of a passage, first read it in sentences to understand the complete thought. Then, analyze the meter and line breaks. Ask yourself *What does Shakespeare want to emphasize by breaking the line here?* Finally, look for rhyme to see how particular lines and ideas are connected. If you reach the end of a passage and don't understand what you've read, go back through the passage slowly, paraphrasing as you go.

DIRECTIONS: *Read this passage from Act II, scene iii. Answer the questions that follow.*

MALCOLM. This murderous shaft that's shot
Hath not yet lighted, and our safest way
Is to avoid the aim. Therefore to horse;
And let us not be dainty of leave-taking,
But shift away. There's warrant in that theft
Which steals itself when there's no mercy left.

1. How many sentences are there in this passage?

   _____

2. Does Shakespeare use a particular meter in this passage? If so, what is it?

   _____

3. What ideas does Shakespeare emphasize with the line breaks he uses in this passage?

   _____

4. How does Shakespeare connect and emphasize ideas with rhyme in this passage?

   _____

5. What is the basic idea of the passage?

   _____

   _____

   As you continue reading *The Tragedy of Macbeth,* use the elements and patterns of organization to analyze the meaning of the text.

The Tragedy of Macbeth, Act II, by William Shakespeare
Vocabulary Builder

Using the Root -voc-

A. DIRECTIONS: *The word root -voc- means "voice" or "calling." Read each definition and then choose the word that best completes each sentence.*

evocative (adj.), calling forth an emotional response
provocative (adj.), serving to provoke or stimulate
vocation (n.), a summons or strong inclination to a particular state or course of action; the work at which a person is regularly employed
vociferously (adv.), marked by or given to insistent outcry
vocalize (adj.), to give voice to

1. The witches speak to Macbeth _____; they will not be quieted.
2. Macbeth finds the witches' predictions very _____.
3. The setting of the first scene in *Macbeth* is _____ of loneliness.
4. Macbeth's _____ at the beginning of the play might be said to be that of a warrior.

Word List

augment   equivocate   multitudinous   palpable   predominance   stealthy

B. DIRECTIONS: *Each question below consists of a pair of words in CAPITAL LETTERS followed by four lettered pairs of words. Choose the pair that best expresses a relationship similar to that expressed in the pair in capital letters.*

___ 1. MULTITUDINOUS : MANY ::
    A. gigantic : large
    B. some : few
    C. up : down
    D. survive : prosper

___ 2. AUGMENT : PREVENT ::
    A. terrify : frighten
    B. beg : plead
    C. hollow : empty
    D. help : hinder

___ 3. STEALTHY : OBVIOUS ::
    A. quiet : healthful
    B. adventuresome : timid
    C. fat : heavy
    D. polluted : filthy

___ 4. PALPABLE : TANGIBLE ::
    A. stealthy : furtive
    B. shy : outgoing
    C. few : multitudinous
    D. ambitious : lazy

___ 5. EQUIVOCATE : DECEPTION ::
    A. whine : exhibit
    B. beautiful : attractive
    C. death : die
    D. sing : song

___ 6. PREDOMINANCE : WEAKNESS ::
    A. valor : courage
    B. success : failure
    C. happiness : gladness
    D. selfishness : miserliness

The Tragedy of Macbeth, *Act II,* by William Shakespeare
Support for Writing

Support for Writing

Use the graphic organizers to record your responses to the Porter's speech in Act II, scene iii, and Thomas de Quincey's responses. Underline or highlight similar responses.

The Tragedy of Macbeth Act II, scene iii Porter's speech	
My Responses	**Thomas de Quincey's Responses**

On a separate page, write an essay comparing your responses to the Porter's speech to Thomas de Quincey's. Use your notes in the chart to help you organize ideas.

The Tragedy of Macbeth, *Act III*, by William Shakespeare
Literary Analysis: Conflict

In literature, as in life, **conflict** is a struggle between two opposing forces. It is an essential dramatic element; it builds tension and holds the reader's interest. Without conflict there can be no drama. The use of **dramatic irony** intersifies the tension, letting readers know things that characters do not. There are many conflicts within Shakespeare's *The Tragedy of Macbeth.* Some of them are external conflicts that take place between characters with opposing goals. Others are internal conflicts that take place within the consciousness of certain characters. Often conflict begins in one scene and escalates throughout a number of scenes that follow.

DIRECTIONS: *Answer the following questions, and then find a quotation from Act III of* The Tragedy of Macbeth *that supports your answer.*

1. In Scene i, what is the conflict between the murderers and Banquo?

   _____

   _____

   _____

   Quotation: _____

2. Why is Banquo in conflict with Macbeth?

   _____

   _____

   _____

   Quotation: _____

3. Why does Macbeth experience an internal conflict at the state dinner?

   _____

   _____

   _____

   Quotation: _____

4. Why is Lady Macbeth in conflict with Macbeth during the state dinner?

   _____

   _____

   _____

   Quotation: _____

5. How does Macbeth use dramatic irony to comment or Banquo's fate?

   _____

   _____

   _____

   Quotation: _____

Name _____ Date _____

The Tragedy of Macbeth, *Act III*, by William Shakespeare
Reading Strategy: Identify Cause-and-Effect Relationships

Identify cause-and-effect relationships in a literary work by looking for connections between two actions or two passages in the work. Your goal is to see how one event or statement (cause) leads to a later one (effect).

In any narrative or drama, the events form a chain of causes and effects. One event causes another, then that second event causes yet another, and so on, from beginning to end. For example, in *Macbeth*, the witches' prediction in Act I that Macbeth will be king leads Macbeth to take the step of killing Duncan in Act II in order to seize the crown. This action, in turn, leads to Macbeth's unstable mental state, which later produces its own effects.

DIRECTIONS: *Fill in the empty boxes in the following series of cause-and-effect relationships. On the lines provided, briefly explain why each event is the effect of the previous one and causes the following one.*

[box]	leads to	[box]	leads to	[box]	leads to	Effect: [box]

Explanation of the First Cause-and Effect Relationship:

_____

_____

Explanation of the Second Cause-and Effect Relationship:

_____

_____

The Tragedy of Macbeth, *Act III*, by William Shakespeare
Vocabulary Builder

Word List

dauntless   indissoluble   infirmity   malevolence   predominant

A. DIRECTIONS: *For each item, choose the lettered word or phrase that is most nearly opposite in meaning to the numbered word. Write the letter of your choice in the blank.*

____ 1. infirmity
   A. bad mood   C. sickness
   B. good cheer   D. good health

____ 2. predominant
   A. special   C. minor
   B. ordinary   D. sleepy

____ 3. indissoluble
   A. easily undone   C. often repeated
   B. not to go forward   D. not to be heard

____ 4. dauntless
   A. agreeable   C. hapless
   B. humorless   D. fearful

____ 5. malevolence
   A. happiness   C. good will
   B. ill feelings   D. desire

B. WORD STUDY: *The prefix mal- means "bad or badly," or "poor or poorly." Rewrite each sentence, replacing the underlined word or words with a word that contains the prefix mal-.*

1. The airplane engine continued to <u>function poorly</u> during a routine inspection.

   _____

2. Sheri was <u>poorly adjusted</u> to her new school environment.

   _____

3. The doctor said my problem with digesting proteins came from <u>improper absorption</u> of certain nutrients.

   _____

4. Every time Tomas comes for a visit, I remember that he is a <u>person who is not content.</u>

   _____

The Tragedy of Macbeth, *Act III,* by William Shakespeare
Support for Writing

Use the graphic organizer to record ideas for your soliloquy in response to the events in Act III, scene iv.

Summary of Key Events:	
Macbeth's Words / Actions	**Your Responses**

On a separate page, write your soliloquy, including your responses to Macbeth's words and actions. Be sure to write your soliloquy in blank verse, mimicking Shakespeare's meter.

Name _____ Date _____

The Tragedy of Macbeth, *Act IV,* by William Shakespeare
Literary Analysis: Imagery

Imagery can create responses from any of the reader's senses: sight, hearing, touch, smell, or taste. Written images can illuminate for the reader the meaning of both individual moments and patterns of meaning that run throughout the text. Many of the images Shakespeare calls upon are **archetypal,** images and symbols that are expressed repeatedly in art and literature across a variety of cultures. These archetypal images have a universal appeal and clearly support the underlying meaning of the text. Look at this imagery-laden quotation from the First Witch in *The Tragedy of Macbeth,* Act IV.

> Pour in sow's blood, that hath eaten
> Her nine farrow, grease that's sweaten
> From the murderer's gibbet throw into the flame.

This passage contains visual imagery: pig's blood; a mother pig eating her nine young. It also contains imagery of touch: grease from the noose that hangs a murderer; grease added to a flame.

Paying attention to imagery can guide you to a deeper understanding of the text. As you read, be on the lookout for repeated imagery; for example, think about the image of blood that runs throughout the entire text of *The Tragedy of Macbeth.* Blood is an archetypal image that can mean many different things: loyalty, guilt, revenge, death, brotherhood, parent-child relationship, royalty, for example. Think about the significance of each of these ideas within the plot of the play.

DIRECTIONS: *Read the following passages from* The Tragedy of Macbeth *and identify the imagery in each. Then write the connection, or what the image makes you think of.*

1. "When shall we three meet again? / In thunder, lightning, or in rain?"

   Imagery: _____

   Connection: _____

2. "Stars, hide your fires; / Let not light see my black and deep desires . . ."

   Imagery: _____

   Connection: _____

3. "I have no spur / To prick the sides of my intent, but only / Vaulting ambition, which o'er-leaps itself / And falls on th' other . . ."

   Imagery: _____

   Connection: _____

4. "But now I am cabined, cribbed, confined, bound in / To saucy doubts and fears . . ."

   Imagery: _____

   Connection: _____

The Tragedy of Macbeth, *Act IV,* by William Shakespeare
Reading Strategy: Analyze Text Structures

Text structures are the parts of a piece of writing that develop and support the theme, plot, and other elements of the writing. Imagery—the language that writers use to re-create sensory experiences—is a type of text structure. Shakespeare uses imagery to develop the theme in *Macbeth.* As you read Act IV, look for ways in which Shakespeare uses imagery related to blood and to babies and children. Notice when he uses these images and how they connect to each other and to characters and events. Then, analyze how the images how convey the play's themes

DIRECTIONS: *Use the following chart to help you recognize how a pattern of images reinforces the themes of the play.*

Image Pattern	Blood	Babies and Children
Examples:	• IV, i 37 •	• IV, i 30 • • •
Relation to Theme:		

The Tragedy of Macbeth, *Act IV,* by William Shakespeare
Vocabulary Builder

Using the Root *-cred-*

A. DIRECTIONS: *Remember that the word root -cred- means "belief." Use the following words to complete the sentences.*

> credibility   credence   credentials

1. The news reporter had to show his _____, or proof of his profession, to get into the crime scene.

2. The mayor's _____ was ruined when it was discovered that he had stolen funds from his office.

3. Those accusations are completely ridiculous; I give them no _____ whatsoever.

Using the Word List

avarice   credulous   intemperance   judicious   pernicious   sundry

B. DIRECTIONS: *Match each word in the left column with its definition in the right column. Write the letter of the definition on the blank next to the word it defines.*

___ 1. pernicious   A. lack of restraint

___ 2. judicious   B. greed

___ 3. sundry   C. tendency to believe readily

___ 4. intemperance   D. showing good judgment

___ 5. avarice   E. various

___ 6. credulous   F. highly injurious or destructive

C. DIRECTIONS: *Use words from the Word List to fill in the blanks.*

1. King Duncan was known as a wise and _____ ruler.

2. When it comes to power and fortune, Macbeth shows great _____.

3. Had Banquo been less _____ about Macbeth's evil intentions, he might have been able to save his own life.

4. Macbeth's control of Scotland had a _____ effect upon the country.

5. The murderers had committed _____ crimes before they killed Banquo.

6. Macbeth's _____ manifested itself when he had Banquo killed.

The Tragedy of Macbeth, *Act IV,* by William Shakespeare
Support for Writing

Use the graphic organizer to record ideas about Macbeth's character and its evolution throughout the play. Focus on the archetypal image of the "fall."

The Tragedy of Macbeth	
Act I	Macbeth's predominant qualities: Major events:
Act II	Macbeth's predominant qualities: Major events:
Act III	Macbeth's predominant qualities: Major events:
Act IV	Macbeth's predominant qualities: Major events:
Act V	Macbeth's predominant qualities: Major events:

On a separate sheet, write an analysis of Macbeth's fall. Use your notes on the evolution of his character and the major events that inspire these changes as a basis for your analysis of the archetype.

The Tragedy of Macbeth, *Act V,* by William Shakespeare
Literary Analysis: Shakespearean Tragedy

People have always been fascinated by tragedy because it allows readers to see themselves and their potential for self-destruction. Each tragedy rests upon the premise that the tragic hero brings about his or her own downfall, often because of an inborn weakness in character, a **tragic flaw.** This flaw can be pride, lust, greed, and so on. In a typical tragedy, the tragic hero begins the play as a respected, usually high-born, member of society. His or her virtues are described at length during the early scenes. In *The Tragedy of Macbeth,* we first meet Macbeth as a hero in battle, a loyal supporter of King Duncan, a good husband, and an excellent friend. With all these wonderful qualities, what could Macbeth want that he does not already possess? What could possibly go wrong? The answer is, of course, human nature. With all the things Macbeth has, he wants most acutely that which he *doesn't* have. His ambition becomes his master, his tragic flaw.Even though Macbeth succumbs to his desire for power, his actions as the end of the play approaches reflect the man whom he used to be. His **tragic impulse** to confront his inevitable tragedy with bravery reminds readers of what makes Macbeth a tragic hero.

DIRECTIONS: *Answer the following questions about Macbeth's character.*

1. If Macbeth had never met the three witches, do you think the events of the play would have turned out the same way? Give reasons for your answer.

   _____

   _____

   _____

   _____

2. Is Macbeth aware of how ambitious he is? Support your response.

   _____

   _____

   _____

   _____

3. Is Lady Macbeth certain of Macbeth's ambition before he kills Duncan? Support your response.

   _____

   _____

   _____

   _____

4. How does Macbeth's tragic impulse manifest itself?

   _____

   _____

   _____

   _____

The Tragedy of Macbeth, *Act V,* by William Shakespeare
Reading Strategy: Infer Beliefs of the Period

The plays of William Shakespeare include many works of dramatic genius with much to say about the course of human events and history. In many ways these plays are universal; they transcend ethnic and cultural boundaries with their tales of fallen heroes, star-crossed lovers, and misguided nobles. But Shakespeare's plays also tell a reader quite a bit about the time period in which Shakespeare himself lived. The playwright applied many of the philosophies, beliefs, and superstitions of his day to illuminate the historical periods about which he wrote. As you look back over *The Tragedy of Macbeth,* ask yourself which ideas might be specific to the time period when William Shakespeare lived and which ones might be said to cross boundaries of time and place.

DIRECTIONS: *You can get more from what you read by analyzing a play or story for its historical perspectives. Use the graphic organizer below to find and keep track of places in the play that reveal something about the time in which the author lived. Two of the boxes are filled in for you. Fill in the rest with other examples from the text.*

Quotation	Meaning
THIRD WITCH: "All hail, Macbeth, that shalt be king hereafter!"	Macbeth seems to take this prophecy as the whole truth. People who lived in Shakespeare's time may have believed that certain individuals could read the future.

The Tragedy of Macbeth, *Act V,* by William Shakespeare
Vocabulary Builder

Word List

antidote   clamorous   harbingers   perturbation   pristine   recoil   vulnerable

A. DIRECTIONS: *Match each word in the left column with its definition in the right column. Write the letter of the definition on the line next to the word it defines.*

  ___ 1. antidote   A. noisy

  ___ 2. clamorous   B. forerunners

  ___ 3. harbingers   C. pure; untouched; unspoiled

  ___ 4. perturbation   D. disorder

  ___ 5. pristine   E. remedy

  ___ 6. recoil   F. weak

  ___ 7. vulnerable   G. draw back

B. WORD STUDY: *Knowing that the word root -turb- means "to disturb," create a sentence using each of the following* italicized *words.*

perturbed, adj., greatly disturbed in mind

turbine, n., a machine that changes the movement of a fluid into mechanical energy

turbojet, n., an airplane powered by turbines

turbid, adj., cloudy, muddy; mixed up or confused

1. _____

2. _____

3. _____

4. _____

The Tragedy of Macbeth, *Act V,* by William Shakespeare
Grammar and Style: Using Adjective and Adverb Clauses

An **adjective clause** is a dependent clause that modifies a noun or a pronoun. Adjective clauses perform the same function as adjectives.

> **EXAMPLE:** *The Tragedy of Macbeth,* <u>which was written by William Shakespeare</u>, tells the story of Macbeth's downfall.

An **adverb clause** is a dependent clause that modifies a verb, an adjective, or an adverb. Adverb clauses perform the same function as adverbs. Adverb clauses tell how, when, where, why, to what extent, or under what conditions.

> **EXAMPLE:** Macbeth's story ends tragically <u>because he succumbs to his tragic flaw of</u> ambition. *(why)*

A. PRACTICE: *Underline each adjective and adverb clause. Identify whether the adverb clauses tell how, when, where, why, to what extent, or under what conditions.*

1. Lady Macbeth begins to plot against King Duncan after she reads Macbeth's letter.

   _____

2. Macbeth, who was loyal and brave, listens to Lady Macbeth's persuasion.

   _____

3. The speech that the Porter makes about knocking on the gate provides comic relief.

   _____

4. Banquo suffers at Macbeth's hands because he knows of the sisters' prophecy.

   _____

B. Writing Application: *Write two sentences about* The Tragedy of Macbeth *using an adjective clause in one and an adverb in the other.*

1. _____

   _____

2. _____

   _____

The Tragedy of Macbeth, *Act V,* by William Shakespeare
Support for Writing

Use the chart to record passages from Macbeth that support the ideas of judgment—either in life or in the afterlife

Earthly Consequences	Fate of Soul in Afterlife

On a separate paper, write a response to Stephen Greenblatt's criticism. Use the quotations you recorded in the prewriting chart above as a basis for your argument.

Name _____ Date _____

from **Oedipus the King** by Sophocles
from **Faust** by Johann Wolfgang von Goethe
Literary Analysis: Tragedy

Tragedy is marked by the inevitability of a hero's downfall. Characters cannot escape the hands of Fate. The **tragic hero** of such a work is usually an example of excellence, in character and breeding, with the exception of one quality—a **tragic flaw.** A tragic flaw might manifest as pride, ambition, greed, or any other excessive and unredeeming quality. The tragic hero inevitably succumbs to the flaw in his or her character, which leads the hero to his or her inevitable demise.

The genre of tragedy originates with the ancient Greeks. The theory behind tragedy suggests that the work should elicit feelings of tenderness, pity, or sorrow in the audience. This quality is called *pathos.* As a result of *pathos,* the audience undergoes *catharsis,* or a sense of purifying the mind through the feeling and release of intense emotions. From the tragedies of ancient Greece through contemporary, realistic tragedy, playwrights work to effect change in an audience through high drama.

DIRECTIONS: *Answer the following questions to analyze the tragedies of* Macbeth, Oedipus, *and* Faust.

1. What role does Fate play in the inevitability of the tragic hero's downfall?
   Macbeth: _____
   Oedipus: _____
   Faust: _____

2. What elements of the work (Fate, tragic flaw, events) elicit feelings of tenderness, pity, or sorrow?
   Macbeth: _____
   Oedipus: _____
   Faust: _____

3. What changes do the tragic heroes undergo to present a message that effects change? What change do the playwrights examine?

   _____

   _____

   _____

from **Oedipus the King** by Sophocles
from **Faust** by Johann Wolfgang von Goethe

Vocabulary Builder

Word List

infamy   insatiableness   reverence   rites   tenacity

DIRECTIONS: *Fill in each blank with the word that correctly completes the sentence.*

1. Faust's _____ was the cause of his making a deal with the devil.

2. No matter how many _____ Oedipus observed, his city was still under siege because of his history.

3. Oedipus will live in _____ for killing his father and marrying his mother.

4. Faust showed his lack of _____ for God by making a deal with Mephistopheles.

5. Oedipus's _____ is evident in the fact that he dedicates his life to suffering for his mistakes.

Name _____ Date _____

Support for Writing

Use the chart to organize your ideas for your comparison of Macbeth, Oedipus, and Faust.

	Macbeth	**Oedipus**	**Faust**
Attributes of a Tragic Hero			
Description of the Tragic Flaw			
Most Sympathetic Character			

On a separate sheet, write your comparison essay examining the tragic heroes Macbeth, Oedipus, and Faust. Use your prewriting notes as a basis for your essay.

Essential Questions Workshop—Unit 2

In their poems, plays, and nonfiction works, the writers in Unit Two express ideas that relate to the three Essential Questions framing this book. Review the literature in the unit. Then, for each Essential Question, choose an author and at least one passage from the author's work that expresses an idea related to the question. Use this chart to complete your work.

Essential Question	Author/Selection	Literary Passage
What is the relationship between place and literature?		
How does literature shape or reflect society?		
What is the relationship of the writer to tradition?		

Name _____ Date _____

Unit 3 Introduction
Names and Terms to Know

A. DIRECTIONS: *Write a brief sentence explaining each of the following names and terms. You will find all of the information you need in the Unit Introduction in your textbook.*

1. Cavaliers and Roundheads: _____

_____

2. Glorious Revolution: _____

_____

3. Agricultural Revolution: _____

_____

4. Elector of Hanover: _____

5. Yorktown: _____

6. Bastille: _____

B. DIRECTIONS: *Use the hints below to help you answer each question.*

1. How did the monarchy's power change from Charles I to George I? *[Hints: What happened to the Stuart kings and why? How did George I come to power? What was his attitude toward ruling England?]*

_____

_____

_____

2. What were the economic and social effects of the Industrial and Agricultural Revolutions? *[Hints: What was the Industrial Revolution? What was the Agricultural Revolution?]*

_____

_____

_____

3. How did the American and French Revolutions help turn the old order "upside-down"? *[Hints: What happened in each of these revolutions? What power shift did they signal?]*

_____

_____

_____

Unit 3 Introduction

Essential Question 1: What is the relationship between place and literature?

A. DIRECTIONS: *Answer the questions about the first Essential Question in the Introduction about the relationship between place and literature. All the information you need is in the Unit 3 Introduction in your textbook.*

I. *London as Literary Capital*

    a. What developments kept London at the center of English culture? _____

    _____

    b. What disasters in London became the focus of literary works, and who were the authors of these works? _____

    _____

II. *Roads Leading to Novels*

    a. The building of roads into the countryside created opportunities for _____

    _____

    b. How did the French author Stendhal define the novel? _____

    _____

III. *Coffeehouses and Literature*

    a. What were coffeehouses, and who met in them? _____

    _____

    b. What were *The Tatler* and *The Spectator?* _____

    c. What is Samuel Johnson's *Dictionary?* _____

    _____

IV. *Influence of the Countryside*

    a. As a result of works like Thomas Gray's *Elegy in a Country Churchyard,* the dominant mood of English poetry became _____

    b. Writers looked to the countryside for _____

    c. The _____ replace the _____ as the preferred setting and subject for English writers.

B. DIRECTIONS: *Answer the questions based on the Essential Question Vocabulary words.*

  1. What are the main advantages of being in a large *city?* _____

  _____

  2. Why might people prefer *country* living to life in the city and the suburbs? _____

  _____

  3. What elements of modern life have increased people's *mobility?* _____

Unit 3 Introduction

Essential Question 2: How does literature shape or reflect society?

A. DIRECTIONS: *On the lines provided, answer the questions about the second Essential Question in the Introduction about the writer and society. All the information you need is in the Unit 3 Introduction in your textbook.*

I. *Milton's Grace and Newton's Gravity*

    a. Why did the English eventually create a separation between church and state?

    _____

    b. What is the theme of Milton's *Paradise Lost?* _____

    c. What view of the world did Isaac Newton present in his *Mathematical Principles of Natural Philosophy?* _____

    _____

    d. On what areas of study was increasing emphasis placed? _____

    _____

II. *Literature and Rationalism*

    a. What is satire, and why did it flourish at this time? _____

    _____

    b. Two examples of satiric writing include _____and _____

    c. What was the original purpose of the essays written by Addison and others?

    _____

    d. Describe the book known as the first English novel. _____

    _____

    e. What did John Wesley do? _____

    _____

B. DIRECTIONS: *Complete the sentence stems based on the Essential Question Vocabulary words.*

    1. *Deism* connected science and religion by _____

    2. Eighteenth-century thinkers favored the *rational* approach to all things, an approach based on _____

    _____

    3. The *values* of the 1700s differ from ours today in that _____

    _____

Unit 3 Introduction

Essential Question 3: What is the relationship of the writer to tradition?

A. DIRECTIONS: *On the lines provided, answer the questions about the third Essential Question in the Introduction about the relationship between the writer and tradition. All the information you need is in the Unit 3 Introduction in your textbook.*

I. *Renaissance and Reformation Traditions*

   a. Why can John Donne be regarded as a child of both the Renaissance and Reformation?
   _____

   b. What is the *carpe diem* theme, and which writers developed it?
   _____

   c. What story did Milton's *Paradise Lost* tell? _____

II. *Milton and the Poet's New Role*

   a. In what sense did Milton take on the role of the prophet? _____
   _____

   b. What later poets followed in Milton's footsteps? _____

III. *New Literary Forms*

   a. What was the heroic couplet, and who perfected it? _____
   _____

   b. Both the essay and the novel require an audience of _____
   _____

   c. What are the modern descendants of the periodical essay? _____

   d. What new genre would become the dominant literary form, and what are its
   characteristics? _____
   _____

B. DIRECTIONS: *Answer the questions based on the Essential Question Vocabulary words.*

1. Why might a popular king strengthen the *monarchy* in general? _____
   _____

2. What kind of subject matter would you expect to see portrayed in an *epic* movie?
   _____

3. Under what circumstances might an ordinary person be called a *prophet*? _____
   _____

Name _____ Date _____

Following-Through Activities

A. CHECK YOUR COMPREHENSION: *Use this chart to complete the Check Your Comprehension activity in the Unit 3 Introduction. In the middle column, list two key concepts for each Essential Question. In the right column, list a key author for each concept. (One set of answers is given for the question about place and literature.)*

Essential Question	Key Concept	Work (Author)
Place and Literature	1. Threats to London 2. _____	1. Samuel Pepys 2. _____
Literature and Society	1. _____ 2. _____	1. _____ 2. _____
Writer and Tradition	1. _____ 2. _____	1. _____ 2. _____

B. EXTEND YOUR LEARNING: *Use this graphic organizer to help you evaluate the debate on the question of the divine right of kings.*

Resolved: That a king rules by divine right and cannot be deposed.	
For the Resolution	**Against the Resolution**

Logical arguments:
  a. _____
  b. _____
  c. _____
	Logical arguments:
	  a. _____
	  b. _____
	  c. _____

Emotional appeals:
  a. _____
  b. _____
  c. _____
	Emotional appeals:
	  a. _____
	  b. _____
	  c. _____

Movements & eye contact _____	*Movements & eye contact* _____
Tone & pitch of voice _____	*Tone & pitch of voice* _____

All-in-One Workbook
103

Works of John Donne
Literary Analysis: Metaphysical Poetry

Metaphysical poetry uses conceits and paradoxes as devices to convey the poet's message. A **metaphysical conceit** is an elaborate metaphor comparing very different ideas, images, or objects. The metaphysical poets used conceits that ranged from elaborate images developed over many lines to simple images presented in only a line or two.

DIRECTIONS: *On the lines following each excerpt, write what is being compared and explain the meaning of the conceit or metaphor expressed.*

1. Death be not proud, though some have called thee
   Mighty and dreadful, for thou art not so;
   For those whom thou think'st thou dost overthrow,
   Die not, poor death, nor yet canst thou kill me.
   From rest and sleep, which but thy pictures be,
   . . .
   One short sleep past, we wake eternally . . .

   _____
   _____
   _____
   _____
   _____

2. If they be two [souls], they are two so
      As stiff twin compasses are two;
   Thy soul, the fixed foot, makes no show
      To move, but doth, if th' other do.

   _____
   _____
   _____
   _____
   _____

All-in-One Workbook
104

Works of John Donne

Reading Strategy: Analyze the Author's Perspective and How It Affects the Meaning

To understand a poem it is helpful to **analyze the author's perspective,** or the view that he is taking, and **how it affects the meaning.** You will find in your reading of Donne's poetry that although the speaker and author are separate, they are closely tied. We can gain insight into the author's perspective by examining the speaker's motivation. What does the poem tell you about the speaker's circumstances? Are the words a cry of the heart? A song? As you read, ask yourself about the speaker's motives and identify the situation that gives rise to the speech.

DIRECTIONS: *The chart records some of the speaker's words from the poem "Song" in one column and an inference about the speaker's situation and motive for speaking in the second column. Continue adding the speaker's words and his possible motives as you read the poem.*

Speaker's Words	Motivation
"Sweetest love, I do not go, For weariness of thee."	He has to leave his beloved. He wants to reassure her that he still loves her and is not tired of her.

Works of John Donne
Vocabulary Builder

Using the Prefix *con-*

A. DIRECTIONS: *Each of the following sentences includes an italicized word that contains the prefix* con-, *meaning "with" or "together." Fill in each blank with a phrase that completes the sentence and reveals the meaning of the italicized word. Consult a dictionary if you need to find out the meaning of a root word.*

1. If a group of people is *convivial,* its members would _____.

2. *Contemporary* art is different from classical art in that it _____.

3. A big company can be a *conglomerate,* which means _____.

4. When two people have a *connection,* they _____.

5. Members of a *concert* band play _____.

6. A *container* is a good place to _____.

7. If you are in *contact* with someone, _____.

8. The *context* of an unfamiliar word _____.

Using the Word List

contention   coveteousness   laity   piety   profanation   trepidation

B. DIRECTIONS: *Write a word or words from the Word List to complete each sentence.*

1. Strong disagreement over the proper role of the congregation caused a problem between the priests and the _____.

2. The congregation approved of George's obvious _____ when he entered the cathedral because they believed it to be evidence of his _____.

3. The guide reminded the tourists to remove their shoes before entering the mosque, explaining that wearing shoes would be a _____.

4. The child gazed at the toy-shop display with undisguised _____.

Works of John Donne
Grammar and Style: Comparative and Superlative Adjectives and Adverbs

Adjectives and adverbs have **comparative** and **superlative** forms.

- When two things are being compared, we use the comparative form. Most comparatives are formed by adding the suffix *-er: bigger, faster, higher*. Some comparatives are formed by using the word *more or less: more beautiful, more slowly, less surprising.*

- When three or more things are being compared, we use the superlative form. Most superlatives are formed by adding the suffix *-est: biggest, fastest, highest*. Some superlatives are formed by using the word *most or least: most beautiful, most slowly, least surprising.*

A. PRACTICE: Identify the italicized adjective or adverb as a comparative or superlative form. Write *comparative* or *superlative* on the line.

1. She played the *most melodious* song on the dulcimer. _____

2. His *happiest* moments were when he was with her. _____

3. He returned *more quickly* than he had expected. _____

4. He was several years *older* than his wife. _____

B. Writing Application: Write the correct form of the adjective or adverb on the line.

1. (easy) Of the two poems, this one is _____ to understand.

2. (interesting) The _____ idea in that piece is "No man is an island."

3. (loud) Of all the bells in the tower, this one is the _____.

4. (sorrowful) This parting made her feel _____ than the last one did.

5. (early) Of the four monks, the one who got up _____ was supposed to ring the bell.

6. (soon) The _____ her husband could return would be in five months.

7. (inspiring) Which of these three selections did you find the _____?

8. (courageously) Who acts _____ —the wife or the husband?

9. (difficult) Which do you think is the _____ stanza in these poems?

10. (fluently) Of the three students, Anthony can read aloud _____.

Works of John Donne
Support for Writing

Use the chart below to help plan your biographical narrative. In the first column, list facts from Donne's biography that you think are significant. In the second column, write relevant information from the background material. In the third column, write lines, passages, or ideas from his poems and "Meditation 17" that you can connect to his biography and the background information.

Biography	Background	Writing

On a separate page, describe your plan for a biographical narrative based on Donne's life and works. Remember that your narrative should be based on a sequence of events, and it should communicate the significance of these events to your audience.

"On My First Son," "Still to Be Neat," and **"Song: To Celia"** by Ben Jonson

Literary Analysis: Epigrams

An **epigram** is a short poem with a **universal theme.** In an epigram, brevity, clarity, and permanence are emphasized. Short epigrams or lines from epigrams are often used as inscriptions on buildings or statues, or as an epitaph for a gravestone. For example, the lines "Rest in soft peace, and, asked, say here doth lie/Ben Jonson his best piece of poetry" is a good epitaph for Jonson's son. The English poet Samuel Taylor Coleridge wrote the following epigram to define epigrams:

What is an epigram? A dwarfish whole,
Its body brevity, and wit its soul.

A. DIRECTIONS: *Read each of the excerpts below and circle those that can be considered epigrammatic.*

1. Mary had a little lamb,
   Its fleece was white as snow.

2. Give me a look, give me a face,
   That makes simplicity a grace;

3. Drink to me only with thine eyes.

4. To err is human, to forgive divine.
   (Alexander Pope, *Essay on Criticism*)

5. What's in a name? That which we call a rose
   By any other name would smell as sweet.
   (Shakespeare, *Romeo and Juliet*)

B. DIRECTIONS: *On the lines below, write two short two- or four-line epigrams: one in praise of friendship and the other as an epitaph.*

_____

_____

_____

_____

_____

_____

_____

_____

_____

"On My First Son," "Still to Be Neat," and **"Song: To Celia"** by Ben Jonson

Reading Strategy: Draw Inferences

When you **draw inferences** and confirm them, you use **text evidence** and your own **experience** to make informed guesses about what you are reading. Drawing inferences helps you better understand what the writer is trying to say. You can draw inferences from the first lines of a poem, and further reading may confirm or disprove your inference. For example, in the first three lines of the poem "Still to Be Neat," Jonson says

Still [always] to be neat, still to be dressed,

As you were going to a feast;

Still to be powdered, still perfumed;

You might infer that the speaker does not appreciate a perfectly groomed woman. Line 6 helps confirm that inference: "All is not sweet, all is not sound." And lines 7 and 8 make clear his preference: "Give me a look, give me a face / That makes simplicity a grace."

DIRECTIONS: *Use the table below to help you draw inferences about passages in the poems and to confirm or disprove your inferences. In the left column, write the lines that lead to an inference. Write your inference in the second column. In the third column, write the phrases or lines that confirm (or disprove) your inference. In the fourth column, confirm your inference, or state a new inference based on the additional information. The first row has been done for you.*

Lines on Which Inference is Based	Inference	Lines Supporting or Disproving Inference	Final Inference
1. "Farewell, thou child of my right hand, and joy;" ("On My First Son," line 1)	Since the poet uses the term *farewell*, this poem is probably about a child who is dying or has died.	Line 3: "Seven years thou wert lent to me" Line 7: "To have so soon scaped world's and flesh's rage" Line 9: "Rest in soft peace"	These lines and phrases verify that the speaker's son has died.
2.			
3.			
4.			

"On My First Son," "Still to Be Neat," and **"Song: To Celia"** by Ben Jonson

Vocabulary Builder

Using the Word *Sound*

In "Still to Be Neat," Ben Jonson uses the word *sound*, a word that has multiple meanings. It can refer to noise, health, security, physical condition, reliability, and a body of water, among other things.

A. DIRECTIONS: *Rewrite each of the following sentences to include the word sound. Consult a dictionary if necessary.*

1. Dan gave Carol advice that she could count on.

   _____

2. The children were tucked, safe and secure, into their beds.

   _____

3. During the night, Amelia heard a noise that frightened her.

   _____

4. The whale dove suddenly downward through the water.

   _____

5. Ted took the boat across the channel from the island to the mainland.

   _____

Using the Word List

divine   fate   lament   presumed   sound   wreath

B. DIRECTIONS: *In each blank, write a word from the Word List to complete the sentence.*

1. The lady's admirer _____ that her makeup hid some flaws.
2. Like everyone in his family, Don enjoyed _____ health.
3. The child's sad _____ was to die young.
4. His family will _____ his passing forever.
5. They hoped for _____ intercession to save the child.
6. Friends sent a lovely _____ made of roses and carnations.

"On My First Son," "Still to Be Neat," and **"Song: To Celia"** by Ben Jonson
Grammar and Style: Using Participles, Gerunds, and Infinitives

A **participle** is a verb form, typically ending in -ed or -ing, used as a modifier, either alone or in a phrase.

Examples: The *grieving* parent wrote a poem about his son.
The woman, *dressed* for the party, wore makeup and jewelry.

A **gerund** is a verb form, typically ending in -ing or -ed, used as a noun, either alone or in a phrase.

Examples: *Seeing* is *believing.*
Writing poetry is what Jonson enjoyed.

An **infinitive** is the form of the verb with *to.* It can function as a noun, an adjective, or an adverb, either alone or in a phrase.

Examples: She wore makeup *to hide* her blemishes.
We have a great deal of *work to do.*

A. PRACTICE: *In each of the following sentences, identify the underlined phrase as a gerund, infinitive, or participial phrase.*

1. To entertain the royal court, Jonson wrote masques. _____
2. The boy, complaining of a stomach ache, had a fever. _____
3. Ben Jonson's followers liked to call themselves the "Sons of Ben." _____
4. After returning to England, Jonson started acting on the stage. _____
5. Suspected of treason, Jonson proved himself innocent. _____
6. Jonson enjoyed visiting with friends at the Mermaid Tavern. _____

B. Writing Application: Write three sentences, using a gerund, infinitive, or participial phrase. Use each type of phrase at least once, and label each one.

1. _____
   _____

2. _____
   _____

3. _____
   _____

"On My First Son," "Still to Be Neat," and **"Song: To Celia"** by Ben Jonson

Support for Writing

Use the chart below to take notes for your critical response. Review the poems, then write notes and cite examples that support or contradict Bush's defense of Jonson's style.

Clarity:

Unity:

"... Jonson demanded . . . the ageless classical virtues of clarity, unity, symmetry, and proportion. . . ."

Symmetry:

Proportion:

On a separate page, write a draft of an essay that responds to Bush's ideas. Begin by summarizing both Bush's point and your position. Then, support your generalizations with quotations from Jonson.

"To His Coy Mistress" by Andrew Marvell
"To the Virgins, to Make Much of Time" by Robert Herrick
"Song" by Sir John Suckling
Literary Analysis: *Carpe Diem* Theme

The **theme** of *carpe diem,* which is Latin for "seize the day," expresses a **universal view** that first appeared in classical literature. Examples of this theme can be found throughout world literature. Robert Herrick's poem "To the Virgins" contains lines that are frequently cited as an example of this theme.

Gather ye rosebuds while ye may,

Old time is still a-flying;

And this same flower that smiles today

Tomorrow will be dying.

The metaphor of the rosebuds is a particularly appropriate symbol for the *carpe diem* theme. The rose is one of the most beautiful of flowers, yet it lives only a short time.

DIRECTIONS: *Answer the following questions.*

1. In the opening lines of "To the Virgins, to Make Much of Time," Herrick uses the image of rosebuds as a symbol of the *carpe diem* theme. What other image does he use as a symbol in the poem?

   _____

   _____

2. In the opening lines from "To His Coy Mistress," the speaker implies that coyness is a crime. How does the speaker use the *carpe diem* theme to justify this implication?

   Had we but world enough, and time,

   This coyness lady were no crime.

   _____

   _____

3. What other lines from "To His Coy Mistress" reinforce the *carpe diem* theme? Give one example.

   _____

   _____

4. In "To His Coy Mistress," what is the speaker's purpose in trying to convince his listener that life is short? Use an example from the poem to support your statement.

   _____

   _____

"To His Coy Mistress" by Andrew Marvell
"To the Virgins, to Make Much of Time" by Robert Herrick
"Song" by Sir John Suckling

Reading Strategy: Analyze and Evaluate Similar Themes

To **analyze and evaluate similar themes** in various selections, think about the particular attitude expressed toward the theme by each writer. For example, Andrew Marvell, Robert Herrick, and John Suckling have all written poems inspired by the theme of *carpe diem*, a Latin phrase that means "seize the day." This theme expresses the idea that life is short, so people should act quickly to enjoy what pleasures they can.

When you analyze poems like this with similar themes, look especially at the following:
- images and other language each poet uses to present the theme
- the poem's speaker—What does he or she seem to think and feel about the theme?
- the poet's view of the theme—for instance, is the poet treating the theme in a serious or humorous way? Is the poet breaking from or sticking with tradition?

Finally, decide whether each poet's approach to the theme is compelling or uninteresting, valid or not valid, and why.

DIRECTIONS: *Complete the chart shown here to help you analyze and evaluate the theme of* carpe diem *in "To His Coy Mistress," "To the Virgins, to Make Much of Time," and "Song." Then, write a statement evaluating the three poets' use of the* carpe diem *theme.*

	Marvell	**Herrick**	**Suckling**
Images / Language			
Speaker's Attitude			
Take on *Carpe Diem* Theme			

Which poem's approach to the *carpe diem* theme did you find most compelling, and why?

_____

_____

_____

"To His Coy Mistress" by Andrew Marvell
"To the Virgins, to Make Much of Time" by Robert Herrick
"Song" by Sir John Suckling
Vocabulary Builder

Using Context to Determine Meaning

A. DIRECTIONS: *Based on contextual meaning, determine if each statement is true or false. Write true or false on the line.*

1. A woman's *coyness* indicates that she is ready to make a commitment.
   _____

2. If a person continues to *languish,* it is clear that he or she needs some help.
   _____

3. To *prevail* over a strong opponent, a team would have to be even stronger.
   _____

4. If you really dislike someone, you might give him or her *amorous* looks.
   _____

5. A man in his *prime* would likely be walking with the aid of a cane. _____

6. A *wan* appearance gives the impression of great weariness, sadness, or weakness.
   _____

Using the Word List

> amorous   coyness   languish   prevail   prime   wan

B. DIRECTIONS: *In each blank, write a word from the Word List to complete the sentence.*

1. At your age, you are just entering your _____.

2. His flirting showed his _____, since he never made a date.

3. She looked with _____ eyes at her new husband.

4. When she left him, he became _____ and went to bed.

5. When her husband left for the army, she began to _____ in despair.

6. After several losses, our team was finally able to _____.

Name _____ Date _____

"To His Coy Mistress" by Andrew Marvell
"To the Virgins, to Make Much of Time" by Robert Herrick
"Song" by Sir John Suckling
Support for Writing

Use the graphic organizer below to develop ideas for your public service announcement. Write your topic in the first box. Then, enter details, such as events or examples, in each box on the left. In the boxes on the right, list vivid words, images, and witty phrases to develop the details.

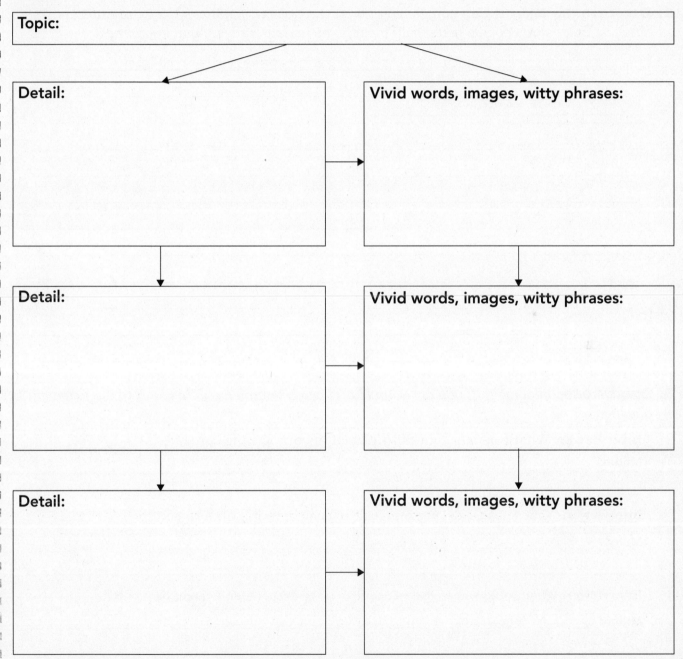

Topic:

Detail:

Vivid words, images, witty phrases:

Detail:

Vivid words, images, witty phrases:

Detail:

Vivid words, images, witty phrases:

On a separate page, write a public service announcement that is informative and interesting.

Name _____ Date _____

Sonnet VII, Sonnet XIX, *from Paradise Lost* by John Milton
John Milton: Biography

A devout Puritan in an age of great religious and political turmoil, John Milton devoted much of his writing time and talent to political polemics supporting the Puritan cause. Nevertheless, he ranks with Shakespeare and Chaucer as one of England's greatest poets. His masterpiece is *Paradise Lost,* considered the finest epic poem in the English language. Amazingly, Milton wrote this brilliant epic after he had gone completely blind.

A. DIRECTIONS: *Imagine that you are creating a chronology of Milton's life for an Internet Web site. List at least ten events you would include, along with dates if you know them.*

_____

_____

_____

_____

_____

_____

_____

_____

_____

_____

_____

B. DIRECTIONS: *Imagine that you are John Milton being interviewed. Respond to the following questions.*

Interviewer: What role has your faith played in your writing career?

Milton:_____

_____

Interviewer: What setbacks did you overcome to achieve your goals as a poet?

Milton:_____

_____

Interviewer: What would you advise someone to do to prepare for a career as a poet?

Milton:_____

_____

All-in-One Workbook
118

Poetry of John Milton
Literary Analysis: Epic Poetry

Milton chose to write *Paradise Lost* in blank verse. The poet rejected the idea of rhymed verse, claiming, "The measure is English Heroic verse without (rhyme), as that of Homer in Greek and of Virgil in Latin; (rhyme) no longer being necessary." Milton thought rhymed verse was "trivial and of no true musical delight" and that the true musical delight in poetry came from the fit of the syllables and the meter of the sentences from one verse to another.

DIRECTIONS: *Scan the following lines of blank verse from Paradise Lost to show the basic iambic pentameter of the verse.*

Of man's first disobedience, and the fruit

Of that forbidden tree, whose mortal taste

Brought death into the world, and all our woe,

With loss of Eden, till one greater Man

Restore us, and regain the blissful seat,

Sing Heav'nly Muse, that on the secret top

Of *Oreb, or of Sinai,* didst inspire

That shepherd, who first taught the chosen seed....

Name _____   Date _____

Poetry of John Milton
Literary Analysis: The Italian Sonnet

Milton's "Sonnet XIX" is an example of an Italian sonnet. The chart shows the similarities and differences between the Italian (or Petrarchan) sonnet and the English (or Shakespearean) sonnet.

Italian Sonnet	English Sonnet
14 lines Divided into an octave (8 lines presenting a problem and a sestet (6 lines responding to the problem) Rhyme scheme of octave is *abba abba;* rhyme scheme of sestet varies.	14 lines Divided into 3 quatrains (4 lines each) and a couplet (2 lines) Rhyme scheme usually *abab cdcd efef gg.*

DIRECTIONS: Prove that this poem is an Italian sonnet by drawing a vertical line between the octave and the sestet and by marking the rhyme scheme.

Sonnet VII

How soon hath Time, the subtle thief of youth,
    Stolen on his wing my three and twentieth year!
    My hasting days fly on with full career,
    But my late spring no bud or blossom showeth.
Perhaps my semblance might deceive the truth.
    That I to manhood am arrived so near,
    And inward ripeness doth much less appear,
    That some more timely-happy spirits endueth.
Yet be it less or more, or soon or slow,
    It shall be still in strictest measure even
    To that same lot, however mean or high,
Toward which Time leads me, and the will of Heaven;
    All is, if I have grace to use it so,
    As ever in my great Taskmaster's eye.

Poetry of John Milton
Reading Strategy: Use a Graphic Organizer to Repair Comprehension

Milton's poetry is sometimes difficult to read and understand because of its long and complex sentence structure. Milton frequently shifts the order of the clauses to add emphasis to certain ideas. The main clause may appear in the middle or at the end of the sentence. One way to repair comprehension of sentences that confuse you is to use a graphic organizer to break them down into the main clause and supporting details.

DIRECTIONS: *Use the table below to help break down confusing sentences and decipher their meaning. The following passage has been used as a model.*

There the companions of his fall, o'erwhelmed
With floods and whirlwinds of tempestuous fire,
He soon discerns, and welt'ring by his side
One next himself in power, and next in crime,
Long after known in Palestine, and named Beelzebub. . . .

Main Clause	Supporting Ideas
1. "He soon discerns"	His companions are overwhelmed with floods and whirlwinds of fire. One of them is weltering by his side. Beelzebub is next to Satan in power and crime.
2.	
3.	
4.	

Poetry of John Milton
Vocabulary Builder

Using the Root -lum-

A. DIRECTIONS: *Each of the following sentences includes an italicized word that contains the word root -lum-, which comes from the Latin word meaning "light" or "lamp." Fill in each blank with a word or phrase that completes the sentence and reveals the meaning of the italicized word.*

1. When you flip the switch to *illuminate* the room, you _____.

2. When the physicist described the star's *luminance,* she was talking about its
_____.

3. Because the face of the watch is *luminescent,* the hands and numbers are
_____ enough to be read in the dark.

Using the Word List

    guile   ignominy   illumine   obdurate

    semblance   tempestuous   transcendent   transgress

B. DIRECTIONS: *Write the word from the Word List that best completes each analogy.*

1. *Trickery* is to _____ as *judgment* is to *wisdom.*

2. _____ is to *yielding* as *agitated* is to *peaceful.*

3. *Happiness* is to *joy* as *appearance* is to _____.

4. _____ is to *dishonor* as *pride* is to *conceit.*

5. *Ignorant* is to *educated* as _____ is to *calm.*

6. _____ is to *darken* as *love* is to *hate.*

7. *Obey* is to *comply* as *violate* is to _____.

8. *Curious* is to *inquisitive* as _____ is to *exceeding.*

Poetry of John Milton

Grammar and Style: Avoiding Misplaced and Dangling Modifiers

A **misplaced modifier** is one that seems to modify a word that it should not or cannot sensibly modify. These constructions can be confusing and unintentionally humorous.

Example: *Grazing peacefully in the meadow*, we saw a herd of cattle. (The participial phrase seems to modify *we*.)

To correct a misplaced modifier, rewrite the sentence so the modifier is close to the word it modifies.

Example: We saw a herd of cattle *grazing peacefully in the meadow*. (The participial phrase clearly modifies *cattle*.)

A **dangling modifier** is one that refers to a word that is implied rather than actually stated in the sentence.

Example: *After reading four books*, the subject was still not clear. (Who did the reading?)

To correct a dangling modifier, rewrite the sentence to include the word to which the modifier refers.

Example: *After reading four books*, I still did not understand the subject.

A. PRACTICE: *Read each sentence and decide whether the italicized modifier is misplaced or dangling. Write misplaced or dangling on the line.*

1. *Regarded as one of the greatest poets of the English language*, his poems are still studied.

   _____

2. *Tutored at home*, Milton's parents saw to his education. _____

3. *Dressed in Puritan clothing*, the painting shows an older Milton. _____

4. *Cast into a fiery pit*, Milton describes the story about the fallen archangel.

   _____

B. Writing Application: *Rewrite each sentence so it does not include a misplaced or dangling modifier.*

1. Sensing that the nation needed an anchor, <u>Paradise Lost</u> helped define a culture.

   _____

   _____

2. Unable to see, darkness set in.

   _____

   _____

3. Mastering many ancient and modern languages, college was the next step.

   _____

   _____

4. Thrown into prison, Andrew Marvell helped arrange Milton's release.

   _____

   _____

Poetry of John Milton
Support for Writing

Use the graphic organizer below to develop ideas and write notes about villains from stories, books, and movies. Write at least two characteristics of each villain.

Villain's name:

Characteristics:

Villain's name:

Characteristics:

Villains

Villain's name:

Characteristics:

Villain's name:

Characteristics:

On a separate page, use your notes to draft an essay that explains why villains, such as Milton's Satan, are interesting to us as readers. Begin your draft by discussing why his character is engaging, and add your observations about the appeal of other villains.

Name _____   Date _____

from Paradise Lost by John Milton
from The Inferno by Dante
Literary Analysis: Comparing Epics Around the World

Epic poems are long narrative poems about the exploits of heroic figures. Epics usually express the ideals of the culture from which they spring. **Comparing epics** from different parts of the world will give you a feeling for the oldest beliefs and traditions of the people who lived in those places.

Epic poems are marked by certain features:

- They always present important subjects and events, such as battles or quests.
- The main characters of epics are always larger than life, and the narratives usually include supernatural creatures who influence human affairs.
- Thematically, epics express the beliefs and values of their cultures.
- The style of an epic is usually elevated, with a serious tone and poetic language.

When you compare epics from different areas of the world, look for examples of these features. Comparing particular examples of the events, characters, themes, and style in several epics will help you see what the epics have in common. In addition, such analysis can help you discover how the epics and their cultures differ.

DIRECTIONS: *Complete the chart shown here to help you compare the English epic* Paradise Lost *with* The Inferno, *the first poem in the Italian epic* The Divine Comedy.

	Paradise Lost	*The Inferno*	**Similarities / Differences**
Subject			
Character(s)			
Theme(s): Values/ Beliefs			
Style (description and one example)			

Comparing Literary Works: Milton and Dante
Vocabulary Builder

Using the Word List

awe   cowered   nimble   shrill   writhes

A. DIRECTIONS: *Write the word from the box that best completes each sentence.*

1. With a _____ step, the narrator follows his guide down the winding path.

2. The narrator looks with _____ on the amazing sight before him.

3. Meanwhile, a suffering soul _____ in pain and terror.

4. The _____ sound of a scream breaks the silence.

5. Even though they _____ in the shadows, they were seen.

B. DIRECTIONS: *Revise each sentence so that the underlined vocabulary word is used in a logical way. Be sure to keep the vocabulary word in your revision.*

Examples: We greeted the <u>insurmountable</u> task with joy.
Revision: We greeted the <u>insurmountable</u> task with dread.

1. Diana looked with <u>awe</u> on her dinner of frankfurters and beans.

_____

2. The elephant <u>writhes</u> as it moves across the plain.

_____

3. The <u>nimble</u> little turtle won the race.

_____

4. The courageous warriors <u>cowered</u> before their weak enemies.

_____

5. The workers could barely hear the <u>shrill</u> whistle that signaled the end of the work day.

_____

Name _____   Date _____

Support for Writing

Use the Venn diagram below to organize information about the setting in the selections. In the left section, write what is unique about the setting in Milton's epic. In the right section write what is unique about the setting in Dante's epic. In the center section, write what is similar about both settings.

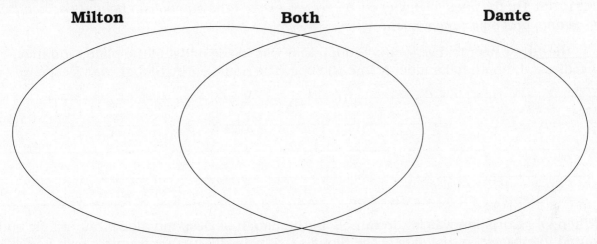

Milton　　　　　　**Both**　　　　　　**Dante**

On a separate page, draft an essay comparing and contrasting the settings in these selections.

Name _____ Date _____

from The Pilgrim's Progress by John Bunyan
Literary Analysis: Allegory

In an **allegory,** the characters, events, settings, and objects are symbols that represent abstract ideas. The purpose of an allegory is to teach a lesson, usually with religious or moral overtones.

DIRECTIONS: *On the lines following each excerpt, explain the symbolism behind each character, event, setting, and object mentioned.*

1. . . . they drew near to a very miry Slough that was in the midst of the plain, and they, being heedless, did both fall suddenly into the bog. The name of the Slough was Despond.

   _____

   _____

   _____

   _____

   _____

2. Wherefore Christian was left to tumble in the Sough of Despond alone; but still he endeavoured to struggle to that side of the Slough that was still further from his own house, and next to the Wicket Gate; the which he did, but could not get out, because of the burden that was upon his back . . .

   _____

   _____

   _____

   _____

   _____

3. It is not the pleasure of the King that this place should remain so bad; his labourers also, have, by the direction of His Majesty's surveyors, been for above this sixteen hundred years, employed about this patch of ground . . .

   _____

   _____

   _____

   _____

   _____

Name _____ Date _____

from **The Pilgrim's Progress** by John Bunyan
Reading Strategy: Interpret Allegory

One purpose for reading an allegory is to find out what it means, what the symbols stand for, and what the lesson is. To **interpret an allegory,** you use your outside knowledge to consider the details and determine what the symbols mean.

DIRECTIONS: *Use the chart below to help you interpret the symbols in this excerpt from* The Pilgrim's Progress.

Interpreting *The Pilgrim's Progress*	
Overall symbolism	
Specific symbols with names that signal their meaning	
Specific symbols not signaled by their names	
Main message or lesson	

from **The Pilgrim's Progress** by John Bunyan
Vocabulary Builder

True or False?

DIRECTIONS: *Determine if each sentence makes a true statement or a false statement. Write true or false on the line.*

1. A person who is *heedless* pays careful attention to everything he or she does.
   _____

2. If you *wallowed* in self-pity, you never gave your own troubles a thought.
   _____

3. A *burden* can weigh you down. _____

4. If you *endeavored* to learn something, you decided it was not worth the effort.
   _____

5. A country's *dominions* include the land under its jurisdiction. _____

6. A family of ten would need a more *substantial* amount of food than a family of four.
   _____

Using the Word List

burden   dominions   endeavored   heedless   substantial   wallowed

B. DIRECTIONS: *Write a complete sentence to answer each question. For each item, use a word from the Word List to replace each underlined word without changing its meaning.*

1. What is one thing you <u>tried</u> to do, worked hard at, and succeeded in accomplishing?
   _____

2. Which part of the <u>governed territories</u> of the United States would you like to visit?
   _____

3. What <u>heavy load</u> has weighed on your mind recently?
   _____

4. What animals do you know about that have <u>rolled about</u> in mud, dirt, water, or dust?
   _____

5. If you were <u>unmindful</u> of where you were going, what might happen?
   _____

6. What might happen if you built a house on a foundation that was not <u>solid</u> enough?
   _____

Name _____ Date _____

Support for Writing: Casting Memo

Your job is to cast the parts for a film based on *The Pilgrim's Progress*. Use the following chart to organize your ideas about suitable actors for the roles. In column 2, describe the qualities each performer will need. In column 3, write the reasons you think a particular actor would be good in the role.

Character	Qualities Needed	Suggested Actor / Reasons
Christian		
Pliable		
Help		
Evangelist		
The King		

from **"Eve's Apology in Defense of Women"** by Amelia Lanier
"To Lucasta, on Going to the Wars" and **"To Althea, from Prison"** by Richard Lovelace
Literary Analysis: Tradition and Reform

Tradition and **reform** go hand in hand. Political and social reformers usually propose ideas that are based on new readings of traditional stories familiar to most everyone in the culture. Bible episodes are often used to inspire reform. For example, Lanier reinterprets the story of Adam and Eve in support of her proposals to reform the treatment of women. Traditional stories, parables, fables, and books have always influenced reform because these stories help to form the basic beliefs of a culture.

DIRECTIONS: *Use the following excerpts from "Eve's Apology in Defense of Women" to answer each of the following questions. Give examples from the selection quoted as evidence to support your interpretation.*

1. In the following excerpt, when Lanier writes "Her fault though great, yet he was most to blame," what "fault" does she refer to? What does she say about the fault?

   But surely Adam cannot be excused,
   Her fault though great, yet he was most to blame;
   What weakness offered, strength might have refused,
   Being Lord of all, the greater was his shame. . . .

   _____

   _____

   _____

   _____

2. According to Lanier, what is the difference between Adam's guilt and Eve's guilt in the following excerpt? Whose is the greater?

   If Eve did err, it was for knowledge sake;
   The fruit being fair persuaded him to fall. . . .

   _____

   _____

   _____

   _____

from "Eve's Apology in Defense of Women" by Amelia Lanier
"To Lucasta, on Going to the Wars" and "To Althea, from Prison" by Richard Lovelace

Reading Strategy: Use Historical Context

The poems by Lanier and Lovelace were inspired by specific social and historical circumstances. Think about the **historical context** when you read these works by asking yourself whether the ideas, assumptions, and beliefs expressed are typical of the era in which the work was written. Ask also if these ideas are a response to events of the period.

Evidence of loyalty and ideas of honor can be found in both of Lovelace's poems. In "To Lucasta, on Going to the Wars," Lovelace says "I could not love thee, Dear, so much,/Loved I not honor more" (lines 11–12). In "To Althea, from Prison," the poet celebrates "The sweetness, mercy, majesty,/And glories of my King" (lines 19–20). By understanding the historical context, you can reach a deeper understanding of the poems and the poets.

DIRECTIONS: *Place the poems of Lanier and Lovelace into historical context using the chart below. Use the biographies and background on pages 559 and 562 of the textbook to learn more about the poets and the events to which they were responding. As you read the poems, look for evidence of the events and circumstances of the era.*

Poem	Historical Event, Assumption, or Belief	Evidence of Historical Context Within Poem
"Eve's Apology in Defense of Women"		
"To Lucasta, on Going to the Wars"		
"To Althea, from Prison"		

from **"Eve's Apology in Defense of Women"** by Amelia Lanier
"To Lucasta, on Going to the Wars" and **"To Althea, from Prison"** by Richard Lovelace
Vocabulary Builder

Using Antonyms

Amelia Lanier uses **antonyms** to make her points in "Eve's Apology in Defense of Women."
Antonyms are words that mean the opposite of each other.

A. DIRECTIONS: *On the lines, write the antonyms in these passages from Amelia Lanier's poem.*

1. What weakness offered, strength might have refused . . .

   _____

2. Yet with one apple won to lose that breath . . .

   _____

Using the Word List

breach   discretion   inconstancy   reprove

B. DIRECTIONS: *The questions below are analogies, with the final term missing. In an analogy, the second pair of words expresses a relationship similar to that in the first pair. Choose the word that best completes each analogy.*

___ 1. COWARDICE : COURAGE : : breach :
    A. break
    B. violate
    C. repair
    D. contract

___ 2. SURE : INDECISIVE : : discretion :
    A. valor
    B. carelessness
    C. indifference
    D. indiscretion

___ 3. APPROVE : REJECT : : reprove :
    A. praise
    B. scold
    C. prove
    D. rebuke

___ 4. TRUE : DISLOYAL : : inconstancy :
    A. fickleness
    B. faithfulness
    C. insolvency
    D. quickness

from **"Eve's Apology in Defense of Women"** by Amelia Lanier
"To Lucasta, on Going to the Wars" and **"To Althea, from Prison"** by Richard Lovelace

Support for Writing

Use the organizer below to make notes that will help you write your "soldier's farewell."

Soldier's feelings about leaving parents:

_____

_____

_____

Soldier's feelings about leaving brothers and sisters:

_____

_____

_____

Soldier's feelings about leaving wife/husband/love interest:

_____

_____

_____

Soldier's feelings about leaving children:

_____

_____

_____

Soldier's feelings about leaving grandparents, aunts, uncles:

_____

_____

_____

Soldier's feelings about the challenges ahead and the meaning of the mission:

_____

_____

_____

On a separate page, draft your "soldier's farewell." The farewell can be addressed to one or more of the people the soldier will be leaving behind.

Name _____ Date _____

Diary: *from* The Diary of Samuel Pepys
Policy Statement: Charles II's Declaration to London, 1666
Primary Sources: Diary and Policy Statement

These two primary sources react to two major crises of Charles II's reign. Reading them can provide valuable historical insights.

DIRECTIONS: *Use the chart below to record and organize the information you learn by applying Who? What? When? Where? Why? and How? questions to the two selections. If a question is not answered in either selection, leave the space blank.*

Question	The Great Plague	The Great Fire
When did the crisis take place?		
Where did the crisis take place?		
Who tried to help remedy the situation?		
What did people do to try to escape the crisis, remedy the situation, and/or prevent it from happening again?		
How did people behave during the crisis?		
Why did the crisis occur?		

Diary: *from* **The Diary of Samuel Pepys**
Policy Statement: Charles II's Declaration to London, 1666
Vocabulary Builder

Using the Cross-Curricular Vocabulary

A. DIRECTIONS: *Using your knowledge of the words in italics, indicate whether these statements are true or false by writing T or F on the line before each statement. Use the lines after the statements to explain your answers.*

___ 1. Wood is a *combustible* material. _____

_____

___ 2. A jury should avoid *deliberation* before reaching a verdict. _____

_____

___ 3. A *magistrate* often entertains audiences by pulling rabbits out of hats. _____

_____

___ 4. A company's bookkeeper is someone who keeps the *accounts*. _____

_____

Using the Word List

abated   apprehensions   eminent   lamentable   malicious   notorious

B. DIRECTIONS: *Write the letter of the definition on the line before the word it defines. Use each definition only once.*

___ 1. abated
___ 2. apprehensions
___ 3. eminent
___ 4. lamentable
___ 5. malicious
___ 6. notorious

a. distressing
b. deliberately harmful
c. worries
d. diminished
e. famous in an unfavorable way
f. noteworthy or high-ranking

Bonus: Using Etymology

C. DIRECTIONS: *On the lines, explain how the meaning of magistrate reflects its Latin origin.*

_____

_____

from **A Journal of the Plague Year** by Daniel Defoe
Literary Analysis: Point of View

Point of view is the perspective from which a story is told. In a story told from the **first-person** point of view, the narrator is a character in the story and uses the words *I* and *me*. In a story told from the **third-person** point of view, the narrator is an observer who describes the characters and action. **Third-person omniscient** point of view means that the narrator knows everything about the characters and events and reveals details that the characters themselves may not know. **Third-person limited** point of view means that the narrator reveals events as only one character experiences them. An **objective** point of view is that of a narrator who relates a story in a completely impersonal way, not getting into the minds or emotions of any character but only describing external aspects of characters and events.

DIRECTIONS: *Identify the point of view of each of the following passages.*

1. David looked out over the quiet city, wondering why no one was out in the streets. In the next apartment, Alice was rocking her sick child to sleep and trying to hold back her tears. "When will this plague end?" she wondered. _____

2. David looked out over the quiet city, wondering why no one was out in the streets. He began to plan his day, thinking that it would be pleasant to take a stroll along the river.

   _____

3. David looked out over the quiet city. No one was out in the streets.

   _____

4. I looked out over the quiet city and saw that no one was out in the streets. From the next-door apartment, I could hear Alice singing a lullaby for her child. I felt terrible for her. I knew that her child would not survive, and I also knew that Alice could not face the truth.

   _____

from **A Journal of the Plague Year** *by Daniel Defoe*
Reading Strategy: Generate and Answer Questions

To monitor your comprehension of a work of literature, you can **generate and answer questions** about it. For example, you might ask yourself questions like these:

- Who is this character?

- What is the author saying?

- When does this event take place?

- Where are these characters going?

- Why does this character act this way?

- How will the character get out of this situation?

Once you have generated questions about the text, you can reread or read ahead to answer them.

DIRECTIONS: *Read this passage from the selection. Write a list of six questions you could ask about it. Then, based on what you know about the selection, answer the questions.*

There was nobody, as I could perceive at first, in the churchyard, or going into it, but the buriers, and the fellow that drove the cart, or rather led the horse and cart; but when they came up to the pit they saw a man go to and again, muffled up in a brown cloak, and making motions with his hands under his cloak, as if he was in a great agony, and the buriers immediately gathered about him, supposing he was one of those poor delirious or desperate creatures that used to pretend, as I have said, to bury themselves. He said nothing as he walked about, but two or three times groaned very deeply and loud, and sighed as he would break his heart.

1. _____
   _____

2. _____
   _____

3. _____
   _____

4. _____
   _____

5. _____
   _____

6. _____
   _____

from **A Journal of the Plague Year** by Daniel Defoe
Vocabulary Builder

Using the Prefix *dis-*

A. DIRECTIONS: *The prefix* dis- *can mean "apart," "not," "opposite of," or "absence of." The words below all contain the prefix* dis-. *The parentheses contain information about the word root for each word. Fill in each blank with a form of the word from the list.*

dispel (*pellere* = "to drive")   distribute (*tribuere* = "to allot")
disgrace (*grazia* = "grace")   disheveling (*chevel* = "hair")
disinfect (*infecter* = "to infect")   disgust (*gustus* = "a taste")

1. The wind blew fiercely, _____ Rob's neatly combed hair.

2. Anita groaned as her teacher began to _____ the test.

3. The first thing Albert did after moving into his new apartment was to clean and _____ the bathroom.

4. Gazing at his sister's messy room, Leroy could feel nothing but _____.

5. Because he had broken the law, the president resigned in _____.

6. Nancy posted a sign to _____ the rumors that school would be closed Friday.

Using the Word List

delirious   distemper   importuning   lamentations   prodigious   resolution

B. DIRECTIONS: *Use the context, or surrounding words, to determine which word from the Word List correctly completes the sentence. Write the word on the line.*

1. Crazed with fear and suffering from pain, the _____ woman seemed out of her mind.

2. It was clear from his enormous size that the man had a _____ appetite.

3. The sighs, wails, and other _____ from the next apartment continued for days after the funeral.

4. The officers stopped _____ the man to go home when they realized their pleas would have no effect.

5. When forty percent of the population came down with the fever, we knew the _____ was out of control.

6. The man was firm in his _____ to do all he could to save his children.

Name _____ Date _____

from **A Journal of the Plague Year** by Daniel Defoe
Support for Writing

Use the graphic organizer below to organize your thoughts for a reflective essay on a time of change.

What are the causes of the change?
_____
_____
_____

How do the changes affect the average person?
_____
_____
_____

How do the changes impact social services, such as law enforcement and education?
_____
_____
_____

How will these changes affect the future?
_____
_____
_____

What are some negative results of the change?
_____
_____
_____

What are some positive results of the change?
_____
_____
_____

On a separate page, draft your essay. Use details from your notes to support your thesis statement.

from **Gulliver's Travels** and **"A Modest Proposal"** by Jonathan Swift
Literary Analysis: Satire, Irony, and Style

Style refers to the individual qualities that distinguish a writer's work. It includes word choice, tone, and use of characteristic elements such as figurative language, sentence length, and methods of organization. It can also include the use of satire and irony.

Satire uses wit and humor to ridicule vices, follies, and abuses. The intent, however, is rooted in a hope for reform: Satirists hope their work will open people's eyes to the real state of affairs in a society so that they will do something about it. **Irony** and sarcasm are important tools of satirists, whose tone may be gentle and amused, or bitter and vicious. Jonathan Swift is one of the most famous and widely read satirists in English and *Gulliver's Travels* and "A Modest Proposal" are among his most enduring works.

DIRECTIONS: *Plan a satire in your own style by writing out the following steps:*

1. Name an institution or custom you believe merits criticism. It may be an organization or custom within your community, your state, the nation, or the world.

   _____

   _____

2. What aspect of this institution or custom deserves criticism? What vice or folly do you want to reveal?

   _____

   _____

3. Describe a setting that could be used in a satire about your subject. The setting can be the actual one, humorously disguised or, like Jonathan Swift's in *Gulliver's Travels*, it can be highly fanciful.

   _____

   _____

4. Name and briefly describe a character or two who will represent ordinary people who must deal with the institution or custom.

   _____

   _____

5. Practice using verbal irony. Describe the institution or custom you are satirizing, or have a character comment on it, making sure the comment says the opposite of what is really meant. Make a statement that seems to defend the institution or custom but actually reveals the institution's shortcomings.

   _____

   _____

   _____

   _____

   _____

Name _____   Date _____

from **Gulliver's Travels** and **"A Modest Proposal"** by *Jonathan Swift*
Reading Strategy: Analyze and Evaluate Information

Good satire is packed with social and political references, but writers of satire are also concerned with telling a good story. They wrap their satirical observations inside the story to comment in a humorous way, using irony as a part of their style. To **analyze and evaluate** satire, the reader needs to know the historical context of the time it was written.

Satirical works that survive their own historical time period, such as *Gulliver's Travels,* do so because they address questions of universal human interest. For example, Gulliver describes the effects of gunpowder to the king of Brobdingnag. To ingratiate himself with the king, Gulliver proudly tells him about the enormous destruction that can be perpetrated by mixing a few simple ingredients and discharging the mixture with the help of a small spark. To Gulliver's surprise, the king is horrified by this notion. In fact, the king becomes so upset by the "evil genius, enemy to mankind" who must have first conceived of gunpowder, that he tells Gulliver never to mention the subject again. Swift uses this discussion to point up the problem of unbridled violence and the need for pacifism in the world. Since violence continues to be a societal and political problem to this day, Swift's satirical commentary retains its relevance.

DIRECTIONS: *To analyze and evaluate satirical works, you must look for the author's intended meaning. Use this graphic organizer to analyze and evaluate material from* Gulliver's Travels *or* "A Modest Proposal". *One example has been completed for you.*

Quotation	Meaning	Relevance Today
1. "He observed, that among the diversions of our nobility and gentry I had mentioned gaming."	It is clear by the questions the king asks that Swift thinks of gambling as a disease and an addiction that ruins lives.	The problem of gambling addiction still exists today.
2.		
3.		
4.		

from **Gulliver's Travels** and **"A Modest Proposal"** by Jonathan Swift
Vocabulary Builder

Using the Root *-jec-*

A. DIRECTIONS: *Each of the following sentences includes an italicized word that contains the word root -jec- meaning "throw." Fill in the blank with a word or phrase that completes the sentence and reveals the meaning of the italicized word.*

1. The criminal hung his head in *abject* misery; he looked completely _____.

2. The last time my grandmother had an *injection* was when she got _____.

3. My uncle liked to *interject* things into the conversation; he always had something to _____.

Using the Word List

censure   commodity   conjecture   expedient   schism   sustenance

B. DIRECTIONS: *The questions below consist of a related pair of words in CAPITAL LETTERS followed by four lettered pairs of words. Choose the pair that best expresses a relationship similar to that in the pair in capital letters.*

___ 1. SCHISM : GROUPS ::
    A. whole : pieces
    B. storm : clouds
    C. division : parts
    D. separation : separate

___ 2. CONJECTURE : INFERENCE ::
    A. confer : talk
    B. speak : statement
    C. relate : relative
    D. go : leave

___ 3. EXPEDIENT : USELESS : :
    A. expense : cost
    B. advantage : win
    C. help : aid
    D. asset : liability

___ 4. SUSTENANCE : FOOD : :
    A. money : cash
    B. drink : eat
    C. water : milk
    D. sustain : weaken

___ 5. COMMODITY : SELL : :
    A. save : interest
    B. scene : see
    C. purchase : dollars
    D. wheat : corn

___ 6. CENSURE : APPROVE : :
    A. condemn : blame
    B. guilt : burden
    C. praise : criticize
    D. error : mistake

Name _____   Date _____

from Gulliver's Travels and **"A Modest Proposal"** by Jonathan Swift
Support for Writing

Use the chart below to generate ideas for your multimedia satire. First, write the behavior, trend, or attitude you want to satirize in the center circle. In the surrounding circles, list characteristics of that subject.

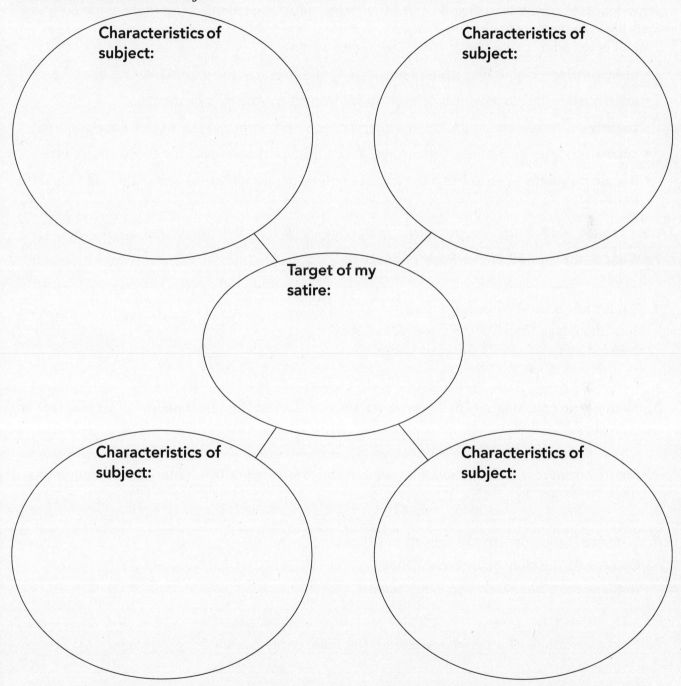

On a separate page, write a description of your multimedia satire. Use the details you have collected on the target of your satire, and exaggerate each of the characteristics. Discuss how you will use different media (photographs, drawings, charts, film, recordings, diagrams, and so on) to present your satire.

Name _____   Date _____

from An Essay on Man and from The Rape of the Lock by Alexander Pope
Literary Analysis: Mock Epic

A **mock epic** uses the epic form for humorous effect. The key feature of a mock epic is its treatment of a trivial subject in an elevated style, thus showing how ridiculous it is. A mock epic tells a story of "heroes" doing "great deeds," but the heroes and deeds are actually petty. A mock epic, like a true epic, may use gods and other supernatural elements. *The Rape of the Lock* is a masterpiece of mock epic.

Mock epics often make use of the following elements:

- **epic similes**—elaborate comparisons that sometimes use the words *like, as,* or *so*
- **antithesis**—the placement side by side of strongly contrasting elements
- **parody**—a humorous imitation of a literary work, pointing out the work's shortcomings
- **satire**—comments, usually humorous, about human flaws, ideas, or social customs
- **heroic couplets**—pairs of rhymed lines in iambic pentameter that work together to make a point

DIRECTIONS: *Explore the characteristics of the mock epic by answering these questions.*

1. What is the subject of *The Rape of the Lock*?

   _____

2. What makes these lines humorous?

   Here, thou, great Anna! whom three realms obey,
   Dost sometimes counsel take—and sometimes tea.

   _____

3. As in a true epic, mighty forces "draw forth to combat on the velvet plain." What war is then described in detail?

   _____

4. Figures from mythology take an interest in the events described. Quote a line that shows their involvement.

   _____

5. Why are these lines an example of antithesis?

   One speaks the glory of the British Queen,

   And one describes a charming Indian screen

   _____

6. Find an example of a heroic couplet in *The Rape of the Lock*.

   _____

from **An Essay on Man** and *from* **The Rape of the Lock** by Alexander Pope
Reading Strategy: Recognize Author's Purpose

In *The Rape of the Lock*, Pope satirizes high society by focusing his wit and poetic talents on a petty incident that takes place among members of the wigged and powdered London upper-crust set. With elevated language and allusions to mythology, Pope deflates London society, exposing its silliness and shallowness. In the following passage, Pope appears to compliment the depth and grandeur of upper-class London society, but he is really ridiculing such people by exposing their pettiness and the shallowness of their conversations.

> Hither the heroes and the nymphs resort,
> To taste awhile the pleasures of a court;
> In various talk th' instructive hours they passed,
> Who gave the ball, or paid the visit last;
> One speaks the glory of the British Queen,
> And one describes a charming Indian screen;
> A third interprets motions, looks, and eyes;
> At every word a reputation dies.

DIRECTIONS: *Use the chart below to interpret the author's purpose in examples from the* The Rape of the Lock. *The left column contains a quote from the poem. In the right column, interpret the meaning underlying the author's words. The first one has been done for you.*

Quotation	**Author's Purpose**
"To arms, to arms!" the fierce virago cries, / And swift as lightning to the combat flies. / All side in parties, and begin th' attack; / Fans clap, silks rustle, and tough whalebones crack . . .	**1.** Pope mocks the high-society ladies and gentlemen whose "arms" are fans, silk dresses and suits, and the whalebone stays of corsets.
Meanwhile, declining from the noon of day, / The sun obliquely shoots his burning ray; / The hungry judges soon the sentence sign, / And wretches hang that jurymen may dine; / The merchant from th' Exchange returns in peace, / And the long labors of the toilet cease.	**2.**
The skillful nymph reviews her force with care: / Let spades be trumps! she said, and trumps they were.	**3.**
The meeting points the sacred hair dissever / From the fair head, forever, and forever!	**4.**
When, after millions slain, yourself shall die; / When those fair suns shall set, as set they must, / And all those tresses shall be laid in dust, / This lock, the Muse shall consecrate to fame, / And midst the stars inscribe Belinda's name.	**5.**

from **An Essay on Man** and from **The Rape of the Lock** by Alexander Pope
Vocabulary Builder

Using Related Words: Words from Political Science

A. DIRECTIONS: *Read each of these lines from* The Rape of the Lock. *Describe the political significance of the underlined word. Use a dictionary if necessary.*

1. To taste awhile the pleasures of a <u>court</u> . . .

   _____

2. Now to the <u>baron</u> fate inclines the field.

   _____

3. The <u>peer</u> now spreads the glittering forfex wide . . .

   _____

4. But this bold <u>lord</u> with manly strength endued . . .

   _____

Using the Word List

   assignations   destitute   disabused   obliquely   plebeian   stoic

B. DIRECTIONS: *Write the word from the Word List that best completes each sentence.*

1. If Sir Plume thought he could get away with a lock of Belinda's hair, she certainly
   _____ him of that notion.

2. In Pope's time beggars lived on the street and were completely _____.

3. Sometimes ladies and gentlemen made secret _____ with one another.

4. If a person gives you a sidewise glance, he or she is looking at you _____.

5. The nobleman was considered by many to be haughty because he rarely spoke to those whom he considered _____, or lower class.

6. The _____ remained calm and collected while others reacted to the news emotionally.

Name _____ Date _____

from An Essay on Man and from The Rape of the Lock by Alexander Pope
Support for Writing

Use the chart below to take notes for your **mock epic.** First, identify the conflict you will describe. Then, use the chart to jot down ideas for boasting speeches of your heroes and heroines, descriptions of warriors and their weapons, how gods and goddesses may enter the action, and epic similes you may use.

Conflict: _____

Epic Elements	
Boasts of heroes and heroines	
Descriptions of warriors and weapons	
Actions of gods and goddesses	
Elaborate comparisons (epic similes)	

from The Preface to A Dictionary of the English Language and *from* **A Dictionary of the English Language** by Samuel Johnson
from **The Life of Samuel Johnson** by James Boswell

Literary Analysis: Dictionary

Samuel Johnson's *Dictionary* was not the first to attempt to include all the English words in one volume. However, it was the first dictionary to set a standard for how all English words should be used. Today's English dictionaries list and define words and provide information about their pronunciation, history, and usage. A modern dictionary entry may also contain a word's syllabication, part(s) of speech, and the definitions for the word in each part of speech. Some dictionaries have synonym studies, which help users achieve the precise **diction** and **tone** they are seeking. Some entries contain a history of the word, correct grammatical usage of the word, illustrations, antonyms, idioms, and foreign words and phrases. Modern dictionaries may also contain roots and other combining forms, abbreviations, and bibliographic and geographic entries. Some even have a section containing brief **biographies,** or information about the lives of well-known people. Electronic dictionaries on computers have expanded the capabilities of dictionaries. If you are unsure of a spelling, you can enter an approximation of the word and be given choices of possible entries. When looking for a word that fits a particular meaning, you can search the dictionary by entering key words that might be found in its definition.

DIRECTIONS: *Read the entry for* gang *in Johnson's dictionary and list the different pieces of information he supplies about the word; then look up the word* gang *in a modern dictionary and note the similarities and differences in the kinds of information supplied. Fill in the Venn diagram to show the similarities and differences between Johnson's dictionary and a modern dictionary.*

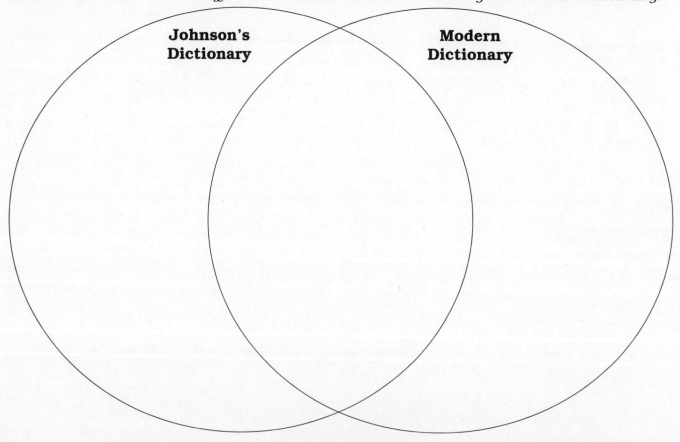

Name _____ Date _____

from The Preface to A Dictionary of the English Language
from A Dictionary of the English Language by Samuel Johnson
from The Life of Samuel Johnson by James Boswell
Reading Strategy: Analyze the Author's Purpose

You **analyze the author's purpose,** or goal in writing, in order to get a clearer idea of the work's meaning. Every writer has a reason for sitting down to compose something. That purpose may be to express a certain idea, to persuade people to accept an opinion, to change a situation, to inform his or her readers, to entertain them, or to figure something out. Once you understand that purpose—the *why* of the work—you will understand the author's meaning—the *what*.

An author's purpose shapes the meaning of what he or she writes. For example, James Boswell's purpose in writing *The Life of Samuel Johnson* was to capture on paper the greatness of a very contradictory and large personality, someone whom Boswell dearly loved. As you read Boswell's work, you will notice that he gives examples of Johnson's admirable and less admirable traits. Understanding Boswell's purpose allows you to understand why Boswell included these examples. You know that he was writing to shed light on a man who was so memorable—and lovable—because his personality was so rich and complex.

Selection	Author's Purpose or Perspective	Example from Text	Effect on Meaning
from The Preface to *A Dictionary of the English Language*			
from *A Dictionary of the English Language*			
from *The Life of Samuel Johnson*			

from **The Preface to A Dictionary of the English Language** and *from* **A Dictionary of the English Language** by Samuel Johnson
from **The Life of Samuel Johnson** by James Boswell
Vocabulary Builder

Using the Root *-dict-*

A. DIRECTIONS: *The words that follow each contain the word root -dict-, from the Latin for "to say." Information about the prefix or suffix of each word is contained in parentheses. On the line, write the word that best completes each sentence.*

> dictate (*-ate* = "act on")
> dictator (*-or* = "one that does something")
> diction (*-ion* = "action or process")
> predict (*pre-* = "before")

1. When the _____ seized power, he immediately censored the newspapers.

2. Because their scientific instruments were precise, the meteorologists were able to _____ accurately the arrival of the storm.

3. The executive began to _____ her speech into the tape recorder.

4. The actor's good _____ enhanced his reading of the short story.

Using the Word List

> abasement   adulterations   caprices   credulity   malignity   risible

B. DIRECTIONS: *Match each word in the left column with its definition in the right column. Write the letter of the definition on the line next to the word it defines.*

___ 1. adulterations
___ 2. risible
___ 3. caprices
___ 4. abasement
___ 5. malignity
___ 6. credulity

A. condition of being put down or humbled
B. tendency to believe too readily
C. strong desire to harm others
D. prompting laughter
E. whims
F. impurities

from The Preface to A Dictionary of the English Language and *from* **A Dictionary of the English Language** by Samuel Johnson
from **The Life of Samuel Johnson** by James Boswell

Support for Writing

Use the graphic organizer below to record your ideas on features that tend to give "personality" to a dictionary. Then, write a thesis statement for your editorial on dictionaries with personality.

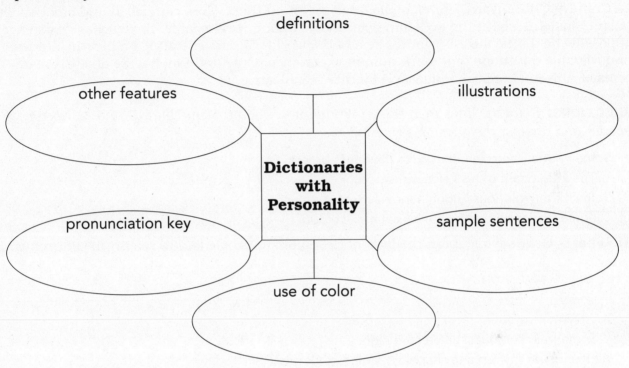

Thesis statement about dictionaries with personality: _____

_____

Name _____ Date _____

"Elegy Written in a Country Churchyard" by Thomas Gray
"A Nocturnal Reverie" by Anne Finch, Countess of Winchilsea
Literary Analysis: Pre-Romantic Poetry

The poems of Thomas Gray and Anne Finch celebrate the formal style of eighteenth-century poetry while at the same time ushering in the emotional expressiveness of the coming Romantic movement. Unlike many other poets of the time, Gray and Finch managed to create poems that stirred not only readers' minds but their emotions. In poems such as Gray's "Elegy Written in a Country Churchyard," for example, readers found themselves compelled and emotionally drawn to insights about the lives and deaths of common rural people, those whose existence supposedly held little meaning for the rest of the world. By concentrating on life's mysteries, the unanswerable questions that mark human experience, Gray and Finch were able to create poems of universal appeal and lasting literary significance.

DIRECTIONS: *Read the lines from "Elegy Written in a Country Churchyard" and "A Nocturnal Reverie" and answer the questions that follow.*

> Some village Hampden, that, with dauntless breast,
>   The little tyrant of his fields withstood,
> Some mute inglorious Milton here may rest,
>   Some Cromwell guiltless of his country's blood.

1. What is Gray saying about the lives of the common people laid to rest in the churchyard?

   _____

   _____

> Yet even these bones from insult to protect
>   Some frail memorial still erected nigh,
> With uncouth rhymes and shapeless sculpture decked,
>   Implores the passing tribute of a sigh.

> Their name, their years, spelt by the unlettered Muse,
>   The place of fame and elegy supply:
> And many a holy text around she strews,
>   That teach the rustic moralist to die.

2. What statement does Gray make about the importance of honoring the dead?

   _____

   _____

"Elegy Written in a Country Churchyard" by Thomas Gray
"A Nocturnal Reverie" by Anne Finch, Countess of Winchilsea
Reading Strategy: Paraphrase

Poetry presents readers with challenges different from those presented by prose. Poetry often uses dense language and imagery, which some readers find difficult to follow. **Paraphrasing** is a useful tool to help guide you through complex poetic passages. Look at the following example from Gray's "Elegy."

Original:
Full many a gem of purest ray serene
The dark unfathomed caves of ocean bear:
Full many a flower is born to blush unseen,
And waste its sweetness on the desert air.

Paraphrase:
Many precious gems are never seen by human eyes because they exist deep in the ocean. Many flowers bloom without ever being seen; their sweet smells dissipate in the desert.

DIRECTIONS: *Use the chart below to help you break down difficult passages in Thomas Gray's "Elegy Written in a Country Churchyard." When you encounter complex material, read it over twice; then try to paraphrase the meaning of the words. Continue reading to make sure that your paraphrase makes sense with regard to the rest of the poem. An example has been completed for you.*

Original	Paraphrase
1. "The boast of heraldry, the pomp of power,/ And all that beauty, all that wealth e'er gave,/ Awaits alike the inevitable hour./The paths of glory lead but to the grave." ("Elegy," lines 33–36)	Having a noble birthright, power, wealth, and beauty doesn't matter; in the end, everyone dies.
2.	
3.	
4.	
5.	

"Elegy Written in a Country Churchyard" by Thomas Gray
"A Nocturnal Reverie" by Anne Finch, Countess of Winchilsea
Vocabulary Builder

Using the Prefix *circum-*

A. DIRECTIONS: *Each of the following sentences includes an italicized word that contains the prefix* circum- *(or* circ-*), meaning "around." Fill in the blank with a word or phrase that completes the sentence and reveals the meaning of the italicized word.*

1. When a path is *circuitous*, it _____.

2. When a person *circulates* at a party, he or she _____
   _____.

3. A *circus* takes place in _____.

4. If a patient is *circumambulating* the grounds, he or she is _____
   _____.

Using the Word List

circumscribed   ingenuous   nocturnal   penury   temperate   venerable

B. DIRECTIONS: *Write a word or words from the Word List to complete each sentence. Then, explain your choice.*

1. It is so cold here that I'm tempted to move someplace where the weather is
   _____.
   _____

2. Finch's poem describes _____ phenomena such as moonlight.
   _____

3. Gray describes the churchyard occupants as _____ regardless of their
   _____, or poverty.
   _____

4. The judge described the ex-senator as lowly and evil for taking advantage of his
   _____, unsuspecting constituents.
   _____

5. The teacher _____ the topics for the final essay by requiring that they focus
   on plot.
   _____

Name _____ Date _____

"Elegy Written in a Country Churchyard" by Thomas Gray
"A Nocturnal Reverie" by Anne Finch, Countess of Winchilsea

Support for Writing

Reread each selection and consider how best to deliver an oral interpretation of one of them or of a passage from one of them. Then organize your ideas on the chart below.

Feature of Oral Presentation	Ideas, Hints, and Tips
Loudness/softness	
Pitch	
Emphasis	
Pace	
Eye Contact	
Body Language	
Sound Effects or Music	

Use a separate page to draft your directions for an oral interpretation. In your draft, mention the ideas you have gathered, and clearly link these ideas to one of the selections.

All-in-One Workbook
157

from "The Aims of *The Spectator*" by Joseph Addison
Literary Analysis: Essay

Historical Context: An **essay** is a piece of short prose that explores a single topic. The word *essay* comes from a French word meaning an "attempt" or "a test." The word was first applied to the writing of Montaigne (1533–1592), a Frenchman whose essays dealt with the questions of life. Although Montaigne's essays were "attempts" to find answers to these enduring questions, they did not always end with definite answers. Montaigne wrote on a number of subjects, but he said that his aim was always to learn about himself.

In "The Aims of *The Spectator*," Addison is "trying" to express his goals for the periodical by describing its usefulness to different types of people. The essay causes the reader to reflect on his or her own relationship to the given topic.

DIRECTIONS: *Read the following excerpts from the essay and answer the questions on another sheet of paper. Give quotations from the essay to support your interpretation.*

from "The Aims of *The Spectator*"

I shall be ambitious to have it said of me that I have brought philosophy out of closets and libraries, schools and colleges, to dwell in clubs and assemblies, at tea tables and in coffeehouses.

1. What is Addison's ultimate goal for *The Spectator*? Give evidence to support your ideas.

from "The Aims of *The Spectator*"

As they lie at the mercy of the first man they meet, and are grave or impertinent all the day long, according to the notions which they have imbibed in the morning, I would earnestly entreat them not to stir out of their chambers till they have read this paper, and do promise them that I will daily instill into them such sound and wholesome sentiments as shall have a good effect on their conversation for the ensuing twelve hours.

2. How would you describe the type of person Addison is writing about in this passage? How does Addison believe *The Spectator* will benefit this type of person?

"**The Aims of *The Spectator***" by Joseph Addison

Reading Strategy: Analyze the Author's Implicit Philosophical Assumptions and Explicit Assumptions

Authors' **philosophical assumptions** rest underneath and support their words. For example, Joseph Addison writes that he wants it said of him that he "brought philosophy out of closets and libraries, schools and colleges, to dwell in clubs and assemblies, at tea tables and in coffeehouses." One **implicit assumption** of this sentence is that it is a good thing to make philosophy more accessible, as Addison hoped to do. An **explicit assumption** of the passage is that a publication like *The Spectator* will be able to take lofty ideas and express them in terms that the general reading public can understand.

Recognizing an author's assumptions—both implicit and explicit—will help you understand the author's viewpoint more fully. It will also make you able to judge that viewpoint more objectively.

DIRECTIONS: *Fill in the second and third columns with one implicit philosophical assumption and one explicit assumption for the passage in the first column. Then, on the lines provided, briefly describe Addison's viewpoint in this essay.*

Passage	Implicit Assumption	Explicit Assumption
"I hope to increase the number of these [women of more elevated life and conversation] by publishing this daily paper, which I shall always endeavor to make an innocent if not an improving entertainment, and by that means at least divert the minds of my female readers from greater trifles."		

What viewpoint do you think Addison expresses about his female readers here? _____

_____

_____

_____

_____

_____

from **"The Aims of *The Spectator*"** by Joseph Addison
Vocabulary Builder

Using the Root *-spec-*

A. DIRECTIONS: *Each of the following sentences includes an italicized word which contains the word root -spec- from a Latin word meaning "to look." Fill in the blank with a word or phrase that completes the sentence and reveals the meaning of the italicized word.*

1. When the detective *inspected* the room, he _____.

2. If she studied every *aspect* of the problem, she _____.

3. If you behold a *spectacle*, you _____.

Using the Word List

    affluence   assiduous   contentious   embellishments   transient   trifles

B. DIRECTIONS: *Synonyms* are words that mean the same or almost the same as each other. On the line, write the word from the box that is a synonym for the underlined word.

1. I like her painting because she manages to describe a place or person without <u>adornments</u>.
   _____

2. He was concerned that too much time was being spent on <u>trivialities</u>. _____

3. The houses in Great Neck were large and hinted at the <u>wealth</u> of the neighborhood.
   _____

4. After the season, the pitcher realized how <u>fleeting</u> were the joys of playing.
   _____

5. Because of their bickering, the partners' relationship could be described as <u>argumentative</u>.
   _____

6. Sheila practiced her violin in a <u>diligent</u> fashion, determined to master the instrument.
   _____

from "**The Aims of *The Spectator***" by Joseph Addison
Support for Writing

Use the chart and lines below to take notes about human behavior. Note the type of behavior you will write about at the top. Then, take notes about your observations of this behavior. Finally, briefly compare and contrast the examples of human behavior.

Type of human behavior:	
Observed examples:	1.
	2.
	3.
	4.

How examples are alike: _____

_____

_____

How examples are different: _____

_____

_____

Use a separate page to write a draft for your letter to the editor about human behavior. Focus your essay on a few examples, and offer conclusions about what the behavior represents.

Contemporary Commentary
Richard Rodriguez Introduces from *Days of Obligation*:
"In Athens Once"

DIRECTIONS: *Use the space provided to answer the questions.*

1. **A.** According to Richard Rodriguez, what do the best journalists achieve?

   B. What noun would Rodriguez like to adopt from Joseph Addison as Rodriguez presents himself to the reader?

   _____

   _____

   _____

2. Briefly explain how Joseph Addison invented a "fictionalized persona."

   _____

   _____

   _____

3. What are some of the similarities Rodriguez sees between eighteenth-century London and modern-day Tijuana?

   _____

   _____

   _____

   _____

4. How does Rodriguez define his "journalistic obligation" to the reader?

   _____

   _____

5. How does the writer describe his "journalistic impulse"?

   _____

   _____

6. Why does Tijuana remind Rodriguez of himself?

   _____

   _____

   _____

   _____

Richard Rodriguez
Listening and Viewing

Segment 1: Meet Richard Rodriguez
- How did Richard Rodriguez's connection with language help him define who he is?
- Why do you think language is an important tool?

_____

_____

_____

_____

Segment 2: Richard Rodriguez on Addison
- What are some characteristics of Joseph Addison's writing?
- How does Richard Rodriguez try to incorporate Addison's writing style in his own work?
- Why do you think that journalism is important to society?

_____

_____

_____

_____

Segment 3: The Writing Process
- How does Richard Rodriguez prepare to begin writing a piece?
- What writing techniques of Richard Rodriguez's would you most likely use in your own writing? Why?

_____

_____

_____

_____

Segment 4: The Rewards of Writing
- Why does Richard Rodriguez think it is important for students to read literature?
- What do you think you can learn by exploring literature?

_____

_____

_____

_____

Essential Questions Workshop—Unit 3

In their poems, epics, and nonfiction works, the writers in Unit Three express ideas that relate to the three Essential Questions framing this book. Review the literature in the unit. Then, for each Essential Question, choose an author and at least one passage from his or her writing that expresses an idea related to the question. Use this chart to complete your work.

Essential Question	Author/Selection	Literary Passage
What is the relationship between place and literature?		
How does literature shape or reflect society?		
What is the relationship of the writer to tradition?		

Name _____ Date _____

Names and Terms to Know

A. DIRECTIONS: *Write a brief sentence explaining each of the following names and terms. You will find all of the information you need in the Unit Introduction in your textbook.*

1. Waterloo: _____

2. Robert Fulton: _____

3. St. Peter's Field: _____

4. The Regency: _____
_____

5. Duke of Wellington: _____
_____

6. Reform Act of 1832: _____

B. DIRECTIONS: *Use the hints below to help you answer each question.*

1. Explain how new inventions added momentum to the Industrial Revolution during this time. *[Hints: What did the steam engine make possible? What did the locomotive do? What industry was transformed by the spinning jenny?]*
_____
_____
_____

2. How did English political reforms affect the period? *[Hints: What conflicts involving the working class came to a head during this period? What were the terms of the Reform Act of 1832? What happened in 1833?]*
_____
_____
_____

3. Describe the state of the monarchy before the arrival of Victoria on the throne. *[Hints: What problems are associated with George III? Who succeeded George III and what was the reputation of his reign? When and how did Victoria become the monarch?]*
_____
_____
_____

Unit 4 Introduction

Essential Question 1: What is the relationship between place and literature?

A. DIRECTIONS: *Answer the questions about the first Essential Question in the Introduction about the relationship between place and literature. All the information you need is in the Unit 4 Introduction in your textbook.*

1. *Romantic Emphasis on Strange, Faraway Places*

    a. Romanticism defined itself by opposition to _____

    b. Who were the Ancient Mariner and Kubla Khan? _____
_____

    c. Who was Ozymandias? _____

2. *Real and Imaginary Refuges*

    a. How did Wordsworth turn the Lake District into a refuge from "dark satanic mills"?
_____

    b. Shelley's skylark and Keats's nightingale are not ordinary birds because they lure
_____

    c. Wordsworth presented nature not as an imaginary, ideal world, but as _____

    d. In what ways had London been improved? _____
_____

    e. In what ways was the image of the city still bleak?
_____

B. DIRECTIONS: *Answer the following questions based on the Essential Question Vocabulary words.*

1. If you could choose an *exotic* vacation spot, what place would you select? _____

2. *Fantastic* can mean "great" or "wonderful," but the word also describes things that are outside _____

3. Where do *urban* populations live? _____

Unit 4 Introduction

Essential Question 2: How does literature shape or reflect society?

A. DIRECTIONS: *On the lines provided, answer the questions about the second Essential Question in the Introduction about the writer and society. All the information you need is in the Unit 4 Introduction in your textbook.*

1. *Political and Industrial Revolutions*

    a. In what terms did Wordsworth describe the French Revolution? _____

    _____

    b. What hard lesson did Napoleon's reign teach the idealists? _____

    c. What hard lesson did the revolutions teach the ruling class? _____

    _____

2. *Writers' Reactions to Revolutionary Changes*

    a. In *The Vindication of the Rights of Woman*, Mary Wollstonecroft urged _____

    b. In "The Chimney Sweeper," William Blake spoke against the practice of _____

    c. What writings of Byron and Shelley took up the cause of the lower classes? _____

    _____

    d. What role for nature did Wordsworth advocate? _____

    _____

B. DIRECTIONS: *Complete the sentence stems based on the Essential Question Vocabulary words.*

1. A *revolution* is a series of events that changes _____

2. In a *power* struggle, two sides fight each other in order to _____

3. *Rebellious* elements in a group make agreement difficult because _____

Unit 4 Introduction

Essential Question 3: What is the relationship of the writer to tradition?

A. DIRECTIONS: *On the lines provided, answer the questions about the third Essential Question in the Introduction, about the relationship between the writer and tradition. All the information you need is in the Unit 4 Introduction in your textbook.*

1. *Rejecting Previous Traditions*

   a. What 18th century literary forms did the Romantics reject, and why?

   _____

   b. Why did numerous writings in this period use ordinary speech? _____

   _____

   c. Against what political views did the Romantic writers rebel? _____

   _____

2. *Reviving Poetical Traditions*

   a. Give examples of Romantic writers who revived the sonnet form or used it in a new way.

   _____

   b. The _____ is a classic form perfected by the Romantic poet John Keats.

3. *Mysterious Literary Figure*

   a. Who is the "Byronic hero," and how was he invented? _____

   _____

   b. Examples of the Byronic hero in the 21st century include _____

   _____

4. *Romantic Prose Inventions*

   a. On what subjects did the novels of Jane Austen focus? _____

   b. On what subjects did Sir Walter Scott's novels focus? _____

   c. What is the "Gothic novel," and how does Mary Shelley's *Frankenstein* use Gothic elements? _____

   _____

B. DIRECTIONS: *Answer the following questions, which are based on the Essential Question Vocabulary words.*

1. How would someone who hates *artificiality* feel about wearing a wig, and why?

   _____

2. If a movie were described as "an *authentic* Western," what kind of setting would it have?

   _____

3. What kinds of feelings would an *outcast* be likely to have? _____

Name _____ Date _____

Following-Through Activities

A. CHECK YOUR COMPREHENSION: *Use this chart to complete the Check Your Comprehension activity in the Unit 4 Introduction. In the middle boxes, fill in a key concept for each of the Essential Questions. In the right boxes, fill in a key author relevant to each concept you list. (The third Essential Question has been done for you.)*

Essential Question	Key Concept	Key Author
Place and Literature		
Literature and Society		
Writer and Tradition	Personal feelings, common speech	Wordsworth

B. EXTEND YOUR LEARNING: *Use this graphic organizer to help you evaluate each of the performances of the groups of writers and questioners.*

Questions	Answers	Evaluations
Why do Romantics reject refined language?	_____ _____ _____ _____	Questioners: _____ _____ Writers: _____ _____
Why do they promote dangerous revolutionary ideas ?	_____ _____ _____ _____	Questioners: _____ _____ Writers: _____ _____
Why are Romantics prejudiced against cities?	_____ _____ _____ _____	Questioners: _____ _____ Writers: _____ _____
Additional question: _____ _____ _____	_____ _____ _____	Questioners: _____ _____ Writers: _____ _____
Additional question: _____ _____ _____	_____ _____ _____	Questioners: _____ _____ Writers: _____ _____

"To a Mouse" and **"To a Louse"** by Robert Burns
"Woo'd and Married and A'" by Joanna Baillie
Literary Analysis: Dialect

Robert Burns was one of the first poets to write verse that incorporated the Scottish dialect of English. **Dialect** is the language, chiefly the speech habits and patterns, of a particular social class, region, or group. Usually dialect differs from the standard form of the language because it possesses its own unique grammar, pronunciation, and vocabulary.

In "To a Mouse," Burns's use of dialect adds to the poem's appeal and the reader's appreciation. If the poem had been written in standard English, it would lack the sense of immediacy and the color achieved in such lines as:

That wee bit heap o' leaves an' stibble, / Has cost thee mony a weary nibble!

By using Scottish dialect, Burns succeeded in capturing his people's tenderness for and intimacy with nature and their shared acceptance of the prospect of "nought but grief an' pain" in the wake of "promised joy."

DIRECTIONS: *The following lines are from "To a Mouse." Rewrite each line in standard English and explain the effect that the use of Scottish dialect alone can achieve.*

1. "Wee, sleekit, cow'rin', tim'rous beastie,"

   _____

   _____

   _____

2. "A daimen icker in a thrave / 'S a sma' request:"

   _____

   _____

   _____

3. "An' naething, now, to big a new ane,"

   _____

   _____

   _____

4. "To thole the winter's sleety dribble, / An' cranreuch cauld!"

   _____

   _____

   _____

"To a Mouse" and **"To a Louse"** by Robert Burns

"Woo'd and Married and A'" by Joanna Baillie

Reading Strategy: Analyze Information from Text Features

A **dialect** is the language and speech habits of the members of a particular group, class, or region. Each dialect has its own unique grammar, pronunciation, and vocabulary. Robert Burns and Joanna Baillie wrote their poems in the Scottish dialect of English. Their use of dialect made their poems more accessible and familiar to their contemporaries in Scotland. Modern readers can use a number of different strategies to **analyze information from text features:**

- Read footnotes to get definitions.
- Use context to guess meaning.
- Speak words aloud and listen for similarities to standard English words.
- Look for similarities between printed dialect words and English words.
- Note apostrophes, which often signal that a letter has been omitted.

DIRECTIONS: *After reading the following lines from "To a Mouse," translate each word in italics, identifying the strategy you used to determine each word's meaning.*

1. "I wad be laith to *rin* an' chase thee / Wi' murd'ring pattle."

   _____

   _____

   _____

2. "I doubt na, *whyles,*[8] but thou may thieve;"

   _____

   _____

   _____

3. "Thy wee bit *housie,* too, in ruin!"

   _____

   _____

   _____

4. "An' *lea'e* us nought but grief an' pain,"

   _____

   _____

   _____

[8]whyles: At times.

"To a Mouse" and **"To a Louse"** by Robert Burns
"Woo'd and Married and A'" by Joanna Baillie
Vocabulary Builder

Using the Suffix -some

A. DIRECTIONS: *The following words all contain the suffix* –some, *meaning "having specific qualities." Using the word's context along with what you know about this suffix, write a definition of each* italicized *word in the blank.*

1. At first the jokes were funny, but they became *tiresome*.

   _____

2. When Jerome went to the zoo, he thought the snakes were *loathsome*, but Janelle enjoyed them.

   _____

3. Bees buzzing around your head at a picnic are so *bothersome*, aren't they?

   _____

Using the Word List

> discretion   dominion   impudence   inconstantly   winsome

B. DIRECTIONS: *Write a word from the Word List to answer each question.*

1. Which word means most nearly the opposite of *imprudence?* _____

2. If you observe someone acting rudely toward a stranger, what word might you use to describe such behavior? _____

3. Which word is closest in meaning to *changeably?* _____

4. Which word describes a monarch's authority over his or her subjects?

   _____

5. What word might you use to describe a person who has a charming manner and appearance? _____

Name _____ Date _____

"**To a Mouse**" and "**To a Louse**" by Robert Burns
"**Woo'd and Married and A'**" by Joanna Baillie
Support for Writing

DIRECTIONS: *Answer the following questions about the use of dialect in literature.*

1. In what ways does the use of dialect add richness to a work of literature? _____

_____

_____

2. How does the use of dialect help reinforce details about the setting in a work of literature?

_____

_____

3. How does the use of dialect help reveal details about characters? _____

_____

_____

4. What argument might someone make *against* the use of dialect in literature? _____

_____

_____

5. How would you answer that argument? _____

_____

_____

6. How does the use of dialect in literature help to preserve certain features of a culture? ___

_____

_____

On a separate page, write a draft of your speech about the use of dialect in literature. Refer to your answers on this page for ideas to include in your speech.

"The Lamb," "The Tyger," "The Chimney Sweeper," and **"Infant Sorrow"** by William Blake

Literary Analysis: Archetypes and Social Commentary

Blake's poetry is filled with **archetypes,** or symbols that reveal universal truths. They consist of plot patterns, character types, and themes that transcend time and culture. Archetypes hold strong emotional power—for Blake, archetypes helped put his mystical visions into words.

Moving beyond his dream-like perceptions, Blake also commented on social injustices of his time. He critiqued events and popular belief in his **social commentary.** Historical and political references support his opinions and add credibility to his writing.

DIRECTIONS: *Identify each of the following words or phrases from Blake's poetry as an archetypal symbol or a historical reference. For each archetypal symbol, explain its meaning and source. For each historical reference, explain what it suggests about Blake's intention.*

1. lamb _____

_____

2. fire _____

_____

3. swaddling bands _____

_____

4. child _____

_____

5. anvil _____

_____

6. angel _____

_____

7. "my father sold me" _____

_____

8. "got with our bags & our brushes to work" _____

_____

"The Lamb," "The Tyger," "The Chimney Sweeper," and **"Infant Sorrow"** by William Blake
Reading Strategy: Applying Critical Perspectives

A **critical perspective** is a way of looking at a work of literature. One type of critical perspective is the **archetypal perspective,** or looking at the universal symbols in the work. Archetypes are images, details, and patterns that seem to have a strong emotional charge and appear across many different cultures.

Another type of critical perspective is the **historical perspective,** or looking at the political, economic, and cultural background of the work.

DIRECTIONS: *Complete the following chart by identifying and explaining the archetypal symbols and historical background of each poem, as indicated.*

Poem	Symbol or Background	Explanation
"The Lamb"		
"The Tyger"		
"The Chimney Sweeper"		
"Infant Sorrow"		

"The Lamb," "The Tyger," "The Chimney Sweeper," and **"Infant Sorrow"** by William Blake
Vocabulary Builder

Using the Root *-spir-*

A. DIRECTIONS: *Each of the following sentences includes an italicized word that contains the word root -spir-, which means "breath" or "life." Fill in each blank with a word or phrase to complete the sentence and reveal the meaning of the italicized word.*

1. If the young woman is *spirited,* she _____.

2. If he was *dispirited* by the bad news, he _____.

3. If we waited to see what would *transpire,* we _____.

4. If the council member's term *expired,* it _____.

5. If the poem *inspires* the reader, it _____.

Using the Word List

    aspire   immortal   sinews   sulk   symmetry   vales

B. DIRECTIONS: *Complete each sentence by filling in the blank with one of the words from the Word List.*

1. The rolling hills and grassy _____ were the landscape of his earliest memories.

2. Early on, he learned to appreciate the veins of leaves, the wings of butterflies—in short, all of nature's _____.

3. With all of these influences, it was only natural that he would _____ to become a nature photographer.

4. Caroline tended to _____ when she did not get her way.

5. Perhaps because they have not had much experience with illness, young people often seem to think they are _____.

6. The long-distance runner had strengthened the _____ of every muscle through his extensive training.

Name _____ Date _____

"The Lamb," "The Tyger," "The Chimney Sweeper," and **"Infant Sorrow"** by William Blake
Grammar and Style: Introductory Phrases and Clauses

An **introductory phrase** is a group of words at the beginning of a sentence. It has no verb.
Examples: **Through the forests,** the tiger ran. **At first,** the hunter did not see him.

An **introductory clause** is a group of words at the beginning of a sentence. It has a subject and a verb but cannot stand alone as a sentence.

Examples: **When morning came,** the children started work. **By the time they stopped,** the sun had set.

A. PRACTICE: *Underline the introductory phrase or clause in each of the following sentences. In the blank, identify it as a phrase or a clause.*

1. For a small fee, the shepherd will take care of the flock. _____

2. While the sheep graze, the shepherd keeps an eye on them. _____

3. As he stalks his prey, the tiger remains silent. _____

4. At first, the prey has no idea he is in danger. _____

5. After the boy's mother died, his father sold him as a servant. _____

6. For very little money, the boy works from dawn to dusk. _____

7. After the child was born, he was wrapped in a blanket. _____

8. Every four hours, the baby needs to be fed. _____

B. Writing Application: *Rewrite each sentence, adding an introductory phrase or clause as indicated in parentheses.*

1. The lamb grew larger. (introductory phrase)

   _____

2. The shepherd searched for the lost lamb. (introductory clause)

   _____

3. We saw the tiger exhibit. (introductory phrase)

   _____

4. The poor tiger was very unhappy. (introductory clause)

   _____

5. The chimney sweeper will do a good job. (introductory phrase)

   _____

6. The young boy became very ill. (introductory clause)

   _____

7. The parents welcomed their new child into the world. (introductory phrase)

   _____

8. The child gained weight rapidly. (introductory clause)

   _____

"The Lamb," "The Tyger," "The Chimney Sweeper," and **"Infant Sorrow"** by William Blake
Support for Writing

Use the charts below to take notes for your multi-genre analysis of Blake's political and philosophical associations.

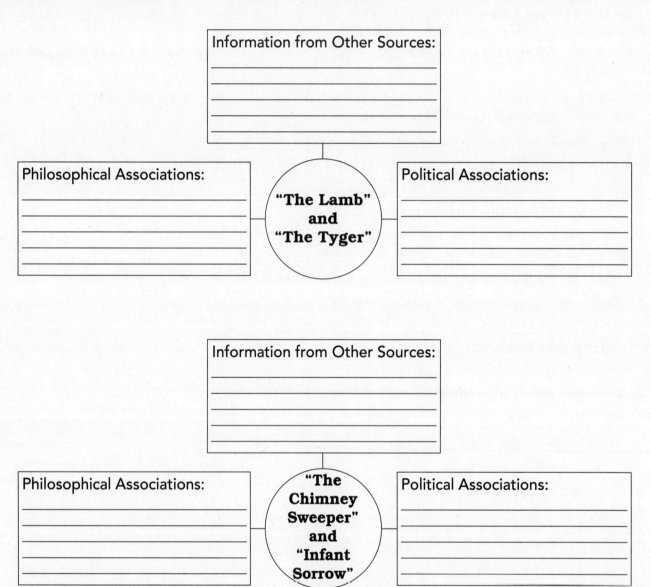

On a separate page, use the information in your charts to write your analysis of Blake's politics and philosophy.

Contemporary Commentary
Elizabeth McCracken Introduces "Introduction" to *Frankenstein* by Mary Shelley

DIRECTIONS: *Use the space provided to answer the questions.*

1. What was McCracken's recurring nightmare when she was a child?

   _____

   _____

   _____

   _____

2. **A.** What does McCracken mean by "the thrill of the terrifying"?

   _____

   _____

   B. Do you agree with McCracken that horror has a strange but widespread appeal to both children and adults? How would you explain this appeal?

   _____

   _____

   _____

   _____

3. According to McCracken, why did her dream about a Frankenstein monster impress her?

   _____

   _____

4. Why did McCracken become a fiction writer?

   _____

   _____

5. What questions about Mary Shelley's *Frankenstein* does McCracken's commentary raise in your mind at this point?

   _____

   _____

   _____

   _____

   _____

   _____

   _____

Elizabeth McCracken
Listening and Viewing

Segment 1: Meet Elizabeth McCracken
- How does Elizabeth McCracken draw on her personal experiences to create characters for her stories?
- Why might real-life experiences be a good starting point for a story?

_____

_____

_____

_____

Segment 2: On Frankenstein
- Why is *Frankenstein* considered a "gothic novel"?
- Although *Frankenstein* was first published in 1818, people are still intrigued by this story today. What do you find timeless about the motivations of Dr. Frankenstein as described by McCracken?

_____

_____

_____

_____

Segment 3: The Writing Process
- How does Elizabeth McCracken "find" her plot?
- Why do you think it is important to be flexible when you develop plot?

_____

_____

_____

_____

Segment 4: The Rewards of Writing
- What advice does Elizabeth McCracken have for young writers?
- Do you agree or disagree with her advice?

_____

_____

_____

_____

Name _____ Date _____

Introduction to Frankenstein by Mary Wollstonecraft Shelley

Literary Analysis: The Gothic Tradition and the Romantic Movement

To the **Romantics** of the early nineteenth century, the **Gothic** elements of mystery, variety, richness, and primitive wildness suggested the natural, free, authentic aspects of life that they valued. The Gothic novel was characterized by mystery, darkness, and horror. The Gothic tradition emphasized setting and plot more than character; often, an atmosphere of brooding and terror pervaded Gothic novels.

DIRECTIONS: *Answer the following questions about how Mary Shelley's Introduction to* Frankenstein *reflects the Gothic tradition.*

1. How might the Swiss setting in which Mary Wollstonecraft Shelley found herself in the summer of 1816 have inspired her to write a Gothic novel?

_____

_____

_____

_____

_____

_____

2. How did the stories that the writers read to amuse themselves help produce a frame of mind conducive to Gothic writing?

_____

_____

_____

_____

_____

_____

3. How is the waking dream that Mary Wollstonecraft Shelley describes characteristic of the Gothic tradition?

_____

_____

_____

_____

_____

_____

Name _____ Date _____

Introduction to Frankenstein by Mary Wollstonecraft Shelley
Reading Strategy: Predict

Making **predictions** about what will happen in a literary work keeps you involved in your reading. Use clues that the writer provides, along with what you learn about the characters and the pattern in which the work is organized. As you read, check your predictions and revise them as necessary.

DIRECTIONS: *In the lines following each excerpt, record what predictions you might make about Mary Shelley's novel* Frankenstein.

1. "'How I, then a young girl, came to think of, and to dilate upon, so very hideous an idea?'"

_____

_____

_____

_____

2. "I busied myself to *think of a story*—a story to rival those which had excited us to this task. One which would speak to the mysterious fears of our nature . . ."

_____

_____

_____

_____

3. ". . . various philosophical doctrines were discussed, and among others the nature of the principle of life and whether there was any probability of its ever being discovered and communicated."

_____

_____

_____

_____

4. "When I placed my head on my pillow, I did not sleep, nor could I be said to think. My imagination, unbidden, possessed and guided me, gifting the successive images that arose in my mind with a vividness far beyond the usual bounds of reverie."

_____

_____

_____

_____

Introduction to Frankenstein by Mary Wollstonecraft Shelley
Vocabulary Builder

Using Related Words: *Phantasm* and *Fantasy*

A. DIRECTIONS: *The word* phantasm *means "supernatural form or shape." It is related to the word* fantasy, *which means "a product of the imagination." Each italicized word in the following sentences is related to* phantasm *or* fantasy. *Replace each one with a synonymous word or phrase. Write the new word or phrase on the line following the sentence.*

1. To Dexter, the shadows looked like a parade of *fantastic* creatures. _____

2. When Sono opened her eyes, the *phantasm* was still there. _____

3. Angela liked to *fantasize* about quitting her job and moving to Alaska. _____

4. Scowling, Greg pronounced, "If you think you're entitled to another week of vacation, you're living in a *fantasy* land!" _____

5. The special effects in that movie were *phantasmagorical*! _____

Using the Word List

acceded	appendage	incitement	phantasm	platitude	ungenial

B. DIRECTIONS: *Fill in each blank with a word from the Word List to complete the sentence.*

1. Alex _____ to Lori's request not to reveal the plans for the surprise party.

2. Without much imagination, the speaker often used a _____ like "All's well that ends well."

3. The shimmering mist in Margo's office turned out to be steam from her teacup, not a _____.

4. The stock market always seems to crash during the _____ weather of October.

5. Tasha's encouragement was all the _____ Li needed to convince her to apply for the job.

6. Dan's pencil looked like an extra _____ growing above his ear.

Name _____ Date _____

Grammar and Style: Avoiding Subject-Verb Agreement Problems

Subjects and verbs must agree in number. Because, except for the verb *be*, English verbs have only two forms in the present tense (the girl *dances*; girls *dance*) and one in the past tense (the girl *danced*), there are few problems with agreement. Here is the basic rule: A singular subject takes a singular verb. A plural subject takes a plural verb.

Example: The <u>worker</u> <u>takes</u> a break at 3:00. The <u>workers</u> <u>take</u> a break at 3:00.

Here is some elaboration on the basic rule: Subjects joined by *and* usually take a plural verb.

Example: <u>Bob and June</u> <u>wash</u> the car together.

Subjects joined by *or, nor, either . . . or,* or *neither . . . nor* sometimes take singular verbs and sometimes plural, depending on the situation.

Examples: <u>One or the other</u> <u>does</u> the drying. (Both subjects are singular and considered as separate, so they take a singular verb.)

<u>Barbara or her brothers</u> <u>arrive</u> in the afternoon. (When one subject is singular and the other is plural, the verb usually agrees with the nearest subject.)

Sometimes, the subject and the verb are separated by a phrase or clause. Determine what the subject is before deciding which form the verb should take.

Example: The <u>students</u> who finish their work early <u>go</u> to lunch first.

A. PRACTICE: *In each sentence below, underline the subject once and the verb twice.*

1. The publishers of the book ask the author for an introduction.
2. The author and her husband go to Switzerland.
3. The rain, which falls incessantly, keeps them indoors for days.
4. Neither the author's husband nor their friend writes a story.
5. The conversations between the author's husband and their friend continue for hours.

B. Writing Application: *Write the correct form of the verb on the line.*

1. Percy Bysshe Shelley, using his unique talents, (write, writes) _____ a poem.
2. Lord Byron and his friend Polidori (begin, begins) _____ stories that fall short of the assignment.
3. Mary Shelley, after placing her head on her pillow, (imagine, imagines) _____ a horrifying creature.
4. Neither Mary Shelley nor her husband (know, knows) _____ how popular her story will become.
5. The members of the group (agree, agrees) _____ that Mary Shelley's idea was the best one of all.

Name _____   Date _____

Introduction to Frankenstein by Mary Wollstonecraft Shelley
Support for Writing: Autobiography of a Monster

Use the cluster diagram below to make notes for your autobiography of a monster. Imagine that you are in the monster's position. What thoughts, experiences, and desires might you have? Write your ideas in the circles.

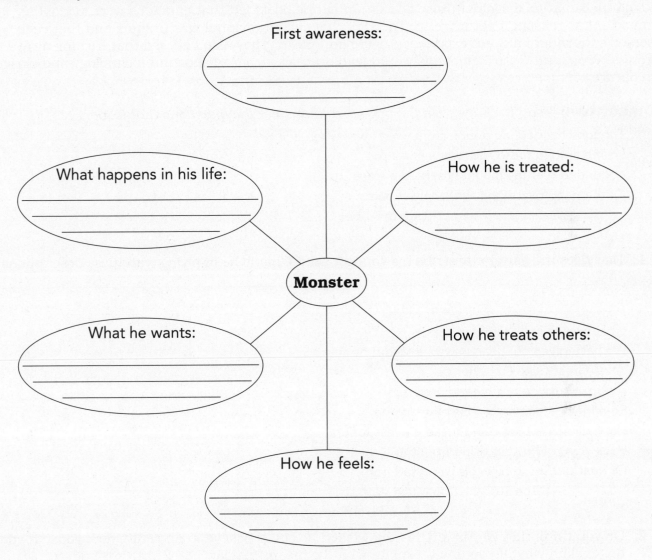

On a separate page, write a draft of your autobiography of a monster. Use the ideas you generated on this page. Remember that an autobiography is the story of a person's life written by that person. Use the pronoun *I* to refer to the narrator.

Poetry of William Wordsworth
Literary Analysis: Romanticism

During the European Enlightenment, a period that preceded Romanticism, writers and poets believed that intellect and reason were the most important aspects of humanity. They also felt that life was a universal experience for all people, no matter their background or living situation. Romanticism argued against those beliefs. Romantic poets felt that emotions were at least as important as reason, if not more so. They felt that each individual was unique, and that each person's individual life and experiences were important. They also believed that turning away from intellect and toward emotions would lead one away from society and technology and closer to nature.

DIRECTIONS: *Read the lines from the poems, and answer the questions that follow.*

> Though changed, no doubt, from what I was when first
> I came among these hills; when like a roe
> I bounded o'er the mountains, by the sides
> Of the deep rivers, and the lonely streams. . . .
>   ("Tintern Abbey")

1. How does the narrator describe his younger self? What is he implying with these descriptions?

   _____

   _____

> Little we see in Nature that is ours;
> We have given our hearts away, a sordid boon! . . .
> . . . —Great God! I'd rather be
> A Pagan suckled in a creed outworn;
> So might I, standing on this pleasant lea,
> Have glimpses that would make me less forlorn;
> Have sight of Proteus rising from the sea;
> Or hear old Triton blow his wreathèd horn.
>   ("The World Is Too Much With Us")

2. Do you think that Wordsworth really wished he could believe in ancient Greek gods? If you do, explain why. If you don't, explain what he meant instead.

   _____

   _____

Name _____   Date _____

Poetry of William Wordsworth
Literary Analysis: Diction

Diction, an important element in a writer's style or "voice," is the writer's choice of words. Skilled writers are very careful with their diction, choosing words that will evoke specific emotions and responses in their readers.

In "Lines Composed a Few Miles Above Tintern Abbey," William Wordsworth uses the words *summers, winters, mountain springs,* and *lofty cliffs* in the first four lines. Ask yourself why he chose these words. Could it be that he was trying to evoke a sense of unity with nature? Then ask yourself what your own emotional response is to these words. Do you want to see those "mountain springs" and "lofty cliffs" for yourself?

DIRECTIONS: *Use this graphic organizer to record significant examples of Wordsworth's choice of words. When you find a passage that evokes an emotional response in yourself, think about what Wordsworth might have been trying to achieve. Write the passage in the chart, underline the words that are especially effective, and explain their emotional effect on you. An example has been done for you.*

Passage	Emotional Effect
1. "Five years have past; five <u>summers</u>, with the length / Of five <u>long winters</u>! And again I hear / These waters, rolling from their <u>mountain springs</u> / With a <u>soft inland murmur</u>." ("Tintern Abbey," lines 1–4)	I wonder why the summers have felt like five long winters. Has he experienced some loss, some sorrow? The description of the waters and their "murmur" is somehow comforting and reassuring.
2.	
3.	
4.	
5.	

Poetry of William Wordsworth
Reading Strategy: Evaluating the Influence of the Historical Period

William Wordsworth lived at a time when great political and social events were sweeping the world. As a young poet when many of these events took place, Wordsworth embraced the excitement and promise of the underlying ideas and felt intense disappointment when certain ideas failed to sustain their promise. Through a careful reading and analysis of his poetry, you will recognize the influence of these events on his poetry and come to a fuller understanding of the meaning of his works.

DIRECTIONS: *Use this graphic organizer to help you record examples of revolutionary political and philosophical influences that colored Wordsworth's view of life in his work. The first example has been provided for you.*

Philosophical and Political Influences

Celebration of Common Folk
"These plots of cottage ground, these orchard tufts / . . . Are clad in one green hue, and lose themselves / 'Mid groves and copses . . . / these pastoral farms, / Green to the very door . . . " ("Tintern Abbey," 11–17)
Love of Nature
Admiration for French Revolution
Loss of Faith in Reasons

Poetry of William Wordsworth
Vocabulary Builder

Using Related Words: *Anatomize*

A. DIRECTIONS: *Answer the following questions about* anatomize *and words related to it.*

1. What does *anatomize* mean? _____

2. What type of tool might an anatomist use? _____

3. If someone were making an anatomic study of mole rats, would she be more interested in the rats' feeding habits or in their internal organs? _____

4. In 1958, Robert Travers wrote a book called *Anatomy of a Murder.* How do you think the book treats the crime in question? _____

Using the Word List

anatomize	presumption	recompense	roused	sordid	stagnant

B. DIRECTIONS: *Each item below consists of a related pair of words in CAPITAL LETTERS followed by four lettered pairs of words. Choose the pair that best expresses a relationship similar to that expressed in the pair in capital letters. Circle the letter of your choice.*

1. EGOTIST : PRESUMPTION ::
   A. traitor : treachery
   B. doctor : stethoscope
   C. coward : bravery
   D. lawyer : summation

2. RECOMPENSE : SALARY ::
   A. fairness : injustice
   B. indebtedness : mortgage
   C. heat : perspiration
   D. interest : payment

3. ROUSED : EXCITED ::
   A. sympathetic : saddened
   B. curious : uninterested
   C. offended : insulted
   D. sleeping : awakened

4. SORDID : FILTHY ::
   A. frigid : lukewarm
   B. amusing : ridiculous
   C. untimely : early
   D. angry : irate

5. SWAMP : STAGNANT ::
   A. ocean : salty
   B. river : flowing
   C. pond : tidal
   D. lake : frozen

6. ANATOMIZE : DISSECT ::
   A. infantilize : mature
   B. categorize : difference
   C. prioritize : equate
   D. analyze : study

Name _____ Date _____

Grammar and Style: Avoiding Pronoun Antecedent Agreement Problems

You will find it easier to understand densely constructed poetry if you learn to recognize pronoun-antecedent agreement. Look, for example, at this excerpt from "London, 1802."

Milton! Thou should'st be living at this hour:

England hath need of thee: she is a fen

Of stagnant waters. . . .

Reading carefully, you will note that the pronouns *Thou* in line 1 and *thee* in line 2 refer to their antecedent, *Milton.* The pronoun *she* in line 2 refers to its antecedent, *England.*

When using pronouns, make sure that the pronoun you choose agrees with its antecedent.

A. PRACTICE: *Circle the word in parentheses that correctly completes each sentence.*

1. The speaker lovingly remembers (his, their) dear sister, who has died.
2. As Wordsworth walks through the woods above Tintern Abbey, he recalls walking through (it, them) with his sister.
3. The Frenchmen had begun a war of conquest, becoming oppressors in (his, their) turn.
4. The speaker complains that we waste our powers rather than using (it, them) wisely.
5. The speaker thinks that if Milton were still alive, (he, they) could inspire the nation.

B. Writing Application: *For each of the antecedents below, write a sentence that uses a correct pronoun. Underline the pronoun in your completed sentence.*

1. The brother and sister _____

_____

2. The green pastoral landscape _____

_____

3. William Wordsworth _____

_____

4. London and Paris _____

_____

5. Poetry _____

_____

Name _____ Date _____

Writing Workshop: Unit 4
Multimedia Presentation: Integrating Media

When developing a multimedia presentation, think about how to provide a balance of types of media, how well each medium works with the other media, and how each medium can help develop your topic.

A. DIRECTIONS: *Use the following chart to evaluate how well each media element works to develop your ideas.*

Media Element	Idea It Expresses or Supports	Is the idea clear? If not, how can you improve it, or should you replace it?

B. DIRECTIONS: *When you make your presentation, do not include all of your media at once, but incorporate them at appropriate points. To think about how to incorporate your media, use the following outline to create an abbreviated outline of your presentation. List the media you will use with each idea.*

Introduction: _____   Media: _____

I. (topic) _____   Media: _____

   A. _____   Media: _____

   B. _____   Media: _____

II. (topic) _____   Media: _____

   A. _____   Media: _____

   B. _____   Media: _____

III. (topic) _____   Media: _____

   A. _____   Media: _____

   B. _____   Media: _____

Comparing Literary Works: Alexander Pushkin, Charles Baudelaire, Tu Fu, and others
Literary Analysis: Lyric Poetry

Lyric poetry expresses the personal thoughts of a single speaker. The first lyric poems were meant to be sung to musical accompaniment. Modern lyric poems are not sung, but they do have a musical quality, with the words and rhythm creating a harmonious effect. Like many songs, they are usually relatively short, express deep feelings, and emphasize the imagination. A lyric poem focuses on creating a single unifying effect.

DIRECTIONS: *Use this chart to identify images from each poem. In sentences, explain how these images relate to the poem's larger meaning.*

Lyric Poetry	Image or Idea
1. "I Have Visited Again"	
2. "Invitation to the Voyage"	
3. "Thick Grow the Rush Leaves"	
4. "Jade Flower Palace"	
5. Tanka #1	
6. Tanka #2	
7. Tanka #3	

Comparing Literary Works: Alexander Pushkin, Charles Baudelaire, Tu Fu, and others
Vocabulary Builder

Using the Word List

> ancestral   imperceptibly   morose   pathos   proffering   scurry

A. DIRECTIONS: *Write the word from the box that best completes each sentence.*

1. The rats _____ across the ruins of the palace.

2. The sailors were _____ tasty tidbits to the albatross, but the sad bird ate nothing.

3. The speaker was overcome with a feeling of _____ as he viewed the crumbling ruins.

4. The speaker felt lonely and _____, thinking sadly about his lost love.

5. Going back to his _____ lands, the speaker was reminded of the past.

6. Each day, the trees grow _____, but over the years their growth is noticeable.

B. DIRECTIONS: *Revise each sentence so that the underlined vocabulary word is used in a logical way. Be sure to keep the vocabulary word in your revision.*

Example: The earthquake <u>imperceptibly</u> jarred the region, toppling buildings.

  Revision: The earthquake <u>imperceptibly</u> hit, barely registering on the Richter scale.

1. The snails <u>scurry</u> about in the yard, busily looking for food.

   _____

2. The <u>pathos</u> of the moment moved the young girl to laughter.

   _____

3. Our <u>ancestral</u> lands have never been owned by our family.

   _____

4. The <u>morose</u> child was happily playing with her friends.

   _____

5. Hal was <u>proffering</u> dessert to his guests, throwing it in the garbage.

   _____

Comparing Literary Works: Alexander Pushkin, Charles Baudelaire, Tu Fu, and others
Support for Writing

Use the Venn diagram below to record your ideas about the two poems you plan to compare and contrast. In the spaces on the top and bottom, record what is unique about each poem. In the space in the middle, record what is similar about the poems.

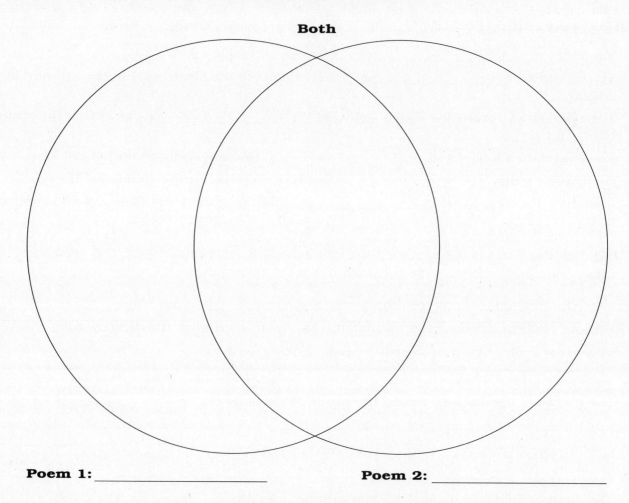

Poem 1: _____   **Poem 2:** _____

On a separate sheet of paper, draft your comparison-and-contrast essay. Draw from the ideas you recorded in your Venn diagram.

All-in-One Workbook
194

Name _____ Date _____

"The Rime of the Ancient Mariner" and **"Kubla Khan"** by Samuel Taylor Coleridge
Literary Analysis: Poetic Sound Devices

   Alliteration is the repetition of a consonant sound at the beginnings of words. **Consonance** is the repetition of consonant sounds in stressed syllables with dissimilar vowel sounds. **Assonance** is repetition of vowel sounds in stressed syllables with dissimilar consonant sounds. **Internal rhyme** is the use of rhyming words within a line. **Slant rhyme** occurs with the use of sounds that are similar but not identical, such as *shore* and *share*.

DIRECTIONS: *In each of the following passages from "The Rime of the Ancient Mariner" and "Kubla Kahn," certain letters are italicized. For each passage, write on the line the **sound device** that is used.*

1. "As who pursued with ye*ll* and b*l*ow" _____

2. "The ice did spl*it* with a thunder-f*it*" _____

3. "*H*e *h*olds *h*im with *h*is skinny *h*and" _____

4. "The ship was ch*eered*, the harbor cl*eared*" _____

5. "'From the fiends that plague thee *thus*!– / Why look'st thou so?' 'With my crossbow / I shot the *Albatross.*'"

6. "And we did spea*k* only to brea*k*" _____

7. "*R*ed as a *r*ose is she" _____

8. "All in a h*o*t and c*o*pper sky" _____

9. "The Wedding G*uest* he beat his br*east*" _____

10. "The death f*ires* danced at n*ight*" _____

11. "The *f*air breeze blew, the white *f*oam *f*lew" _____

12. " 'Through utter drought all dumb we *stood*! / I bit my arm, I sucked the *blood.*' "

13. "His *f*lashing eyes, his *f*loating hair!" _____

14. "A *d*amsel with a *d*ulcimer" _____

15. "For *h*e on *h*oneydew *h*ath fed," _____

16. "And cl*o*se your eyes with h*o*ly dread" _____

17. "And from this chasm, with *c*easeless turmoil s*ee*thing" _____

18. "And 'mid this tumult Kubla heard from *far* / Ancestral voices prophesying *war*!'" _____

"The Rime of the Ancient Mariner" and **"Kubla Khan"** by Samuel Taylor Coleridge
Reading Strategy: Analyze Poetic Effects

One of the primary characteristics that sets verse apart from prose is the range of poetic and sound devices commonly used in poetry. These devices enhance the musical qualities of the language by pleasing the ear, but they also serve to emphasize meaning and create mood. By paying attention to these devices, you can become more sensitive to the nuances and effects of poetic language. The following are several different types of sound devices:

alliteration:	repetition of consonant sounds at the beginnings of words
consonance:	repetition of consonant sounds at the ends of words
assonance:	repetition of vowel sounds in nearby words or syllables
internal rhyme:	rhymes occurring within a poetic line
ordinary repetition:	repetition of entire words

DIRECTIONS: *Use this chart to keep track of poetic effects as you read "The Rime of the Ancient Mariner" and "Kubla Khan." Each time you encounter a poetic sound device, write the example in the left column. Then, in the right column, explain the effect of the device, or how it enhances the text. The first passage has been done for you.*

Line or Phrase	Device	Effect
1. "Water, water, everywhere,/ Nor any drop to drink." ("Rime," lines 121–122)	repetition and alliteration	Repetition of the word *water* and of the *w* sound emphasizes the amount of water. Repetition of the *dr-* sound in *drop* and *drink* also emphasizes the lack of drinking water. The differing alliteration in each line contrasts the amount of water with the lack of drinking water.
2.		
3.		
4.		
5.		

"The Rime of the Ancient Mariner" and **"Kubla Khan"** by Samuel Taylor Coleridge
Vocabulary Builder

Using the Root *-journ-*

A. DIRECTIONS: *Each of the following words contains the Latin root -journ-, which comes from the French and Latin words for "day." For each of the following sentences, choose one of the five words or phrases to replace the italicized word or phrase.*

adjourn   du jour   journal   journey   journalism

1. The long day's *trip* had wiped me out completely. _____

2. I'm not so interested in writing fiction; I prefer *reporting*. _____

3. Kevin wrote all of his secret sorrows in his *diary*. _____

4. At midnight, the council finally decided that it was time for the meeting *to end for the day.*
_____

5. Maggie ordered the radish salad and the soup *of the day.* _____

Using the Word List

averred   expiated   reverence   sinuous   sojourn   tumult

B. DIRECTIONS: *Choose the letter of the description that best fits each word below. Write the letters on the lines provided.*

___ 1. tumult
   A. commotion
   B. height
   C. depth
   D. gathering

___ 2. sinuous
   A. weak
   B. strong
   C. straight
   D. curving

___ 3. averred
   A. expressed ignorance
   B. stated to be true
   C. stated to be false
   D. defended weakly

___ 4. expiated
   A. breathed
   B. blamed
   C. explained
   D. atoned

___ 5. sojourn
   A. stay for a while
   B. visit briefly
   C. travel widely
   D. carry to

___ 6. reverence
   A. sadness
   B. veneration
   C. revisitation
   D. abhorrence

Name _____ Date _____

"The Rime of the Ancient Mariner" and **"Kubla Khan"** by Samuel Taylor Coleridge
Support for Writing

Use the cluster diagram to gather details from "The Rime of the Ancient Mariner" about the albatross and about its effects on the Mariner.

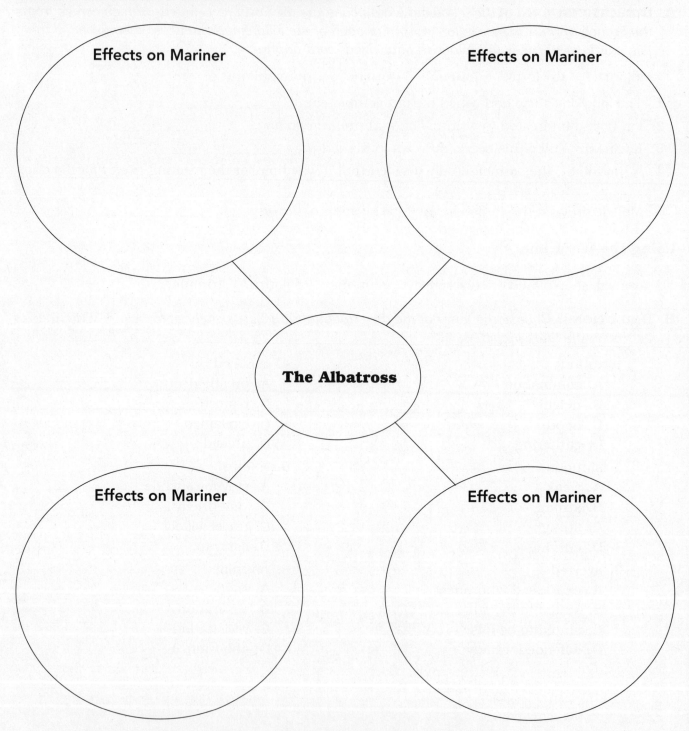

On a separate page, use the information you have gathered in your cluster diagram as you write your essay analyzing the meanings of the albatross as a symbol.

Name _____ Date _____

"She Walks in Beauty," *from* Childe Harold's Pilgrimage, and *from* Don Juan by George Gordon, Lord Byron
Literary Analysis: Figurative Language

To build powerful images, writers use **figurative language,** or figures of speech. Through figurative language, things that might at first seem completely unrelated are linked together.

Similes make comparisons using the word *like* or *as:*

The empty house was like a tomb.

Metaphors make comparisons without using *like* or *as:*

The empty house was a tomb.

Personification gives human characteristics to nonhuman subjects:

The empty house whispered of its past.

A. DIRECTIONS: *Following are passages from various poems. On the line at the right, identify the figure of speech that is used in each passage.*

1. "The lowered pulses of the river beat . . ." _____

2. "I tell you the past is a bucket of ashes." _____

3. The fields "were patched like one wide crazy quilt . . ." _____

4. ". . . drowsy lights along the paths/Are dim and pearled" _____

5. "The twigs are snapping like brittle bones." _____

B. DIRECTIONS: *Following is a series of items beside which are listed various types of figurative language. Describe each item in a sentence using the figure of speech indicated.*

1. storm clouds (personification) _____

_____

_____

2. courage (personification) _____

_____

_____

3. spring rain (simile) _____

_____

_____

4. the motorcycle (metaphor) _____

_____

_____

Name _____ Date _____

"She Walks in Beauty," *from* Childe Harold's Pilgrimage,
and *from* Don Juan by George Gordon, Lord Byron
Reading Strategy: Question

Poetry is meant to be read several times. You might read a poem once to get a general sense of its themes. On another reading, you might focus on the language and rhythm of the poem. Next, you might pay special attention to its images. At least one of your readings should be devoted to achieving a basic understanding of what the poet is trying to communicate. You can do this by reading actively—asking questions about the poem and answering them. Ask questions that use the words *who, what, where, when,* and *why.* For example, consider the excerpt in your textbook from *Childe Harold's Pilgrimage:*

- **Question:** *What* does the speaker hope to communicate? **Answer:** He expresses admiration for the ocean.
- **Question:** *Why* does the speaker admire the ocean? **Answer:** Humans and human activities are insignificant in comparison to the ocean; the ocean is unchanging; it rules its domain and cannot be tamed by humans.

DIRECTIONS: *Read the excerpt in your textbook from* Don Juan. *Write questions about the poem using the words listed below. Then answer your questions.*

1. Who _____

   _____?

   _____

   _____

2. What _____

   _____?

   _____

   _____

3. What _____

   _____?

   _____

   _____

4. Why _____

   _____?

   _____

   _____

5. Why _____

   _____?

   _____

   _____

"She Walks in Beauty," *from* Childe Harold's Pilgrimage, and *from* Don Juan by George Gordon, Lord Byron
Vocabulary Builder

Using the Suffix *-ous*

A. DIRECTIONS: *The following words all contain the suffix* -ous, *meaning "full of." In the blanks, complete each sentence with the appropriate word or words from the list.*

adventurous	delicious	famous	humorous
miraculous	ominous	rebellious	

1. The mushrooms tasted _____; they were not poisonous.

2. The _____ hero walked forward boldly into the storm, undeterred by the

   _____ lightning flashing all around him.

3. The politician was _____ for always beginning his speeches with a

   _____ anecdote.

4. Maude made a _____ recovery following cardiac surgery.

5. Feeling _____, Theo refused to celebrate the holidays.

Using the Word List

    arbiter   avarice   copious   credulous   retort   torrid

B. DIRECTIONS: *Match each word in the left column with its definition in the right column. Write the letter of the definition on the line next to the word it defines.*

___ 1. retort		A. willing to believe
___ 2. credulous		B. plentiful
___ 3. copious		C. greed
___ 4. avarice		D. reply with a wisecrack
___ 5. fathomless		E. too deep to measure
___ 6. arbiter		F. judge

Name _____   Date _____

"She Walks in Beauty," *from* Childe Harold's Pilgrimage, and *from* Don Juan by George Gordon, Lord Byron
Support for Writing: Monologue

Use the chart below to gather and record ideas for your monologue.

Byronic Opinions That Fit Today's World	Byron's Circumstances and Attitude	Words and Phrases That Convey His Attitude

On a separate page, use the information you have gathered to write your monologue.

Name _____   Date _____

"Ozymandias," "Ode to the West Wind," and "To a Skylark"
by Percy Bysshe Shelley
Literary Analysis: Imagery

Poets use vivid **imagery** for many reasons. Appealing to a reader's senses of sight, hearing, taste, smell, and touch can make the poem seem more real to the reader. Certain images may also inspire a reader to respond with feelings of awe, disgust, fear, desire, amusement, or joy, to name just a few. But poets do not use images purely to keep the reader's interest—often, the images in a poem help to develop the poem's theme. For example, in "To a Skylark," Shelley uses imagery to reinforce the theme of creativity. He compares the bird to the moon, a poet, a highborn maiden, a glowworm, and a rose. The subject of each image emits or creates a beautiful thing: The moon and glowworm both emit light, the poet creates poetry, the maiden sings, and the rose emits a pleasant odor.

DIRECTIONS: *Answer the following questions on the lines provided.*

. . . Two vast and trunkless legs of stone
Stand in the desert. Near them, on the sand,
Half sunk, a shattered visage lies, whose frown,
And wrinkled lip, and sneer of cold command . . .
                    ("Ozymandias," lines 2–5)

1. To what senses does this image appeal?

   _____

2. What emotions might this image provoke in a reader?

   _____

   Nothing beside remains. Round the decay
   Of that colossal wreck, boundless and bare,
   The lone and level sands stretch far away.
                    ("Ozymandias," lines 12–14)

3. To what senses does this image appeal?

   _____

4. What emotions might this image provoke in a reader?

   _____

5. How is this image related to the theme of the poem?

   _____

   _____

"Ozymandias," "Ode to the West Wind," and "To a Skylark"
by Percy Bysshe Shelley

Reading Strategy: Compare and Contrast Elements

Poets use descriptive language, or **imagery,** to make their writing seem more real and vivid to the reader. They do this by appealing to a reader's physical senses with visual details, sounds, smells, tastes, and textures. By **comparing and contrasting elements** from different texts, you can get a better sense of how the author uses language in a particular way to create mood and diffuse meaning.

DIRECTIONS: *As you read these poems, copy several passages that contain vivid images in the first column of the graphic organizer below. In the second column, describe the image in your own words. Include details that Shelley implies but may not specifically mention. Remember to include sounds, smells, tastes, and textures, as well as sights, if appropriate. In the third column, write the possible meaning of the image. Think about why the poet chose this image and its effect on the poem as a whole.*

Passage	Description of Image	Meaning
1. "Round the decay / Of that colossal wreck, boundless and bare, / The lone and level sands stretch far away." ("Ozymandias," lines 12–14)	The statue is surrounded by a vast empty desert where it is dry and hot and there is no sound but the wind.	Ozymandias's fearsome power and fame have been leveled to nothingness—mere fragments in the desert sands.
2.		
3.		
4.		
5.		

"Ozymandias," "Ode to the West Wind," and "To a Skylark"
by Percy Bysshe Shelley
Vocabulary Builder

Using the Root -puls-

A. DIRECTIONS: *The word root -puls- means "push" or "drive." Using your knowledge of the word root -puls- and the information in parentheses, replace each italicized word or phrase with a word that includes the word root -puls-. Write the new word on the line that follows the sentence.*

compulsive (*com-* = with)	impulsiveness (*im-* = toward)
pulsar (*-ar* = of or relating to)	repulse (*re-* = against)

1. Astronomers began to pick up waves of electromagnetic radiation that were being emitted from a previously unknown *neutron star.* _____

2. Because he is *a/an obsessive* shopper, Isaiah can't save money. _____

3. Maddie regretted her *spontaneity* after she threw her book out the window. _____

4. The army used tanks to *drive back* the attacking forces. _____

Using the Word List

blithe   impulse   profuse   satiety   sepulcher   verge

B. DIRECTIONS: *Fill in each blank with a word from the Word List.*

1. Mary visited the graveyard to put flowers by her ancestor's _____.

2. It was difficult to stop the flooding because the flow of water was so _____

3. After the pie-eating contest, Harold was beyond _____; he was on the _____ of being sick.

4. José loved his grandmother, but her _____ response to even the most depressing events irritated him.

5. When the rescue ship sailed into the harbor and unloaded the survivors, Sarah obeyed her sudden _____ to kneel and kiss the solid ground.

Name _____ Date _____

"Ozymandias," "Ode to the West Wind," and "To a Skylark"
by Percy Bysshe Shelley
Support for Writing

Use the lines below to record questions and to organize your research into the scientific and political background of one of Shelley's poems.

1. Specific question: _____
_____

   A. General question: _____
_____

   B. General question: _____
_____

2. Specific question: _____
_____

   A. General question: _____
_____

   B. General question: _____
_____

3. Specific question: _____
_____

   A. General question: _____
_____

   B. General question: _____
_____

Use your questions to guide your research into the background of your poem. On a separate page, use the information you gather to support your main points.

Name _____   Date _____

Poetry of John Keats
Literary Analysis: Ode

The **ode** is a long lyric poem with a serious subject. Written in an elevated style, the ode usually honors its subject and addresses it directly. There are three types of odes in English. The **Pindaric ode** is written in sets of three stanzas and is modeled after the odes of the Greek poet Pindar. Pindar's odes were chanted by a chorus onstage, in the Greek dramatic tradition. With the first stanza, or strophe, the chorus moved to the right; with the second, or antistrophe, it moved to the left. For the third and final stanza, or epode, the chorus stood still. In the English Pindaric ode, the strophes and antistrophes have one stanza pattern and the epode has another. The **Horatian ode** is modeled after the odes of the Roman poet Horace. It is homostrophic, or contains only one type of stanza, and tends to be more restrained and meditative in tone. Finally, the **irregular ode** contains no set strophic pattern.

DIRECTIONS: *Fill in the following table to determine which type of odes Keats has written. When analyzing the stanzas, be sure to count out the number of lines, rhyme scheme, and meter for each stanza.*

	"Ode to a Nightingale"	"Ode on a Grecian Urn"
Number of stanzas		
Number of lines per stanza		
Rhyme scheme(s)		
Meter(s)		
Type of ode		

Poetry of John Keats
Reading Strategy: Paraphrase

Keats's nineteenth-century language and complex figures of speech can be difficult to understand. If you come to the end of a stanza and have no idea what you have just read, go back and read each phrase or sentence one at a time. Once you've identified the spots that are giving you trouble, you can **paraphrase** them, or restate them in your own words. Read the following example from Keats's "On First Looking into Chapman's Homer":

> Oft of one wide expanse had I been told
> That deep-browed Homer ruled as his demesne;
> Yet did I never breathe its pure serene
> Till I heard Chapman speak out loud and bold. . . .

Paraphrase:

I had often been told of great works of literature produced by the wise and profound Homer. However, I never appreciated the greatness of his work until I came across Chapman's bold and vivid translation of it.

The paraphrased version uses simple words and phrases in the place of more difficult ones and rearranges the order of the sentence parts. Once you have paraphrased the passage, you can more easily see that the "wide expanse," or "great place," refers to Homer's poetry and that Chapman's speaking of this place refers to his translation of Homer's work.

DIRECTIONS: *Paraphrase the following difficult passages from Keats's poems. Use the footnotes and a dictionary, if necessary, to define difficult words.*

from "When I Have Fears That I May Cease to Be":

1. "When I have fears that I may cease to be
   Before my pen has gleaned my teeming brain . . ."

   _____

   _____

from "Ode to a Nightingale":

2. "Fade far away, dissolve, and quite forget
   What thou among the leaves hast never known,
   The weariness, the fever, and the fret. . . ."

   _____

   _____

   _____

Name _____ Date _____

Poetry of John Keats
Vocabulary Builder

Word Analysis: Multiple Meanings

A. DIRECTIONS: *Write two definitions for the italicized word in each sentence. First write the literal meaning and then a figurative meaning. Finally, place a check mark before the definition that applies to the italicized word in the sentence.*

1. The *crown* of the tree had been struck by lightning.

   _____

   _____

2. The company's *board* met to decide the fate of the business.

   _____

   _____

3. William built a high *fence* around his property to keep out the wolves.

   _____

   _____

4. *Notice* of the meeting appeared in the newspaper this morning.

   _____

   _____

5. She was determined to *walk* in peace and not to give in.

   _____

   _____

Using the Word List

    gleaned   ken   requiem   surmise   teeming   vintage

B. DIRECTIONS: *Fill in the blank in each sentence with the correct word from the Word List.*

1. I _____ that the trouble began long before we got here.

2. He _____ as much information as he could from the newspaper article.

3. The cathedral choir sang a _____ at his funeral.

4. Jack just bought a Model T to add to his collection of _____ cars.

5. The bag of rotten apples was _____ with ants.

6. The secrets of the universe are far beyond my _____.

Poetry of John Keats
Support for Writing

Complete the chart below by writing quotations about dramatic situations and moments where Keats evokes the reader's emotions in his poems. Then, think about the quotations and draw a conclusion.

Quotations Expressing Feelings and Ideas

	Poem title: _____	Poem title: _____
Dramatic Situations	Quotation:	Quotation:
	Quotation:	Quotation:
Evokes Reader's Emotions	Quotation:	Quotation:
	Quotation:	Quotation:

Conclusion: _____

_____

_____

_____

On a separate page, draw on information from the chart to support your analysis of Keats's use of imagery, personification, figures of speech, and sound.

Name _____ Date _____

Primary Sources: Parliamentary Debate and Letter

The primary sources in this grouping debate and discuss the First Reform Bill, which expanded voting rights in Britain. Reading these sources can reveal the thinking of both sides in this important historical debate.

DIRECTIONS: *Record each speaker or writer's position on the Reform Bill and the facts, reasons, and/or examples that he gives to support his position.*

Lord John Russell	
Position	**Support**

Sir Robert Peel	
Position	**Support**

Thomas Babington Macaulay	
Position	**Support**

Parliamentary Debate: Speech by Lord John Russell
Parliamentary Debate: Speech by Sir Robert Peel
Letter: Thomas Babington Macaulay to Thomas Flower Ellis
Vocabulary Builder

Using the Cross-Curricular Vocabulary

A. DIRECTIONS: *Use your knowledge of the word in italics to determine the answer to each question. Circle the letter of the answer.*

1. What is a politician's *constituency*?
   (a) his or her mentor   **(b)** his or her principles   **(c)** those who voted for him or her

2. What sort of people are *electors*?
   (a) people in an elite group   **(b)** people who run for office   (c) people who vote

3. What do people do when they air their *grievances*?
   (a) They complain.   **(b)** They entertain.   (c) They mourn.

4. What is a *measure* passed by lawmakers designed to do?
   (a) indicate the strength of a proposal   **(b)** remedy a situation   (c) continue a debate

5. If a politician expresses an *orthodox* opinion, what sort of opinion is it?
   (a) liberal   **(b)** conservative   (c) radical

Using the Word List

   extravagant   inauspicious   reverence

B. DIRECTIONS: *Complete the sentence with the vocabulary word from the word list that makes the most sense in the context.*

1. Because she is so _____, Carla is sometimes short of money.

2. Was it a good time to invest, or were conditions _____?

3. A bow our curtsey is often a sign of _____.

BONUS: Using Etymology

C. DIRECTIONS: *On the lines, explain how the meaning of orthodox reflects its Greek origin.*

_____

_____

Name _____ Date _____

"On Making an Agreeable Marriage" by Jane Austen
from **A Vindication of the Rights of Woman** by Mary Wollstonecraft
Literary Analysis: Social Commentary

Mary Wollstonecraft and Jane Austen were writers who were enormously gifted in the art of **social commentary.** These women looked closely at the world around them, thought deeply about what they saw, and put their views down on paper for the betterment and enjoyment of others. For example, Austen begins her letter to her niece by gently prodding Fanny to remember all her gentleman friend's wonderful qualities. But Austen's letter slowly transforms into an appeal to consider carefully before accepting a marriage proposal, thereby avoiding a marriage of convenience or a marriage for the sake of money. Her point, in the end, is that there is nothing worse than marriage without mutual affection and respect. Austen, who remained unmarried throughout her brief life, was nonetheless able to view the institution of marriage with great perception and evenhandedness.

DIRECTIONS: *Read the excerpts from the selections, and answer the questions that follow.*

And from the time of our being in London together, I thought you really very much in love.—But you certainly are not at all—there is no concealing it.—What strange creatures we are!—It seems as if your being secure of him (as you say yourself) had made you Indifferent.

(from "On Making an Agreeable Marriage")

1. What point does Austen make about the fickle nature of some human relationships?

   _____

   _____

   _____

   _____

It is acknowledged that they spend many of the first years of their lives in acquiring a smattering of accomplishments; meanwhile strength of body and mind are sacrificed to libertine notions of beauty, to the desire of establishing themselves—the only way women can rise in the world—by marriage. And this desire making mere animals of them, when they marry they act as such children may be expected to act—they dress, they paint, and nickname God's creatures. . . . Can they be expected to govern a family with judgment, or take care of the poor babes whom they bring into the world?

(from A *Vindication of the Rights of Woman*)

2. What point is Wollstonecraft making about women's place in society?

   _____

   _____

   _____

   _____

   _____

   _____

"On Making an Agreeable Marriage" by Jane Austen
from **A Vindication of the Rights of Woman** by Mary Wollstonecraft
Reading Strategy: Determine the Writer's Purpose

It is particularly important to **determine the writer's purpose** when you're reading essays, speeches, or works of social commentary. Authors of these works can have a variety of purposes. Some seek to explain an issue or a process; others attempt to persuade a certain group or society in general to think in a particular way. Still others write to incite their audience to take action.

DIRECTIONS: *Use this graphic organizer to help you record and analyze Mary Wollstonecraft's purpose for writing* A Vindication of the Rights of Woman. *For each paragraph write down clues that reflect the author's tone and attitude. Decide what you think the author's purpose was. Then think about how the paragraph affected your own opinion on the topic. The first paragraph has been analyzed for you.*

Author's Tone/Attitude	Author's Purpose	Personal Reaction
Paragraph 1: The author takes a tone that reveals her to be saddened and frustrated by the way women of her generation are being educated. She feels strongly that women are sacrificing their intellects in order to gain the attentions of men. Wollstonecraft keeps her tone low-key, but it is clear that the situation she is writing about also makes her angry.	The author is attempting to persuade readers that women have been unfairly treated.	Some of the points about society that Wollstonecraft makes are still relevant today. Many women act nice or pretend they're not overly intelligent so that men won't feel threatened.
Paragraph 2:		
Paragraph 3:		
Paragraph 4.		
Paragraph 5:		

"On Making an Agreeable Marriage" by Jane Austen
from **A Vindication of the Rights of Woman** by Mary Wollstonecraft
Vocabulary Builder

Using the Root -fort-

A. DIRECTIONS: *Each of the following sentences includes an italicized word that contains the word root -fort-, meaning "strong." Fill in the blank with a word or phrase that completes the sentence and reveals the meaning of the italicized word.*

1. A musical analogy Mary Wollstonecraft might have used is that while women were expected to play the piano softly and prettily, men could be counted on to play *fortissimo*, _____.

2. The *fortress* stood upon a hill and was _____.

3. Jane Austen wrote to her niece Fanny to provide *fortification* for Fanny to make up her own mind about marriage. Austen wanted to _____ Fanny's resolve.

4. Mary Wollstonecraft put a lot of *effort* into her essay on woman's rights. It was a _____ to put her deepest feelings into words.

Using the Word List

> amiable   fastidious   fortitude   gravity   specious   vindication

B. DIRECTIONS: *In the following paragraph, fill in the blanks using words from the Word List.*

Jane Austen wrote to Fanny out of concern with regard to her niece's future marriage. Austen's argument was certainly not (1) _____, or deceptively attractive. To Austen, choosing the right husband was a matter of great (2) _____. In Austen's mind, there was no need to provide (3) _____ for *not* marrying someone; one either loved the other person or one didn't. She had no regard for women who behaved in a false manner by only pretending to care for someone. Nor did Austen advocate being so (4) _____ as to be pleased by no man. She recommended a clear head, an open heart, and (5) _____ of spirit. Austen's philosophy seemed to be that if one of those things predominates over the others, all is lost. Although she had no hesitation about speaking her mind, Austen's tone remained (6) _____ throughout her letter to Fanny.

"On Making an Agreeable Marriage" by Jane Austen
from **A Vindication of the Rights of Woman** by Mary Wollstonecraft
Support for Writing

Use the chart below to take notes for your e-mail to an author. Review the selection and jot down notes about the author's opinion in the first column. Then, jot down notes about your response in the second column. Include reasons and facts to support your opinion.

Author:

Author's Opinion	My Reaction

On a separate page, use the information in the chart to draft your e-mail to an author.

Name _____ Date _____

Essential Questions Workshop—Unit 4

In their poems, fiction, and nonfiction works, the writers in Unit Four express ideas that relate to the three Essential Questions framing this book. Review the literature in the unit. Then, for each Essential Question, choose an author and at least one passage from the author's writing that expresses an idea related to the question. Use this chart to complete your work.

Essential Question	Author/Selection	Literary Passage
What is the relationship between place and literature?		
How does literature shape or reflect society?		
What is the relationship of the writer to tradition?		

Name _____ Date _____

Names and Terms to Know

A. DIRECTIONS: *Write a brief sentence explaining each of the following names and terms. You will find all of the information you need in the Unit Introduction in your textbook.*

1. Crystal Palace: _____

2. King Edward VI: _____

_____

3. *On the Origin of Species*: _____

_____

4. Suez Canal: _____

5. Irish Potato Famine: _____

6. Empress of India: _____

B. DIRECTIONS: *Use the hints below to help you answer each question.*

1. What did the reign of Queen Victoria come to represent to the English? *[Hints: What values were important to the queen? What was celebrated in the Great Exposition of 1848? What was celebrated in Victoria's Golden and Diamond Jubilees?]*

_____

_____

_____

2. What reforms were legislated during Queen Victoria's reign? *[Hints: What was child labor? What did the Elementary Education Act intend to do? What does "franchise" mean, and how was it extended?]*

_____

_____

_____

3. What problems loomed after the death of Victoria? *[Hints: What was happening in the newly united Germany? What did France want after the war with Germany in 1871? Where was nationalism becoming a strong movement?]*

_____

_____

_____

Name _____ Date _____

Unit 5 Introduction

Essential Question 1: What is the relationship between place and literature?

A. DIRECTIONS: *Answer the questions about the first Essential Question in the Introduction about the relationship between place and literature. All the information you need is in the Unit 5 Introduction in your textbook.*

1. *Extent of the British Empire*

   a. How much of the world was part of the British Empire at its height? _____

   _____

   b. What foreign nations had come under British rule? _____

   _____

2. *Spirit of Exploration and Conquest*

   a. What values were celebrated by Tennyson's hero Ulysses? _____

   _____

   b. How did these values differ from those of the medieval age, as represented by Dante's *Divine Comedy*? _____

   _____

3. *Literature Reflecting Empire*

   a. How was the ordinary British soldier portrayed in the poetry of Rudyard Kipling?

   _____

   b. What does Kipling's "Recessional" warn against? _____

B. DIRECTIONS: *Answer the questions based on the Essential Question Vocabulary words.*

1. What might be the negative results of one people's *conquest* of another? _____

   _____

2. Why might a country be proud of its ability to establish an *empire*? _____

   _____

3. Why would someone near the end of life become concerned with the question of his or her *legacy*? _____

   _____

Unit 5 Introduction

Essential Question 2: How does literature shape or reflect society?

A. DIRECTIONS: *On the lines provided, answer the questions about the second Essential Question in the Introduction about the writer and society. All the information you need is in the Unit 5 Introduction in your textbook.*

1. *Best and Worst of Victorian Society*

    a. What positive attitude characterized the Victorian era, and what good results did this attitude achieve? _____

    _____

    b. What happened during the Irish Famine in the 1840s? _____

    _____

    c. What did the British army do to enemy families during the Boer War near the end of Victoria's reign? _____

2. *Wisdom and Foolishness*

    a. What scientific advances were made by Michael Faraday and Joseph Lister?

    _____

    b. What did the essays of Matthew Arnold urge his countrymen to do? _____

    _____

    c. What military folly was portrayed in Tennyson's "Charge of the Light Brigade"?

    _____

3. *Belief and Unbelief*

    a. What did the Victorians want to believe? _____

    b. What was the effect of the writings of Charles Darwin about evolution? _____

    _____

    c. What was paradoxical about the treatment of children during the Victorian age?

    _____

B. DIRECTIONS: *Complete the sentence stems based on the Essential Question Vocabulary words.*

1. The *spirit* of the Victorian age is different from our own because _____

    _____

2. *Modernization* can make life better by _____

3. "It was the best of times; it was the worst of times" is a *paradox* because _____

    _____

Unit 5 Introduction

Essential Question 3: What is the relationship of the writer to tradition?

A. DIRECTIONS: *On the lines provided, answer the questions about the third Essential Question in the Introduction about the relationship between the writer and tradition. All the information you need is in the Unit 5 Introduction in your textbook.*

1. *Literature Looking Inward*

   a. What problem of his times does Tennyson address in *In Memoriam?* _____

   _____

   b. What warning to his countrymen does Tennyson's *Idylls of the King* offer?

   _____

2. *Sonnets and Dramatic Monologues*

   a. What Victorian notes does Elizabeth Barrett Browning add to the love sonnet? _____

   _____

   b. What do the dramatic monologues of Robert Browning do? _____

   _____

3. *The Victorian Novel*

   a. How were most Victorian novelists published? _____

   _____

   b. Identify three prominent Victorian novelists, along with one of their works. _____

   _____

   c. What twin theme runs through much Victorian literature? _____

B. DIRECTIONS: *Answer the questions based on the Essential Question Vocabulary words.*

1. How do you know when you are making *progress* in learning something? _____

   _____

2. Why would it be necessary to *reform* a system in which small children are sent to work to help support their families?

   _____

3. How could a novel provide a *commentary* about a social problem? _____

   _____

4. Under what circumstances might an ordinary person be called a *prophet?* _____

   _____

All-in-One Workbook
221

Unit 5 Introduction
Following-Through Activities

A. CHECK YOUR COMPREHENSION: *Use this chart to complete the Check Your Comprehension activity in the Unit 5 Introduction. In the middle boxes, fill in a key concept for each of the Essential Questions. In the right boxes, fill in a key author relevant to each concept you list. (The second Essential Question has been done for you.)*

Essential Question	Key Concept	Key Author
Place and Literature		
Literature and Society	England as a world empire	Rudyard Kipling
Writer and Tradition		

B. EXTEND YOUR LEARNING: *Use this graphic organizer to help you prepare a multimedia presentation on the 1851 Crystal Palace and its displays.*

Research questions	Print source	Visuals / Sound source
What did the Crystal Palace look like?		
How was it constructed?		
What are examples of exhibits from England?		
From the Empire?		

from **In Memoriam, A.H.H.,** **"The Lady of Shalott," "Ulysses,"** and *from* **The Princess:**
"Tears, Idle Tears" by Alfred, Lord Tennyson

Literary Analysis: The Speaker in Poetry

We can truly understand a poem only when we understand who is speaking and what motivated him or her to do so. In Tennyson's "Ulysses," the hero is an adventurer who not only reveals his longing to roam "with a hungry heart" but also attempts to persuade his aging followers and subjects that he and his band should leave the kingdom and "sail beyond the sunset."

DIRECTIONS: *On the lines, describe what Ulysses reveals in each quotation about his own thoughts and feelings or how he hopes to persuade his listeners with his words. Remember that both ordinary subjects and Ulysses's fellow adventurers are listening to him speak.*

1. How dull it is to pause, to make an end, / To rust unburnished, not to shine in use!

   _____

   _____

   _____

   _____

2. This is my son, mine own Telemachus, / To whom I leave the scepter and the isle / Well-loved of me, discerning to fulfill / This labor, . . .

   _____

   _____

   _____

   _____

3. . . . My mariners, / Souls that have toiled and wrought, and thought with me— / That ever with a frolic welcome took / The thunder and the sunshine, . . .

   _____

   _____

   _____

   _____

4. 'Tis not too late to seek a newer world. / Push off, and sitting well in order smite / The sounding furrows; . . .

   _____

   _____

   _____

   _____

from In Memoriam, A.H.H., "The Lady of Shalott," "Ulysses," and **from The Princess: "Tears, Idle Tears"** by Alfred, Lord Tennyson

Reading Strategy: Analyze Author's Assumptions and Beliefs

If we look beyond the words and images in poetry, we can often find the author's assumptions and beliefs. Depending on when and where the author lived and his or her experiences, those assumptions and beliefs may or may not be familiar to us. As you read a poem, first try to understand the speaker's meaning. The speaker may be the author of the poem or a fictional character. Once you understand what the speaker is saying, figure out the author's assumptions and/or beliefs that underlie the speaker's words.

DIRECTIONS: *In the following chart, record the poet's message and then what you believe to be the underlying assumption or belief in the message.*

Quote From Poem	Speaker's Meaning	Underlying Assumption/ Belief
1. But who shall so forecast the years/And find in loss a gain to match?/Or reach a hand through time to catch/ The far-off interest of tears? (*In Memoriam, A.H.H.*)		
2. O Death in Life, the days that are no more. ("Tears, Idle Tears")		
3. I am a part of all that I have met;/ Yet all experience is an arch wherethrough/Gleams that untraveled world, whose margin fades/ Forever and forever when I move. ("Ulysses")		

Name _____ Date _____

from In Memoriam, A.H.H., "The Lady of Shalott," "Ulysses," and *from* The Princess:
"Tears, Idle Tears" by Alfred, Lord Tennyson
Vocabulary Builder

A. DIRECTIONS: *Poems rely on figurative language to convey meaning in a fresh way. Underline examples of figurative language used in the following stanza from* In Memoriam, A.H.H. *Write the literal and figurative meanings of two of the words you identify.*

Let Love clasp Grief lest both be drowned,
   Let darkness keep her raven gloss.
   Ah, sweeter to be drunk with loss,
To dance with death, to beat the ground

1. Word _____ Literal Meaning: _____ Figurative Meaning: _____
2. Word _____ Literal Meaning: _____ Figurative Meaning: _____

Using the Word List

   chrysalis   diffusive   furrows   prosper   prudence   waning

B. DIRECTIONS: *Choose the letter of the word or phrase most nearly* similar *in meaning to each numbered word. Write the letter of your choice in the blank.*

___ 1. diffusive
   A. polluted
   B. fervent
   C. dispersed
   D. alternate

___ 2. waning
   A. bathing
   B. waxing
   C. expanding
   D. declining

___ 3. furrows
   A. grooves
   B. ponders
   C. plants
   D. lairs

___ 4. chrysalis
   A. flower bud
   B. cocoon
   C. soil
   D. crystal

___ 5. prosper
   A. sink
   B. play
   C. pretend
   D. thrive

___ 6. prudence
   A. carelessness
   B. carefulness
   C. haughtiness
   D. pettiness

from **In Memoriam, A.H.H., "The Lady of Shalott," "Ulysses,"** and *from* **The Princess:**
"Tears, Idle Tears" by Alfred, Lord Tennyson

Support for Writing

Use the chart below to record information about Tennyson's life and poetry. Write events from Tennyson's life in each box in the left column in the order in which the events occurred. Write his literary achievements in the boxes on the right. Then, circle the arrow that shows whether each literary achievement was an effect or a cause of the corresponding event in his life.

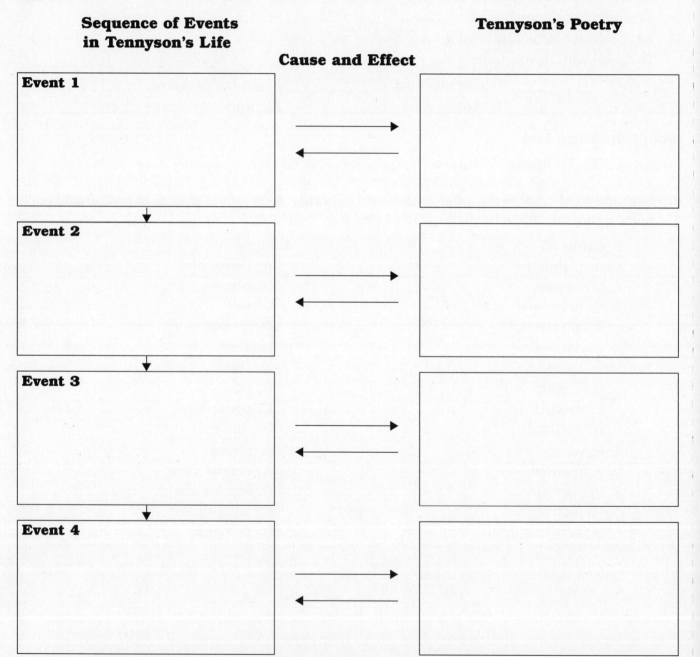

**Sequence of Events
in Tennyson's Life**

Tennyson's Poetry

Cause and Effect

Event 1

Event 2

Event 3

Event 4

On a separate page, use the information you have recorded in the chart as you write a draft of your biographical essay on Tennyson. Discuss the cause-and-effect relationship between his life and his work.

"My Last Duchess," "Life in a Love," and **"Porphyria's Lover"**
by Robert Browning
Sonnet 43 by Elizabeth Barrett Browning
Literary Analysis: Dramatic Monologue

A **dramatic monologue** is a speech, sometimes to a silent listener, in which a character indicates a setting and a dramatic conflict. In the monologue, this character reveals his or her inmost feelings, sometimes without knowing it.

A. DIRECTIONS: *Complete the following chart. Indicate the setting and names or general identities of the speaker and listener, and summarize the conflict in each poem.*

Poem	Setting	Speaker	Listener	Conflict
"My Last Duchess"				
"Life in a Love"				
"Porphyria's Lover"				

A **run-on line** ends where the flow of words forces you to read on without pause. An **end-stopped line** ends just where a speaker would naturally pause.

B. DIRECTIONS: *Identify which lines below are run-on lines and which are end-stopped lines.*

That's my last Duchess painted on the wall,   1. _____

Looking as if she were alive, I call   2. _____

That piece a wonder, now: Fra Pandolf's hands   3. _____

Worked busily a day, and there she stands.   4. _____

Name _____ Date _____

"My Last Duchess," "Life in a Love," and **"Porphyria's Lover"**
by Robert Browning
Sonnet 43 by Elizabeth Barrett Browning

Reading Strategy: Compare and Contrast Speakers in Poems

The poems by Robert Browning and Elizabeth Barrett Browning all deal with the subject of love. However, each speaker has a distinct perspective on love.

DIRECTIONS: *Think about something or somebody you love. Use quotes below to compare and contrast each speaker's view and feelings about love to your own view and feelings about a person or thing that you love. If there is no comparison or contrast, say so, but make sure to explain.*

1. . . . Oh sir, she smiled, no doubt, / Whene'er I passed her; but who passed without/Much the same smile? This grew; I gave commands; Then all smiles stopped together.

⬇

Speaker's view/feeling about love:

⬇ ⬇

This compares to my feelings about: Explain:	This contrasts with my feelings about: Explain:

2. I love thee with the breath,/ Smiles, tears, of all my life!

⬇

Speaker's view/feeling about love:

⬇ ⬇

This compares to my feelings about: Explain:	This contrasts with my feelings about: Explain:

"My Last Duchess," "Life in a Love," and **"Porphyria's Lover"**
by Robert Browning
Sonnet 43 by Elizabeth Barrett Browning
Vocabulary Builder

Using the Suffix -ence

A. DIRECTIONS: *Answer each of the following questions, changing the underlined word to a word with the suffix -ence.*

1. Why was Alan <u>absent</u> from the meeting?
   _____
   _____

2. How did the class behave when there was an observer <u>present</u>?
   _____
   _____

3. Why did the teacher praise the <u>diligent</u> students?
   _____
   _____

4. How did the suspect prove he was <u>innocent</u> of the charge?
   _____
   _____

Using the Word List

countenance	dowry	eludes
munificence	officious	sullen

B. DIRECTIONS: *Match each word in the left column with its definition in the right column. Write the letter of the definition on the line next to the word it defines.*

___ 1. countenance   A. overly eager to please
___ 2. officious   B. state of being generous; lavishness
___ 3. munificence   C. avoids or escapes
___ 4. dowry   D. face
___ 5. eludes   E. morose; sulky
___ 6. sullen   F. natural talent, gift, or endowment

Name _____ Date _____

"My Last Duchess," "Life in a Love," and "Porphyria's Lover"
by Robert Browning
Sonnet 43 by Elizabeth Barrett Browning
Integrated Language Skills: Support for Writing

You are a detective investigating the Duke's history and character for the father of a woman to whom the Duke has proposed. Use the cluster diagram to gather details from "My Last Duchess" about the duke's character and first marriage.

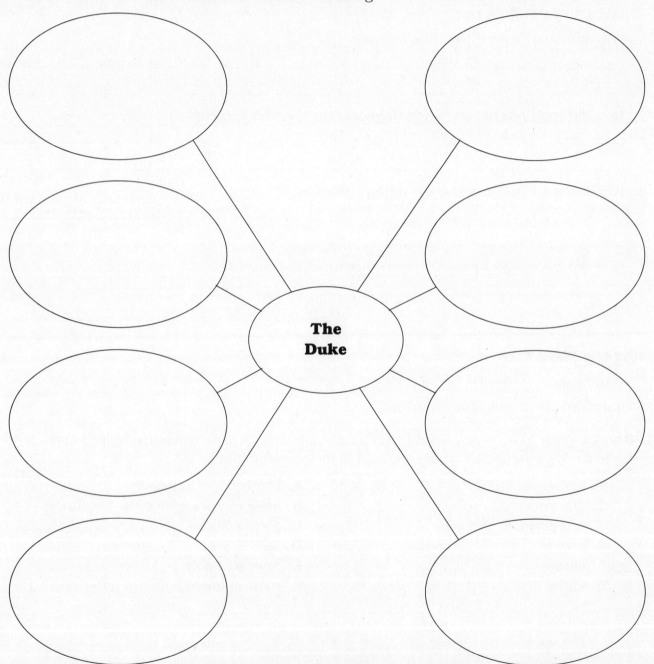

On a separate page, use the information you have gathered in your cluster diagram to help you draft a detective report for the woman's father about the duke's proposal. Start by presenting your position. Then, explain the reasons behind your position.

Name _____   Date _____

from **Hard Times** by Charles Dickens
Charles Dickens: Biography

Charles Dickens, the widely read Victorian novelist, had a miserable childhood. He was left on his own while his father was in debtor's prison. The effects of his childhood lasted throughout Dickens's life and haunted him even after he had established himself as a writer, husband, and father. He wrote: *"My whole nature was so penetrated with grief and humiliation of such considerations, that even now, famous and caressed and happy, I often forget in my dreams that I have a dear wife and children; even that I am a man; and wander desolately back to that time in my life."*

Imagine that you are Charles Dickens, and continue writing each of the following diary entries about important events in his life. Draw from the facts that you know about Dickens's life and use your imagination to fill in the details.

I cannot believe it! My father has been sent to debtor's prison and I am on my own.

I have just woken up from a nightmare, which is always the same.

It is only nine months since *The Pickwick Papers* was published, but boy, how my life has changed!

from **Hard Times** by Charles Dickens
Literary Analysis: The Novel and Social Criticism

A **novel** is a long work of fiction, usually featuring a complex plot, major and minor characters, a significant theme, and several settings. Like many novelists in nineteenth-century England, Charles Dickens created the fictional worlds in his novels to reflect real people and social institutions. Through his novels, he could comment on what he saw as problems and injustices in his society. This type of commentary through fiction is known as **social criticism.**

DIRECTIONS: *Examine the social criticism in* Hard Times *by answering the following questions.*

1. Of Thomas Gradgrind, Dickens writes: ". . . he seemed a kind of cannon loaded to the muzzle with facts, and prepared to blow [the students] clean out of the regions of childhood at one discharge." What is Dickens's attitude toward Thomas Gradgrind's teaching style? Why is this passage an example of social criticism?

   _____

   _____

   _____

2. When Mr. Gradgrind addresses student Sissy Jupe, he refers to her only as "girl number twenty." Why does he refer to her in this way? What viewpoint is Dickens criticizing by drawing attention to this? What aspect of the school is he criticizing?

   _____

   _____

   _____

3. Bitzer responds to a question about horses as follows: "Quadruped. Graminivorous. Forty teeth, namely twenty-four grinders, four eye-teeth and twelve incisive. . ." What aspect of school is Dickens criticizing?

   _____

   _____

   _____

4. Dickens describes Mr. M'Choakumchild as one of "one hundred and forty other schoolmasters, had been lately turned out at the same time, in the same factory, on the same principles, like so many pianoforte legs." What is Dickens's opinion of teachers?

   _____

   _____

   _____

from **Hard Times** by Charles Dickens
Reading Strategy: Recognize the Writer's Purpose

A **writer's purpose** is his or her reason for writing a literary work. An author might write a novel for one or more of the following reasons: to address a social problem, to satirize a particular institution, or to entertain readers with humor or adventure. To understand a writer's purpose, pay close attention to the details he or she uses to describe characters, events, and ideas. These details reveal the writer's attitude, or feelings, toward what he or she is describing. The writer's attitude, in turn, suggests his or her purpose.

DIRECTIONS: *As you read the selection, try to determine the writer's purpose by answering the following questions.*

1. In Chapter 1 of *Hard Times*, what details does Dickens use to describe the schoolroom? What details does he use to describe the physical appearance of "the speaker" in the schoolroom? What might these details say about the author's attitude and purpose?

   _____

   _____

   _____

2. What details does Dickens use to create a contrast between Sissy Jupe and Bitzer? Why does Sissy clash with her teachers? What might the incident surrounding Sissy indicate about the author's attitude and purpose?

   _____

   _____

   _____

DIRECTIONS: *Write a short essay answering the following question:*

3. If Dickens's purpose had been to praise the educational system, many details in the story would be different. Choose a paragraph in the story and rewrite it here with different details to reflect the author's purpose of praising the educational system.

   _____

   _____

   _____

   _____

   _____

   _____

   _____

Name _____ Date _____

from Hard Times by Charles Dickens
Vocabulary Builder

Using the Prefix mono-

The Greek word prefix *mono-* means "single" or "alone." This meaning appears in *monotonous*, meaning "having a single tone" or "dull and unwavering."

A. DIRECTIONS: *Complete each sentence with a word shown below.*

monogram   monolithic   monophony   monosyllabic

1. The old library was a _____ stone structure.
2. His initials formed a _____ on his writing paper.
3. The song was a simple _____, without harmonizing parts.
4. The teacher repeated the _____ word *facts*.

Using the Word List

adversary   approbation   deficient   etymology
indignant   monotonous   obstinate   syntax

B. DIRECTIONS: *For each numbered word, choose the word that is most similar in meaning.*

___ 1. monotonous
    A. alone
    B. quiet
    C. exciting
    D. dull

___ 2. obstinate
    A. approving
    B. displeased
    C. stubborn
    D. slow

___ 3. adversary
    A. opponent
    B. partner
    C. student
    D. teacher

___ 4. indignant
    A. thoughtful
    B. displeased
    C. agreeable
    D. strict

___ 5. approbation
    A. punishment
    B. lesson
    C. approval
    D. plan

___ 6. deficient
    A. containing
    B. unfortunate
    C. lacking
    D. well-supplied

___ 7. etymology
    A. word study
    B. science of birds
    C. ecology
    D. historical study

___ 8. syntax
    A. sentence
    B. grammar
    C. word origins
    D. dictionary

Name _____   Date _____

from **Hard Times** by Charles Dickens
Grammar and Style: Avoiding Shifts in Verb Tense

The following is a list of **proper verb tenses** for the word "learn."

Present:	I learn
Past:	I learned
Future:	I will learn
Present perfect:	I have learned
Past perfect:	I had learned
Future perfect:	I will have learned

A. PRACTICE: *Correct the following sentences so that they avoid shifts in verb tense. Use the verb tense in parentheses in your rewritten sentence.*

1. Sissy learned that Mr. Gradgrind likes only facts and would not have appreciated original thought. *(past)*

   _____

   _____

2. The students in the class will grow up and understand that Mr. Gradgrind is wrong about his philosophy on education, and they will have lost respect for him. [future]

   _____

   _____

3. Bitzer appreciated the discussion on horses because it is amusing and it will distract the class from the math homework. [present]

   _____

   _____

B. Writing Application: *What is the most important thing for students to learn, and why? Write a short paragraph discussing your view of education. In your writing, use one of the "perfect tenses" and circle it.*

   _____

   _____

   _____

   _____

   _____

   _____

   _____

   _____

   _____

from **Hard Times** by Charles Dickens
Support for Writing

Use the chart below to record information about each source.

Bibliographic information for print sources should include the title, author's name, place of publication, publisher, and date of publication. Internet sources should have as much of the print information as you can find plus the Internet address and the date the site was researched.

Primary or Secondary	Bibliographic Information	Content and Comments

On a separate page, use the information in your chart to prepare your annotated bibliography. Include annotations that explain why each source was useful.

Name _____   Date _____

from **Hard Times** by Charles Dickens
"**An Upheaval**" by Anton Chekhov
Literary Analysis: Comparing Social Criticism in Fiction

Social criticism in fiction is woven into a story and is not necessarily stated directly in the work, though sometimes it is stated through the thoughts, words, and actions of characters in the work. Social criticism in fiction often takes any of the following four forms:

1. The criticism is woven into a **realistic** story that shows life as it is to reveal social ills.
2. Social ills are **exaggerated**, which forces readers to see them more clearly.
3. The fictional story takes place in a **utopian**, or perfect, society to allow readers to draw conclusions about the ills in their own society.
4. The fictional story takes place in a **dystopian**, or dreadful, society, which leads readers to see what would happen if the social ills were allowed to continue.

DIRECTIONS: *Use the chart to compare and contrast the forms of criticism used in Dickens's and Chekhov's works.*

Hard Times by Charles Dickens

Social Criticism	How is it conveyed? (Quote from story or explanation)	Form (Realism; Exaggeration; Utopian; Dystopian)	Is there a character who sees the problem?
1.			
2.			

"An Upheaval" by Anton Chekhov

Social Criticism	How is it conveyed? (Quote from story or explanation)	Form (Realism; Exaggeration; Utopian; Dystopian)	Is there a character who sees the problem?
1.			
2.			

Name _____ Date _____

Vocabulary Builder

Using the Word List

ingratiating   kindred   palpitation   rummaging   turmoil

A. DIRECTIONS: *For each sentence, choose a word from the word list that best completes its meaning.*

1. Mashenka had no_____ who would take care of her when she left her job.

2. When Mashenka arrived, she found people _____ through her belongings.

3. Madame Kushkin was prone to heart _____s because of her nervous condition.

4. What was the use of all that work _____ herself to her employers if they would never trust her anyway?

5. The house was filled with _____ because of the missing brooch.

B. DIRECTIONS: *Match each word in the left column with its definition in the right column. Write the letter of the definition next to the word it defines.*

___ 1. turmoil   A. relatives

___ 2. rummaging   B. trying to win favor

___ 3. kindred   C. upheaval

___ 4. palpitation   D. searching

___ 5. ingratiating   E. rapid flutter of one's heart

Name _____ Date _____

Integrated Language Skills: Support for Writing

Chekhov and Dickens both use their fiction to criticize aspects of their societies. To compare the way each author gets his message across, the reader must first carefully analyze each selection's message and the way it is conveyed.

DIRECTIONS: *Use the graphic organizer below to help you organize your thoughts to write a compare-and-contrast essay about the means each author uses to convey his message.*

	Hard Times	*Upheaval*
1. Chief Social Criticism in the Selection		
2. Use of Realism? (If so, give examples.)		
3. Use of Satire? (If so, give examples.)		
4. Effectiveness of Social Criticism? (Give your opinion, with support.)		

Name _____ Date _____

from **Jane Eyre** by Charlotte Brontë
Literary Analysis: Author's Political and Philosophical Assumptions

Everybody makes assumptions when they speak and when they write. Some of your assumptions are a product of where you live and the time period in which you live. For example, a woman in the Victorian era may assume that her place in society is less than that of a man. Much of what she says may contain this underlying assumption.

Example: *I couldn't wait for my husband to return home so that I could ask him if I could accept the invitation to the party.* The assumption in this sentence is that the husband is in charge of the wife's actions.

In a novel that contains social criticism, the author may make **political and philosophical assumptions** that are typical of the time in which he or she lives and may also make some **political and philosophical assumptions** that are new or different from the predominant ones at the time.

DIRECTIONS: *After each of the following quotes from the excerpt from* Jane Eyre, *record the political or philosophical assumption that underlies the statement.*

1. "Miss Smith put into my hands a border of muslin two yards long, together with a needle, thimble, etc., and sent me to sit in a quiet corner of the school room, with directions to hem the same."

   Assumption:

   _____

2. "Hardened girl!" exclaimed Miss Scatcherd, "nothing can correct you of your slatternly habits: carry the rod away."

   Assumption:

   _____

3. "Yes, in a passive way: I make no effort; I follow as inclination guides me. There is no merit in such goodness."

   Assumption:

   _____

4. ". . . like Felix, I put it off to a more convenient season."

   Assumption:

   _____

Name _____   Date _____

from **Jane Eyre** by Charlotte Brontë
Reading Strategy: Analyze an Author's Assumptions

In a novel, an author's assumptions can be conveyed through characters, dialogue, and situations. In a novel that contains social criticism, some of the characters may reflect the "old system" that the author feels should be changed while others reflect the "new system," or the new ideas for change. When the reader examines the characters, dialogue, and situations, he or she can analyze them to understand both the author's assumptions and the philosophical and political ideas for change

DIRECTIONS: *Fill in the chart below to reflect the assumptions that Brontë makes in* Jane Eyre. *In the last column, decide whether Brontë approves of the assumption or feels it needs to change.*

Situation/Character/ Dialogue	Underlying Assumption	Brontë's Position
1. Helen Burns is subject to abuse by her teacher.		
2. " 'And if I were in your place, I should dislike her: I should resist her; if she struck me with that rod, I should get it from her hand; I should break it under her nose.' "		
3. "Helen's head, always drooping, sank a little lower as she finished this sentence."		
4. " ' . . . it is weak and silly to say you *cannot bear* what it is your fate to be required to bear.' "		

from **Jane Eyre** by Charlotte Brontë
Vocabulary Builder

A. DIRECTIONS: *Write a sentence with each of the vocabulary words. Make sure that your sentence shows that you know the meaning of the word.*

1. obscure:

_____

_____

2. comprised:

_____

_____

3. sundry:

_____

_____

4. tumult:

_____

_____

5. truculent:

_____

_____

Using the Word List

comprised   obscure   sundry

B. DIRECTIONS: *For each numbered word, choose the word that is most similar in meaning.*

___ **6. obscure**
   A. vague
   B. correct
   C. clear
   D. lonely

___ **7. comprised**
   A. organized
   B. taught
   C. argued
   D. contained

___ **8. sundry**
   A. few
   B. angry
   C. ridiculous
   D. various

Name _____ Date _____

from **Jane Eyre** by Charlotte Brontë
Support for Writing

DIRECTIONS: *Reread the selection to find information you will need to write a school report on Helen Burns from the perspective of Miss Scatcherd. Use the charts below to record the information. Use this information to create your school report.*

Helen Burns

Schoolwork	
Effort	
Personal Hygiene	
Posture	

Miss. Scatcherd

Dialogue/ Actions	What it says about her character

Contemporary Commentary
James Berry Introduces "From Lucy: Englan' Lady," "Time Removed," and "Freedom"

DIRECTIONS: *Use the space provided to answer the questions.*

1. Briefly describe the author's roots, mentioned by James Berry in the first paragraph of his essay.

    _____

    _____

2. Why is Rudyard Kipling's poem "Recessional" significant for Berry?

    _____

    _____

3. According to Berry, what is Lucy's attitude toward the Queen of England? What does Lucy's outlook represent?

    _____

    _____

    _____

    _____

4. When James Berry returned to Jamaica after a long absence, how did he feel when he saw his homeland again?

    _____

    _____

5. According to Berry, how did England contrast with Jamaica?

    _____

    _____

    _____

6. What explanation does Berry offer for the title of his poem "Time Removed"?

    _____

    _____

7. What seems to be Berry's attitude toward the pain and suffering of the past? How do you evaluate this attitude? Briefly explain your answer.

    _____

    _____

    _____

    _____

    _____

James Berry
Listening and Viewing

Segment 1: Meet James Berry
- As a young boy, how did James Berry use his interests as the basis of his writing?
- What interests have you pursued as writing topics, and why?

_____

_____

_____

_____

Segment 2: James Berry Introduces "Lucy: Englan' Lady"
- What inspired James Berry to write the poem "Lucy: Englan' Lady"?
- How does James Berry's reading of this poem change the way you might understand it if you read the poem yourself?

_____

_____

_____

_____

Segment 3: The Writing Process
- What process does James Berry follow when he develops a character?
- As a writer, do you think you would rather create characters from your own imagination or base them on real people? Explain your answer.

_____

_____

_____

_____

Segment 4: The Rewards of Writing
- James Berry believes that literature helps "widen the human vision of experience." What do you think he means by this?
- What do you think you can learn about yourself by reading and writing?

_____

_____

_____

_____

Name _____ Date _____

"**Dover Beach**" by Matthew Arnold
"**Recessional**" and "**The Widow at Windsor**" by Rudyard Kipling

Literary Analysis: Mood as a Key to Theme

The feelings that a poem creates in the reader make up the **mood** of the poem. How you feel after you read a poem can give you a hint as to the poem's central idea, or **theme.**

If you finish reading a poem feeling happy, the poem likely expressed an optimistic outlook or a pleasing image. If, however, a poem's theme has to do with the evils of imperialism, for example, it probably will not contain optimism or pleasing images. A reader might come away from such a poem feeling threatened, sober, or scared. Those feelings can be a clue that the poem's central idea is to be taken seriously.

To create mood, poets use vivid images and words that have emotional appeal. Notice how Matthew Arnold creates a rhythm that imitates the sound of the ocean. Notice, too, the vivid verbs and adjectives he uses, which have more emotional appeal than less colorful language.

> Listen! you hear the grating roar
> Of pebbles which the waves draw back, and fling,
> At their return, up the high strand,
> Begin, and cease, and then again begin,
> With tremulous cadence slow, and bring
> The eternal note of sadness in.

DIRECTIONS: *Following each passage, describe the mood of the passage—the feelings the passage creates in you—and indicate the words or phrases that create that mood. Then, interpret those feelings in connection with the theme of that poem.*

1. lines 9–14 from "Dover Beach" (see above)

_____

_____

_____

_____

2. lines 13–18 from "Recessional":

> Far-called, our navies melt away—
> On dune and headland sinks the fire—
> Lo, all our pomp of yesterday
> Is one with Nineveh and Tyre!
> Judge of the Nations, spare us yet,
> Lest we forget—lest we forget!

_____

_____

_____

_____

Name _____ Date _____

"Dover Beach" by Matthew Arnold
"Recessional" and "The Widow at Windsor" by Rudyard Kipling
Reading Strategy: Relate Mood and Theme to Historical Period

The Victorian Era in England was marked by change. Progress in science led to the questioning of religious faith. There was a huge disparity between rich and poor. The expansion of the British Empire brought much anxiety and tension. All of these factors are present in the **mood and theme** of literature written during this **historical period.** A reader can better understand the poems in this section by keeping the historical context in mind while reading the poems.

DIRECTIONS: *Use the chart below to record lines of poetry that show how different aspects of the historical period relate to the mood and theme of each poem. If you do not find a relationship between a poem and an aspect of the historical period, you may leave a box blank.*

	Questioning of Religious Faith	Disparity of the Classes	Tensions of War and Expansion
"Dover Beach"	1.	2.	3.
"Recessional"	4.	5.	6.
"The Widow at Windsor"	7.	8.	9.

All-in-One Workbook
247

"Dover Beach" by Matthew Arnold
"Recessional" and **"The Widow at Windsor"** by Rudyard Kipling
Vocabulary Builder

Using the Root -*domi*-

A. DIRECTIONS: *From the Latin* dominus, *English acquires several words whose meanings relate to the word's meaning of "lord" or "master." Keep this in mind as you answer questions about some words that include the -domi- root. Use a dictionary if you wish.*

1. How is someone who *dominates* different from someone who *domineers*?

   _____

2. Portuguese and Brazilian royalty are allowed to add the word *Dom* to their names, as a sign of their status. What, in your opinion, does this signify?

   _____

3. What is an *indomitable* enemy?

   _____

Using the Word List

   awe   cadence   contrite   dominion   tranquil   turbid

B. DIRECTIONS: *Match each word in the left column with its definition in the right column. Write the letter of the definition on the line next to the word it defines.*

___ 1. cadence   A. repenting for sin
___ 2. contrite   B. murky
___ 3. dominion   C. reverence, fear, and wonder
___ 4. tranquil   D. free from disturbance
___ 5. turbid   E. rhythmic sequence
___ 6. awe   F. power

Name _____ Date _____

"Dover Beach" by Matthew Arnold
"Recessional" and **"The Widow at Windsor"** by Rudyard Kipling
Integrated Language Skills: Support for Writing

Use the charts below to gather details for your response to critic Walter E. Houghton's statement that the Victorian Age was characterized by "widespread doubt about the nature of man, society, and the universe." Then, use your information to write a thesis statement.

"Dover Beach"

	Images	Moods	Themes
Doubt			
Self-Confidence			

"Recessional"

	Images	Moods	Themes
Doubt			
Self-Confidence			

"The Widow at Windsor"

	Images	Moods	Themes
Doubt			
Self-Confidence			

Thesis Statement (agree or disagree with Houghton's statement): _____

_____

On a separate page, use the thesis statement to help you write your response.

Name _____ Date _____

Primary Sources: "Progress in Personal Comfort" and Cook's Railroad Advertisement
Primary Sources: Persuasion in Advertisements

    Advertisements always use persuasion in order to convince consumers to purchase a product and/or service. An article in a newspaper may or may not use persuasion depending on the topic and the author's purpose. Articles in which an author shares his or her opinion are often intended to convince the reader that the writer's point of view is correct.

    The four modes of persuasion are:

1. logical: presents factual evidence and arguments that make sense
2. faulty: presents arguments that do not make sense
3. deceptive: presents intentionally misleading information
4. emotional: uses status symbols, peer pressure, patriotism, humor, or appeals to reader's emotions

DIRECTIONS: *Use the table below to identify and compare the means of persuasion used in the primary source selections. Some boxes may be blank.*

	Progress in Personal Comfort	Cook's Railroad Advertisement
1. Logical		
2. Faulty		
3. Deceptive		
4. Emotional		

5. What differences do you notice in persuasion techniques used in each primary source?

_____

_____

_____

Primary Sources: "Progress in Personal Comfort" and **Cook's Railroad Advertisement**
Vocabulary Builder

Using the Word List

bilious	depredation	fracture	gout
macadam	privations	pulp	

A. DIRECTIONS: *On the line, write the Word List word that best completes each sentence.*

1. The man fell on the dark streets, causing a _____ in his knee.
2. _____ was an untreatable disease before the invention of calomel.
3. Streets in Victorian England were often made of _____.
4. Smith lists the _____ of his life when he was young.
5. Cook's trip would not be enjoyable if a traveler was _____.
6. Smith's hat was reduced to a _____ in the rain.
7. Smith describes the old times as dangerous because of the _____.

B. DIRECTIONS: *Match each word in the left column with its definition in the right column. Write the letter of the definition on the line next to the word it defines.*

___ 1. depredation   A. losses
___ 2. macadam   B. having a digestive ailment
___ 3. fracture   C. soft, formless mass
___ 4. pulp   D. type of arthritis
___ 5. gout   E. broken bone
___ 6. bilious   F. road surfacing
___ 7. privations   G. robbing

Name _____ Date _____

"Remembrance" by Emily Brontë
"The Darkling Thrush" and "Ah, Are You Digging on My Grave?"
by Thomas Hardy
Literary Analysis: Stanza Structure and Irony

A **stanza** usually contains a certain number of lines arranged to show a recurring pattern, rhythmic structure, and rhyme scheme. **Irony** is a deliberate contradiction between expectation and reality. Poets can establish certain expectations in their readers through a regular stanza structure. When poets then inject surprising events or ideas within the stanza structure, they create irony. The contrast between expectation and reality can make a poem more memorable.

DIRECTIONS: *Write your answers to the following questions on the chart.*

Questions for Analysis	"Remembrance"	"The Darkling Thrush"	"Ah, Are You Digging on My Grave?"
1. How many stanzas are in the poem?			
2. What is the stanza type (number of lines, meter, rhyme scheme)?			
3. What expectation is established by the stanza structure?			
4. What change or surprise occurs in the poem?			
5. What is the irony in the poem?			

"Remembrance" by Emily Brontë
"The Darkling Thrush" and **"Ah, Are You Digging on My Grave?"**
by Thomas Hardy
Reading Strategy: Reading Stanzas as Units of Meaning

Like paragraphs in prose, stanzas in poetry are usually a unit of meaning—they convey a main idea. Sometimes, a stanza will create a unified mood. Taken together, the stanzas of a poem express a larger theme or idea. As you read, analyze the stanzas in a poem for a progression of thoughts, a sequence of events, or a building of an argument or mood within the poem.

A. DIRECTIONS: *On the lines, write your answers to the following questions.*

1. In "Remembrance," what progression of thoughts or sequence of events does the speaker describe in stanzas one through five?

   _____

2. What change in the speaker's attitude occurs in stanzas six through eight?

   _____

3. What pattern is established in the first four stanzas of "Ah, Are You Digging on My Grave"?

   _____

B. DIRECTIONS: *On the flow chart, write a summary of each stanza in "The Darkling Thrush."*
Then write a sentence stating how the stanzas work together to create meaning.

Stanza 1:

↓

Stanza 2:

↓

Stanza 3:

↓

Stanza 4:

↓

Overall Meaning:

"Remembrance" by Emily Brontë
"The Darkling Thrush" and **"Ah, Are You Digging on My Grave?"** by Thomas Hardy
Vocabulary Builder

Using the Root -terr(a)-

A. DIRECTIONS: *Match each word in the left column with its definition in the right column. Write the letter of the definition on the line next to the word it defines.*

____ 1. territorial

____ 2. terrace

____ 3. subterranean

____ 4. terra-cotta

____ 5. terrarium

A. beneath the earth

B. fired clay used as building material

C. a glass container containing a garden of small plants and perhaps some small land animals

D. relating to a geographical area

E. a flat roof or paved outdoor space

Using the Word List

gaunt   languish   obscured   prodding   rapturous   terrestrial

B. DIRECTIONS: *On the line, write the Word List word that best completes the meaning of the sentence as a whole.*

1. The thrush in Hardy's poem sings a _____ song.

2. While in mourning, the woman refused to eat and became _____ and pale.

3. Who was _____ the dead woman's grave?

4. When a casket is buried, it is _____ by the soil above it.

5. The turn of the century causes the speaker to _____ rather than celebrate.

6. Unable to fly, the ostrich is a more _____ creature than other birds.

C. DIRECTIONS: *Fill in the blank with one of the vocabulary words to complete the analogies.*

1. _____ is to clear as night is to day

2. chubby is to _____ as tall is to short

3. happy is to _____ as sad is to miserable

"Remembrance" by Emily Brontë
"The Darkling Thrush" and **"Ah, Are You Digging on My Grave?"**
by Thomas Hardy
Grammar: Using Active Voice

When it is appropriate to the meaning of your sentence, use the active voice to lend vitality to your writing. The active voice can also help you cut down on unnecessary words. Consider the following example:

There was a deafening noise coming from the refrigerator.

A deafening noise came from the refrigerator.

DIRECTIONS: *Rewrite the following letter, using the active voice where appropriate.*

Dear Ms. Satchel,

    Your history class was enjoyed by me this semester. In fact, I think it was enjoyed by all of your students. Liveliness and a great atmosphere in the classroom were created by your sense of humor. Learning history has never been enjoyed by me until now. History was brought alive for me with your teaching. There is sadness in me because the year is ending.

    Your future students are envied by me to have you as a teacher. Hopefully, your summer will be great.

                    Your Student,

                    Nigel

"Remembrance" by Emily Brontë
"The Darkling Thrush" and "Ah, Are You Digging on My Grave?"
by Thomas Hardy
Support for Writing

Use the chart below to gather information for your comparison of literary sources. Use a variety of sources, such as an encyclopedia, an online review, or an article written by a scholar.

Title of work analyzed: _____

Source	Contents	Analysis

Choose two of the sources to draft your analysis. On a separate page, use details from the chart as you compare them to each other and analyze their literary value.

"God's Grandeur" and **"Spring and Fall: To a Young Child"**
by Gerard Manley Hopkins
"To an Athlete Dying Young" and **"When I Was One-and-Twenty"**
by A. E. Housman

Literary Analysis: Rhythm and Meter

Rhythm is the alternation of strong and weak—or stressed and unstressed—syllables, which creates a flow or movement. **Meter** describes or "measures" rhythm when it follows a regular pattern. When poets or readers examine the meter of a poem, they "scan" the poem, marking stressed syllables with a ′ mark and unstressed syllables with a ˘ mark.

The meter of a poem is measured in feet. A foot is a combination of two or more syllables, at least one of which is typically stressed. There are specific kinds of feet. Here are two examples.

Metrical Foot	Pattern of Syllables	Example
iamb	one unstressed, one stressed (˘′)	The time you won your town the race
trochee	one stressed, one unstressed (′˘)	It will come to such sights colder

Another way to measure and label meter is to count how many feet are in a line. In the iambic example in the chart, the line contains four iambic feet. Thus, the line is said to be in iambic *tetrameter*. The words *trimeter* and *pentameter* refer to lines of poetry with three feet and five feet, respectively.

Hopkins is known for experimenting with rhythm. He uses counterpoint rhythm, which consists of two opposing rhythms in one line of poetry. He also uses what he called "sprung rhythm," which he felt closely imitates the flow of natural speech. In sprung rhythm, each foot begins with a stressed syllable, which may then be followed by any number of unstressed syllables. Scanning a poem written in sprung rhythm reveals its lack of conventional meter.

DIRECTIONS: *Follow the instructions given to examine the meter of Hopkins's and Housman's poems. (Scansion is not an exact science, but you should be able to find general patterns.)*

1. Scan the second stanza of "To an Athlete Dying Young." Then, identify the meter of each line.

   Today, the road all runners come,
   Shoulder-high we bring you home,
   And set you at your threshold down,
   Townsman of a stiller town.

2. Scan these two lines from "God's Grandeur."

   And for all this, nature is never spent:
       There lives the dearest freshness deep down things; . . .

   What effect does the meter have on the meaning of these lines? _____

   _____

"God's Grandeur" and **"Spring and Fall: To a Young Child"**
by Gerard Manley Hopkins
"To an Athlete Dying Young" and **"When I Was One-and-Twenty"**
by A. E. Housman

Reading Strategy: Analyze Author's Beliefs

Analyzing an author's beliefs can help readers understand that person's poetry more fully. Even simple details, such as knowing whether a poet is a man or a woman, can make a poem's meaning more clear. Whenever you read an author's **biography** in a textbook or anthology, be sure to apply what you learn to that person's writings.

Perhaps the most significant and startling fact about Gerard Manley Hopkins, for example, is that he was a Jesuit priest for all of his adult life. As you read his poems, look for signs of his religious beliefs. You may also see signs of the conflict he felt between his vocation and his other interests.

DIRECTIONS: *Use the charts on this page to record what you learn about each poet from the biographies on pages 1087 and 1091. Then look for evidence of each man's character or personality in his poems. Quote lines or phrases from the poems that reveal the poets' backgrounds. An example entry has been provided.*

Characteristic of Hopkins	Where Characteristic Is Seen in Poems
strong religious beliefs	"The world is charged with the grandeur of God." ("God's Grandeur," line 1)

Characteristic of Housman	Where Characteristic Is Seen in Poems

"God's Grandeur" and **"Spring and Fall: To a Young Child"**
by Gerard Manley Hopkins
"To an Athlete Dying Young" and **"When I Was One-and-Twenty"**
by A. E. Housman

Vocabulary Builder

Using Coined Words

A. DIRECTIONS: *In "Spring and Fall," Hopkins uses* unleaving *to describe the falling of the leaves from the branches. This coined word concisely and descriptively expresses the poet's idea. For each of the following phrases, either coin a noun that names the idea or image in a descriptive way, or coin an adjective that would suit the subject.*

1. a puddle _____

2. the first leaf buds of spring _____

3. puppies _____

4. a playground full of children _____

Using the Word List

blight   brink   grandeur   lintel   rue   smudge

B. DIRECTIONS: *Choose the letter of the word or phrase most nearly* similar *in meaning to each numbered word below. Write the letters on the lines provided.*

___ 1. blight
   A. disease
   B. rotten
   C. dim
   D. understandable

___ 2. grandeur
   A. more grand
   B. larger
   C. magnificence
   D. haughtiness

___ 3. rue
   A. mourn
   B. rejoice
   C. blush
   D. regret

___ 4. smudge
   A. thought
   B. wipe
   C. stain
   D. work of art

___ 5. brink
   A. edge
   B. death
   C. sadness
   D. thought

___ 6. lintel
   A. soup
   B. legume
   C. wooden frame
   D. bar above a door

Name _____ Date _____

"God's Grandeur" and "Spring and Fall: To a Young Child"
by Gerard Manley Hopkins
"To an Athlete Dying Young" and "When I Was One-and-Twenty"
by A. E. Housman
Integrated Language Skills: Support For Writing: Letter of Recommendation

You are Robert Bridges, and you are writing a letter to a British publishing company to recommend that it publish a book of Hopkins's poetry. Use the following chart to help you organize your thoughts on what is unique about Hopkins's poetry. Remember to describe these aspects of Hopkins's poetry in a positive way so that you will persuade the publisher to publish a book.

Hopkins's Innovative Style	What does it mean?	Examples from Hopkins's Poems	How will you describe it in your letter?
1. Sprung Rhythm			
2. Inscape			
3. Coined Words			

Name _____   Date _____

Essential Questions Workshop—Unit 5

In their poems, fiction, and nonfiction works, the writers in Unit Five express ideas that relate to the three Essential Questions framing this book. Review the literature in the unit. Then, for each Essential Question, choose an author and at least one passage from the author's writing that expresses an idea related to the question. Use this chart to complete your work.

Essential Question	Author/Selection	Literary Passage
What is the relationship between place and literature?		
How does literature shape or reflect society?		
What is the relationship of the writer to tradition?		

Name _____ Date _____

Names and Terms to Know

A. DIRECTIONS: *Write a brief sentence explaining each of the following names and terms. You will find all of the information you need in the Unit Introduction in your textbook.*

1. Lenin: _____

2. Royal Air Force: _____
   _____

3. Iraq: _____
   _____

4. Winston Churchill: _____

5. Treaty of Versailles: _____
   _____

6. Sir Edward Grey: _____

B. DIRECTIONS: *Use the hints below to help you answer each question.*

1. What long-term effects did World War I have on later world events? *[Hints: How was the war related to the Bolshevik revolution? What was the connection between Irish nationalism and the war? How did the treaty ending World War I pave the way to new German aggression?]*

   _____

   _____

   _____

2. What was England's "finest hour"? *[Hints: What did England do when German troops invaded European countries? What protected England? What was the outcome?]*

   _____

   _____

3. How did the two World Wars lead to the end of the British Empire? *[Hints: What was England's condition after World War I? What happened to London during World War II? Why was it impossible for the British to sustain their old empire?]*

   _____

   _____

   _____

Unit 6 Introduction

Essential Question 1: What is the relationship between place and literature?

A. DIRECTIONS: *Answer the questions about the first Essential Question in the Introduction about the relationship between place and literature. All the information you need is in the Unit 6 Introduction in your textbook.*

1. *Three Englands*

    a. What were the "three Englands" in the twentieth century? _____

    _____

    b. What contradictions exist among these three Englands? _____

    _____

2. *The Changing Landscape*

    a. How did the English countryside change after World War I? _____

    b. What did the German Blitz do to the English landscape? _____

    _____

3. *Divisions in England*

    a. What divide developed between the northern and southern parts of England in the twentieth century? _____

    _____

    b. What racial divides in England developed after the British Empire fell apart? _____

    _____

4. *Legacies*

    a. What cultural legacies did England give the world in the twentieth century? _____

    _____

    b. What idea about England is expressed in the writings of Nadine Gordimer and V.S. Naipaul? _____

B. DIRECTIONS: *Answer the questions based on the Essential Question Vocabulary words.*

1. Why might it be especially hard to *rebuild* a reputation after it is injured? _____

    _____

2. How might a country's natural resources be connected with its *economic* well being? _____

    _____

3. Why would *consciousness* of nationality be especially strong during wartime? _____

    _____

Name _____ Date _____

Unit 6 Introduction

Essential Question 2: How does literature shape or reflect society?

A. DIRECTIONS: *On the lines provided, answer the questions about the second Essential Question in the Introduction about the writer and society. All the information you need is in the Unit 6 Introduction in your textbook.*

1. *New Freedoms in the New Century*

    a. How did the bicycle lead to new freedom in women's clothing? _____
    _____

    b. What did the Suffragettes do? _____
    _____

    c. What happened to the old Victorian ways during the early twentieth century? _____
    _____

2. *Difficult Times*

    a. What made the 1930s a "low, dishonest decade," according to poet W. H. Auden? _____
    _____

    b. What was required of the British during World War II? _____
    _____

    c. How did British society change immediately after World War II? _____
    _____

3. *A New Monarch*

    a. How did Queen Elizabeth II contribute to the revival of English spirit? _____
    _____

    b. What changes occurred during the "swinging sixties"? _____
    _____

4. *Thatcher, Blair, and Beyond*

    a. What did Prime Minister Margaret Thatcher succeed in reversing?
    _____

    b. What was the state of England during the Tony Blair years?
    _____

B. DIRECTIONS: *Complete the sentence stems based on the Essential Question Vocabulary words.*

1. Social *trends* can be hard to _____

2. Improving the *welfare* of everyone in a nation _____

3. An up-to-the-minute, *contemporary* example of slang is _____

All-in-One Workbook
264

Name _____ Date _____

Unit 6 Introduction

Essential Question 3: What is the relationship of the writer to tradition?

A. DIRECTIONS: *On the lines provided, answer the questions about the third Essential Question in the Introduction about the relationship between the writer and tradition. All the information you need is in the Unit 6 Introduction in your textbook.*

1. *Expanding Tradition*

    a. How have the Internet and the availability of inexpensive books expanded people's access to traditional British literature? _____

    b. What new kinds of writers are now included in the British tradition? _____

    _____

2. *Twentieth-Century Poetry*

    a. What earlier poets does Yeats's "The Second Coming" recall?

    _____

    b. What twentieth-century writers have found new uses for the sonnet? _____

    _____

3. *The Short Story and Nonfiction*

    a. Give examples of the writers who have turned the British short story into a "global genre" in the twentieth century. _____

    _____

    b. Which writers deal with the problems of a fading empire? _____

    _____

4. *Connecting Present and Past*

    a. What happens to literary traditions in tumultuous times? _____

    _____

    b. What affirmation did T.S. Eliot express in his poem "Little Gidding"? _____

    _____

B. DIRECTIONS: *Complete the sentence stems based on the Essential Question Vocabulary words.*

1. *Idealism* can have a positive effect when _____

    _____

2. While some people welcome new *technology*, others fear it because _____

    _____

3. The twentieth century was marked by *conflict* of many kinds: _____

    _____

Unit 6 Introduction
Following-Through Activities

A. CHECK YOUR COMPREHENSION: *Use this chart to complete the Check Your Comprehension activity in the Unit 6 Introduction. In the middle boxes, fill in a key concept for each of the Essential Questions. In the right boxes, fill in a key author relevant to each concept you list. (The first Essential Question has been done for you.)*

Essential Question	Key Concept	Key Author
Place and Literature	Bombing of England WWII	Winston Churchill
Literature and Society		
Writer and Tradition		

B. EXTEND YOUR LEARNING: *Use this graphic organizer to help you prepare a book talk on authors from former British colonies.*

BOOK TALK WORKSHEET

Author Information
Name (phonetic pronunciation): _____

Date of birth: _____ Native country_____

- -

Works
Title + Summary: _____

_____

Title + Summary: _____

_____

_____

- -

Country's Influence
Style: _____

_____

Subject matter: _____

_____

_____

- -

Recitation
Identify excerpt: _____

Reason for choice: _____

Performance details: _____

   Vocalizations: _____

   Gestures/ Movements: _____

Poetry of William Butler Yeats
Literary Analysis: Symbolism

A **symbol** is a word, character, object, or action that stands for something beyond itself. To determine whether a word has symbolic meaning, consider it within the context of the poem. For example, the city of Byzantium, which symbolically represents the poetic imagination, is central to the meaning of "Sailing to Byzantium." It is in Byzantium that the speaker finds "the singing masters of (his) soul." That Byzantium is part of the title is another clue to its significance.

The following is an anonymous poem. Read the poem and answer the questions that follow.

In the Garden

In the garden there strayed

A beautiful maid

As fair as the flowers of the morn;

The first hour of her life

She was made a man's wife,

And buried before she was born.

1. The "maid" of this poem is an allusion to Eve in the Biblical story of creation. What evidence in the poem indicates that "maid" is symbolic?

   _____

   _____

   _____

   _____

   _____

   _____

2. According to the Bible, God created Adam's mate, Eve, by fashioning her from one of Adam's ribs. This means that Eve was never actually "born" in the normal sense of the word. Given this information, how can Eve be interpreted as a symbol for women in general?

   _____

   _____

   _____

   _____

   _____

   _____

   _____

Poetry of William Butler Yeats
Reading Strategy: Apply Literary Background

Most people approach life with a particular set of beliefs about the way things work and the importance of particular ideas, such as freedom, truth, and justice. People form their philosophies of life through personal experience and from information they gather. William Butler Yeats structured his own philosophical system through his experiences in life and through study.

Yeats used his opportunity as a writer to share his philosophical system with his readers. Even through poetry, Yeats expressed his philosophical assumptions. His philosophy becomes evident through the analysis of his imagery and symbolism.

DIRECTIONS: *Read each poem and describe a symbol or image from that poem. Explain how that symbol or image relates to Yeats's philosophical assumption that conflicting forces are at work in most aspects of life. An example has been completed for you.*

Conflicting forces are at work in most aspects of life.		
Poem	**Image or Symbol**	**Relationship to Philosophy**
"When You Are Old"	Love fleeing	Love is a force of attraction, yet it flees from the subject and hides; thus, a force of attraction acts in repulsion.
"The Lake Isle of Inisfree"		
"The Wild Swans at Coole"		
"The Second Coming"		
"Sailing to Byzantium"		

Poetry of William Butler Yeats
Vocabulary Builder

Using the Root -archy

A. DIRECTIONS: *The Greek root -archy- means "ruler." Read each sentence and decide if it is true or false. Write T or F and explain your answers.*

1. The king is the head of the *monarchy*.

_____

2. You are more likely to have power in a *patriarchy* if you are female.

_____

Using the Word List

anarchy   artifice   clamorous   conquest   conviction   paltry

B. DIRECTIONS: *Each item consists of a word from the Word List followed by four lettered words. Choose the word that is most nearly a synonym of the Word List word. Circle the letter of your choice.*

1. clamorous
   A. miserable
   B. joyful
   C. noisy
   D. timid

2. conquest
   A. victory
   B. plunder
   C. strategy
   D. battle

3. anarchy
   A. faith
   B. disorder
   C. power
   D. hope

4. conviction
   A. freedom
   B. doubt
   C. weakness
   D. certainty

5. paltry
   A. simple
   B. meager
   C. clear
   D. kind

6. artifice
   A. destruction
   B. ingenuity
   C. cleverness
   D. incivility

Name _____   Date _____

Grammar and Style: Sentence Fragments and Run-ons

A **sentence fragment** is a group of words that does not express a complete thought but is punctuated as if it were a sentence. A **run-on sentence** is two or more independent clauses that are not correctly joined or separated.

You can correct a sentence fragment by adding the words needed to make a complete sentence.

Sentence Fragment: Knowledge that the world will go on without you.

Corrected: "The Wild Swans at Coole" speaks of the knowledge that the world will go on without you.

You can correct a run-on sentence by using a comma and a coordinating conjunction or a semicolon to connect two independent clauses.

Run-on Sentence: Yeats thought that history runs in cycles this theory is especially apparent in "The Second Coming."

Corrected: Yeats thought that history runs in cycles; this theory is especially apparent in "The Second Coming."

A. PRACTICE: *Separate the independent clauses in these run-on sentences as indicated in parentheses.*

1. "In "When You are Old," the speaker talks of a woman he once loved he now speaks of her sadly and with longing. (comma + *but*)

   _____

   _____

2. The speaker of "The Lake Isle of Innisfree" longs for the peace of the isle he is confined to gray pavements and roadways. (comma + *but*)

   _____

   _____

3. The speaker wants to build a cabin at Innisfree, he wants to plant beans and keep bees. (semicolon)

   _____

   _____

B. WRITING APPLICATION: *Correct these sentence fragments and run-on sentences, rewriting them on the lines provided.*

4. The swans wheeling and turning on their great wings.

   _____

   _____

5. "The Second Coming" speaks of the end of one cycle of history, a new cycle is beginning.

   _____

   _____

6. Yeats's belief in the two-thousand-year cycle of history.

   _____

   _____

Name _____   Date _____

Poetry of William Butler Yeats
Support for Writing

Review Yeats' poetry to find examples of "the world of change" and "changelessness." Write specific examples in the chart below. Think about whether your examples support Ellman's thesis that Yeats' poetry is based on the opposition between these worlds. Write your opinion below.

World of Change	Changelessness

My opinion:

_____

_____

_____

On a separate page, use the statement of your opinion to write a thesis statement for your analysis of a theme. Then use details from the chart to support your thesis statement as you write.

Name _____ Date _____

"Preludes," "Journey of the Magi," and "The Hollow Men" by T. S. Eliot
Literary Analysis: Modernism

Modernism was a literary movement of the early-to-mid twentieth century in which writers attempted to break away from traditional forms and styles of the past. Modernist literature was highly influenced by industrialization and by World War I, which many writers felt left the world chaotic, fragmented, and sad. Modernism in poetry had several main features:

- Objectivity or impersonality, in which images or allusions take the place of direct statements

- A rejection of realistic depictions of life in favor of images

- Critical attention to social conditions and spiritual troubles

DIRECTIONS: *Connect the elements of Modernism with the following excerpts from the Modernist poems you have read.*

1. The morning comes to consciousness . . . From the sawdust-trampled street / With all its muddy feet that press / To early coffee-stands. / With the other masquerades / That time resumes, / One thinks of all the hands / That are raising dingy shades / In a thousand furnished rooms.
   In what way is the style and theme of this excerpt from "Preludes" uniquely Modernist?

   _____

   _____

   _____

2. And the night-fires going out, and the lack of shelters, / And the cities hostile and the towns unfriendly / And the villages dirty and charging high prices: / A hard time we had of it. / At the end we preferred to travel all night. / Sleeping in snatches, / With the voices singing in our ears, saying / That this was all folly.
   In what way is the style of this excerpt reflective of the Modernist movement? In what way does the subject matter of "The Journey of the Magi," and the faithful dedication of the Magi revealed in this excerpt, set it apart from the strictly Modernist viewpoints expressed in the other two poems?

   _____

   _____

   _____

3. The eyes are not here / There are no eyes here / In this valley of dying stars / In this hollow valley / This broken jaw of our lost kingdoms / In this last of meeting places / We grope together / And avoid speech / Gathered on this beach of the tumid river
   What attitude toward people and the modern world is expressed in this excerpt from "The Hollow Men"? In what way is its style and theme similar to that of "Preludes"?

   _____

   _____

   _____

Name _____   Date _____

Reading Strategy: Relating Literary Works to Historical Period

In order to understand the themes in T. S. Eliot's poetry, you must find meaning in repeated images, words, and phrases. By noting these patterns, you can find the meanings they suggest about the historical period in which Eliot wrote. For example, notice the images Eliot presents of urban life in "Preludes." If you put these images together, what do you learn about Eliot's view of the modern world?

DIRECTIONS: *As you read the poems, use the following questions as a guide to search for meaning in the images and patterns of Eliot's poems.*

1. What images does Eliot use to describe the city in "Preludes"? What feeling is created by these images? What do these images say about his perception of modern, urban life?

_____

_____

_____

2. What images in "Preludes" relate directly to the actions of humans in the urban setting? What does the pattern of these images suggest about the lives of the people?

_____

_____

_____

3. In "Journey of the Magi," what images does Eliot give of the journey? That relate to Eliot's own time? What effect do the images have?

_____

_____

_____

4. What words and phrases in "Journey of the Magi" reflect modern language? What do they suggest about the Magi's journey?

_____

_____

_____

5. What images in "The Hollow Men" describe specific limitations of the hollow men? What do these details reveal about the men's situation in life?

_____

_____

_____

Name _____ Date _____

"Preludes," "Journey of the Magi," and "The Hollow Men" by T. S. Eliot
Vocabulary Builder

Using the Root *-fract-*

In "Journey of the Magi," T. S. Eliot describes camels as "sore-footed and *refractory.*" The word *refractory* means "stubborn" or "hard to manage." It contains the root *-fract-*, meaning "to break." A *refractory* camel is one that breaks away from the path which you want to take.

A. DIRECTIONS: *Complete each sentence with a word from the following list.*

refract   fractional   fractious

1. He ate only a _____ portion of his meal.
2. Guards were trying to control the loud and _____ crowd.
3. A prism hanging in a window will _____ sunlight into different colors.

Using the Word List

dispensation   galled   refractory   supplication   tumid

B. DIRECTIONS: *Choose a lettered pair that best expresses a relationship similar to that expressed in the numbered pair. Circle the letter of your choice.*

1. GALLED : FRICTION ::
   A. worked : accomplishment
   B. consume : food
   C. rested : sleep
   D. injury : sore

2. REFRACTORY : STUBBORN ::
   A. generous : unselfish
   B. organize : arrange
   C. ancient : contemporary
   D. quietly : whisper

3. DISPENSATION : BELIEF ::
   A. creation : invent
   B. theory : philosophy
   C. operation : machine
   D. thought : concentrate

4. SUPPLICATION : PRAYER ::
   A. organization : society
   B. belief : knowledge
   C. education : lesson
   D. instruction : learn

5. TUMID : SHRIVELED ::
   A. pester : annoy
   B. heat : scorching
   C. massive : miniature
   D. simple : plain

Name _____ Date _____

"Preludes," "Journey of the Magi," and **"The Hollow Men"** by T. S. Eliot

Grammar and Style: Transitional Expressions

Transitional expressions are words and phrases that connect independent clauses. Conjunctive adverbs are one kind of transitional expression. A transitional expression is always followed by a comma.

Here are some common transitional expressions:
- Cause-effect: consequently, because of this
- Time: in time, afterward, at present
- To illustrate: in other words, for instance
- To add to: also, moreover, in addition
- Compare: similarly, in a like manner
- Contrast: however, on the contrary

A. PRACTICE: *Combine each pair of independent clauses with a transitional element that serves the purpose given in parentheses.*

1. "Preludes" creates images of futile modern life in the city. "The Hollow Men" uses images to create a mood of futility. (compare)

_____

_____

2. In "Journey of the Magi," Eliot refers to a long-ago event. He uses modern language to describe it. (contrast)

_____

_____

3. The modern age has taken the life out of people. They are left hollow and paralyzed. (cause-effect)

_____

_____

B. WRITING APPLICATION: *Add a transitional expression and an independent clause to each sentence. Write the new sentence.*

1. The city in "Preludes" is dirty and soulless.

_____

_____

2. The speaker in "Journey of the Magi" misses his home.

_____

_____

3. Eliot reveals regret for the past in "The Hollow Men.

_____

_____

"Preludes," "Journey of the Magi," and **"The Hollow Men"** by T. S. Eliot
Support for Writing

Review Eliot's poems to find imagery, rhythms, and themes that reflect modernism. Use the Venn diagram to compare and contrast them to the techniques and themes in one or two works of modernist art. In the parts of the circles that do not overlap, write how the poems and works of art are different. In the parts that do overlap, write how they are similar.

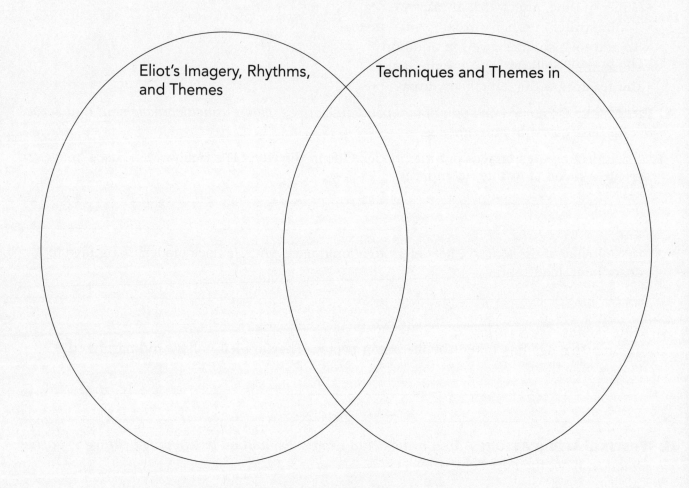

Look at the differences and similarities between Eliot's poems and the works of art. On a separate page, state whether you think the similarities outweigh the differences or the reverse. Then write a report that supports your opinion.

"In Memory of W. B. Yeats" and **"Musée des Beaux Arts"** by W. H. Auden
"Carrick Revisited" by Louis MacNeice
"Not Palaces" by Stephen Spender

Literary Analysis: Influence of Subgenres: Allegory and Pastoral

In an **allegory,** a writer uses symbolic characters to represent abstract qualities or traits. In a **pastoral,** a writer celebrates nature and those who live in the natural world.

DIRECTIONS: *State whether each set of lines is an allegory or a pastoral, or both. Explain your answer.*

1. The provinces of his body revolted,
   The squares of his mind were empty,
   Silence invaded his suburbs...

   _____

   _____

2. But the green banks are as rich and the lough as hazily lazy
   And the child's astonishment not yet cured.

   _____

   _____

3. ...the ploughman may
   Have heard the splash, the forsaken cry,
   But for him it was not an important failure....

   _____

   _____

"In Memory of W. B. Yeats" and **"Musée des Beaux Arts"** by W. H. Auden
"Carrick Revisited" by Louis MacNeice
"Not Palaces" by Stephen Spender

Reading Strategy: Compare and Contrast Elements

You can gain a greater understanding of a poet's use of allegory and the pastoral by comparing and contrasting those elements in their poems. Read the pairs of lines below. Describe how they are similar and different.

1.

From "In Memory of W.B. Yeats"	from "Musee des Beaux Arts"
With the farming of a verse Make a vineyard of the curse, Sing of human unsuccess In a rapture of distress….	…the ploughman may Have heard the splash, the forsaken cry, But for him it was not an important failure…
Similarities:	
Differences:	

2.

From "Carrick Revisited"	from "Not Palaces"
Back to Carrick, the castle as plumb assured As thirty years ago…	Not palaces, an era's crown Where the mind dwells, intrigues, rests: Architectural gold-leaved flower From people ordered like a single mind, I build…
Similarities:	
Differences:	

"In Memory of W. B. Yeats" and **"Musée des Beaux Arts"** by W. H. Auden
"Carrick Revisited" by Louis MacNeice
"Not Palaces" by Stephen Spender
Vocabulary Builder

Using the Root -top-

A. DIRECTIONS: *Knowing that the word root -top- means "place" and drawing upon your knowledge of other word roots, circle the letter of the best answer for each question.*

1. What does a *topographer* do?
   A. designs buildings
   B. plans cities
   C. records geographical features
   D. studies the use of electricity
2. Where would you find a *utopia*?
   A. in someone's imagination
   B. in the ocean
   C. on a plain
   D. in a distant galaxy

Using the Word List

affinities   intrigues   prenatal   sequestered   topographical

B. DIRECTIONS: *Choose the phrase that is the most appropriate description for each numbered word. Circle the letter of your choice.*

1. sequestered
   A. a small fish in a big pond
   B. a knight on a mission
   C. a dancer on a stage
   D. a patient in quarantine
2. topographical
   A. a political map of Britain
   B. a spinning carnival ride
   C. a relief chart of a park
   D. a featureless, grassy plain
3. affinities
   A. a group of total strangers
   B. a network of interpersonal relationships
   C. an endless universe
   D. a structure made of building blocks

4. prenatal
   A. a ship being repaired
   B. a poet's first book
   C. a check-up for a mother-to-be
   D. a cat lapping up a large saucer of cream
5. intrigues
   A. conspirators' plots
   B. pilots' instruments
   C. students' textbooks
   D. priests' vestments

"In Memory of W. B. Yeats" and "Musée des Beaux Arts" by W. H. Auden
"Carrick Revisited" by Louis MacNeice
"Not Palaces" by Stephen Spender
Support for Writing

Write the details and images about the artwork you chose in the chart below. Then, list words and phrases to describe these details. Try to think of vivid and precise words and phrases that will help the reader "see" the details in the painting.

Images and Details	Vivid Words and Phrases

On a separate page, use the ideas you have gathered to draft your poem about the artwork. Try to get across one main impression in your work. Use either the free verse and conversational style of Auden or the more rhythmic style of Spender.

Name _____ Date _____

"The Lady in the Looking Glass: A Reflection," *from Mrs. Dalloway*, "Shakespeare's Sister" by Virginia Woolf
Literary Analysis: Point of View

The **point of view** of a story is the perspective from which the story is told.

- A **first-person** narrator tells his or her own story. With this technique, authors can probe the thoughts of the narrator—but not those of other characters.
- A **third-person** narrator tells what happened to others. An **omniscient third-person** has the ability to reveal the thoughts of several characters. A narrator with **limited omniscience** only sees into the mind of one or few characters. An **objective narrator** describes what happens and cannot reveal character's thoughts.

In the chart, write the point of view from which each selection is told. Explain your answer.

Selection	Point of View	Reason
"The Lady in the Looking Glass"		
from *Mrs. Dalloway*		
"Shakespeare's Sister"		

Name _____ Date _____

"The Lady in the Looking Glass: A Reflection," *from Mrs. Dalloway,* "Shakespeare's Sister" by Virginia Woolf
Literary Analysis: Stream of Consciousness

In "The Lady in the Looking Glass" and the excerpt from *Mrs. Dalloway,* Virginia Woolf uses **stream-of consciousness** narration, which attempts to convey the random flow of thoughts in a character's mind. She includes word associations in her stream-of-consciousness narration, in which words or phrases a character thinks lead to other words and thoughts and reveal truths about the character.

DIRECTIONS: *Write your answers to the following questions.*

1. Identify a stream-of-consciousness passage in "The Lady in the Looking Glass." Explain what elements of stream of consciousness it demonstrates.

   _____

   _____

   _____

2. Does the narrator in "The Lady in the Looking Glass" convey reliable information about Isabella? Why or why not?

   _____

   _____

   _____

3. Why might Woolf have chosen this type of narrator?

   _____

   _____

   _____

4. Identify the elements of stream of consciousness in the excerpt from *Mrs. Dalloway.*

   _____

   _____

5. What word associations does Clarissa Dalloway make? What do they reveal about her?

   _____

   _____

   _____

"The Lady in the Looking Glass: A Reflection," *from Mrs Dalloway,*
"Shakespeare's Sister" by Virginia Woolf

Reading Strategy: Repairing Comprehension by Questioning

When reading experimental works like those of Virginia Woolf, you can repair **comprehension by questioning** to find your way through each story and determine its meaning. Two areas of focus are *who* is narrating and *why* the narrator emphasizes an incident. For example, as you begin "The Lady in the Looking Glass," you must ask who the narrator is. Questioning and suggesting possible answers can help you determine the story's meaning.

DIRECTIONS: *Write a question and answer for each of the following passages.*

"The Lady in the Looking Glass: A Reflection"

1. As for facts, it was a fact that she was a spinster; that she was rich; that she had bought this house and collected with her own hands . . . the rugs, the chairs, the cabinets, which now lived their nocturnal life before one's eyes. Sometimes it seemed as if they knew more about her than we, who sat on them, wrote at them, and trod on them so carefully, were allowed to know.

    Question: _____

    Answer: _____

2. At last there she was, in the hall. She stopped dead. She stood by the table. She stood perfectly still. At once the looking glass began to pour over her a light that seemed to fix her; that seemed like some acid to bite off the unessential and superficial and to leave only the truth. It was an enthralling spectacle.

    Question: _____

    Answer: _____

from *Mrs. Dalloway*

3. She stiffened a little on her kerb, waiting for Durtnall's van to pass. A charming woman, Scrope Purvis thought her (knowing her as one does know people who live next door to one in Westminster); a touch of the bird about her, of the jay, blue-green, light, vivacious, though she was over fifty, and grown very white since her illness.

    Question: _____

    Answer: _____

"Shakespeare's Sister"

4. She made up a small parcel of her belongings, let herself down by a rope one summer's night and took the road to London. She was not seventeen. The birds that sang in the hedge were not more musical than she was.

    Question: _____

    Answer: _____

"The Lady in the Looking Glass: A Reflection," *from Mrs. Dalloway,* "Shakespeare's Sister" by Virginia Woolf
Vocabulary Builder

Using the Prefix *trans-*

A. DIRECTIONS: *Knowing that* trans- *means "through" or "across," use the following words to complete the sentences.*

transatlantic   translucent   transom   transmutation

1. The glass panel is _____, allowing light to shine through it.

2. Opening the _____ above the door allowed the breeze to pass through.

3. The scientific experiment caused a _____ of the chemical substance.

4. During World War I, how many days did a _____ crossing require?

Using the Word List

evanescence   escapade   irrevocable   reticent
suffused   transient   upbraidings   vivacious

B. DIRECTIONS: *Match each word in the left column with its definition in the right column. Write the letter of the definition on the line next to the word it defines.*

___ 1. suffused   A. temporary; passing through quickly
___ 2. transient   B. gradual disappearance, especially from sight
___ 3. upbraidings   C. silent; reserved
___ 4. evanescence   D. adventure
___ 5. reticent   E. filled
___ 6. vivacious   F. unchangeable
___ 7. irrevocable   G. stern words of disapproval for an action
___ 8. escapade   H. lively; fun-loving

"The Lady in the Looking Glass: A Reflection," *from Mrs. Dalloway,*
"Shakespeare's Sister" by Virginia Woolf

Grammar and Style: Using Parallel Structure

Parallel structure is the repeated use of the same grammatical form or pattern. Writers may use parallel structure to create a natural rhythm or flow in their writing or to emphasize an idea. In the following lines from "The Lady in the Looking Glass," the parallel structures are underlined:

As for facts, it was a fact <u>that she</u> was a spinster; <u>that she</u> was rich; <u>that she</u> had bought the house . . . .

A. PRACTICE: *Rewrite the italicized words to make the sentence structures parallel.*

1. Mrs. Dalloway looked out the door and *was remembering* her youth.

   _____

2. Though Shakespeare could achieve fame and prosperity, a woman in his time *was not able to.*

   _____

3. Isabella wore the finest clothes and *she was the owner of* the finest furnishings.

   _____

4. The mirror showed a woman without thoughts and *who had no* friends.

   _____

B. Writing Application: *Rewrite each of the following sentences, incorporating parallel sentence structure.*

1. Shakespeare studied, wrote, and was able to become a success because he was a man.

   _____

   _____

2. Men laughed at Shakespeare's sister, and they were quickly dismissing her.

   _____

   _____

3. Scrope Purvis observed that Mrs. Dalloway was birdlike, light, and she was vivacious.

   _____

   _____

4. Mrs. Dalloway loved London, including its motor cars and listening to brass bands.

   _____

   _____

"The Lady in the Looking Glass: A Reflection," *from Mrs. Dalloway,*
"Shakespeare's Sister" by Virginia Woolf
Support for Writing

Review "The Lady in the Looking Glass" or the excerpt from *Mrs. Dalloway*. Choose a passage that clearly illustrates the technique of stream-of-consciousness and copy it in the chart. Then write your own "translation" of the passage as if it were expressed by a traditional omniscient narrator.

Stream-of-Consciousness Passage	Omniscient Narrator Translation

On a separate page, use your translation to write an essay comparing and contrasting the two techniques. Use examples from the chart to support your ideas.

"The Lady in the Looking Glass" by Virginia Woolf, *from* **Pedro Páramo** by Juan Rulfo, *from* **The Nine Guardians** by Rosario Castellanos

Literary Analysis: Stream of Consciousness

Many writers in the nineteenth-century focused their efforts on accurately and vividly portraying their characters' thoughts and behaviors. This was sparked by the increased attention to psychology at that time in social history. As popularity in that science grew, psychoanalysis became popular; dreams, memories, impulses, perceptions, and associations were classified as stream-of-consciousness. In the early twentieth-century, more writers attempted to refine the art of revealing these intricacies within their characters to show the characters' motivations, as well as their deepest thoughts. Within **stream-of-consciousness narration**, there are specific traits:

- The external world is presented through one or more characters' impressions in the first- or third-person point of view.

- The writing switches abruptly to new mental associations.

- Memories and/or flashbacks can be used, shifting time.

- Dreams and/or fantasy elements may be present.

- Details as symbols may be interpreted to reveal character.

- Long sentences or irregular grammar or punctuation may be employed to capture the flow of thoughts racing through the character's brain.

DIRECTIONS: *Complete the chart below by citing specific examples or passages from each work that correspond to features of steam-of-consciousness writing. Some boxes may remain blank.*

	Castellanos: *The Nine Guardians*	Rulfo: *Pedro Páramo*	Woolf: "The Lady in the Looking Glass" and/or *Mrs. Dalloway*
Abrupt switches to new associations			
Time shifts			
Presence of dreams and/or fantasy			
Symbolic details			

"The Lady in the Looking Glass" by Virginia Woolf
from **Pedro Páramo** by Juan Rulfo
from **The Nine Guardians** by Rosario Castellanos

Vocabulary Builder

A. DIRECTIONS: Revise each sentence so that the underlined vocabulary word is used logically. Be sure not to change the vocabulary word.

Example: When they <u>decapitated</u> the queen, the audience laughed.
When they <u>decapitated</u> the queen, the audience turned away.

1. Adrian's constant <u>palpitations</u> caused her to schedule a dental appointment.

   _____

2. Countless <u>tendrils</u> of rocks masked the facade of the house.

   _____

3. Since Connor had been so <u>diligent</u> about organizing the fundraiser, his boss fired him.

   _____

4. Fifi's French Cafe gives me memories of bland food and feeling <u>sated</u> after the meal.

   _____

5. <u>Furtively</u>, Nik announced his candidacy for Student Council.

   _____

Using the Word List

diligent   furtively   palpitations   sated   tendrils

B. DIRECTIONS: *For each numbered word, choose the word or phrase that is the most similar in meaning. Circle the letter of your choice.*

1. palpitations
   A. aftershocks from an earthquake
   B. rhythmic drum taps
   C. rapid heartbeats
   D. waves with whitecaps forming

2. tendrils
   A. plants' stemlike parts
   B. droplets of cool water
   C. carved wood pieces
   D. warm desert winds

3. diligent
   A. persevering
   B. curious
   C. distinct
   D. elated

4. sated
   A. temporary
   B. overjoyed
   C. highly anticipated
   D. full from eating

5. furtively
   A. acting shy
   B. in a sneaky manner
   C. on cue
   D. about to explode

Name _____ Date _____

"The Lady in the Looking Glass" by Virginia Woolf
from **Pedro Páramo** by Juan Rulfo
from **The Nine Guardians** by Rosario Castellanos
Support for Writing Worksheet

DIRECTIONS: *Complete the following table with details from each of the three selections that reveal contrasting points.*

	"The Lady in the Looking Glass"	from *Pedro Páramo*	from *The Nine Guardians*
What point of view is used to depict setting?			
What memories or associations occur due to aspects of setting?			
Identify details that make the setting vivid.			
How is character conveyed through setting details?			

DIRECTIONS: *Identify similarities that are shared among the stories by completing the chart below.*

	from *Pedro Páramo*/ from *The Nine Guardians*/ "The Lady in the Looking Glass"
Similarity #1	
Similarity #2	
Similarity #3	

Use the information you have gathered in the graphic organizers as you write your comparison/contrast essay.

"The Lagoon" by Joseph Conrad
"Araby" by James Joyce
Literary Analysis: Plot Devices and Theme

In "The Lagoon," Conrad uses a **story within a story,** a plot device in which a character in a fictional narrative tells a story. Conrad's plot device focuses attention on Arsat's story by framing it with another narrative. In "Araby," Joyce uses an **epiphany,** a plot device in which a character has a sudden and profound revelation in an ordinary moment, to heighten the story's climax.

The plot devices in both selections are closely tied with each story's main concern, or **theme**. In "The Lagoon," Conrad juxtaposes the two points of view from which the story unfolds (e.g., narrator and first-person account). This technique highlights the theme of relating passion to the process of storytelling. Similarly, contrasting the point of view within the story, Joyce uses the epiphany in "Araby" to relate the difference in intensity between the narrator's passion at the time of the story, with his separation and detachment from it years later, when he is actually revealing it.

DIRECTIONS: *Write your answers to the following questions.*

1. As you read "The Lagoon," what clues signal the beginning and the end of the story within the story?

   _____

   _____

   _____

2. In what way does the brothers' escape plan contribute to the theme of "The Lagoon," that death is inescapable?

   _____

   _____

   _____

3. Would Arsat's story in "The Lagoon" have the same effect if it had been told on its own? Explain.

   _____

   _____

   _____

4. What is the epiphany in "Araby"?

   _____

   _____

   _____

5. In "Araby," what is the boy doing or looking at when he has an epiphany?

   _____

   _____

   _____

6. How do the effects of time contribute to the overall theme in "Araby"?

   _____

   _____

   _____

"The Lagoon" by Joseph Conrad
"Araby" by James Joyce

Reading Strategy: Identify Cause-and-Effect Relationships

The relationships between the sequence of events in a story comprise the plot. Each event directly or indirectly impacts another event in some form, often causing yet another event. Until the story concludes and the action ceases, this sequence continues. Identifying and comprehending the **cause-and-effect relationships** within a story helps the reader have a better understanding of not only the plot, but also the story's theme. For example, in "The Lagoon" once the reader understands the cause of Arsat's exile, the effects of his pain and the reason for others' attitudes toward him become apparent.

DIRECTIONS: *Read the following passages from the stories. For each, identify either the cause or effect of the situation in a few short sentences.*

1. "Therefore I shall speak to you of love. Speak in the night. Speak before both night and love are gone—and the eye of day looks upon my sorrow and my shame; upon my blackened face; upon my burntup heart."

   _____

   _____

   _____

2. "I heard him calling my name again with a great shriek, as when life is going out together with the voice—and I never turned my head. My own name! . . . My brother! Three times he called—but I was not afraid of life. Was she not there in that canoe? And could I not with her find a country where death is forgotten—where death is unknown!"

   _____

   _____

   _____

3. At last she spoke to me. When she addressed the first words to me I was so confused that I did not know what to answer. She asked me was I going to *Araby*. I forget whether I answered yes or no. It would be a splendid bazaar, she said; she would love to go.

   _____

   _____

   _____

"The Lagoon" by Joseph Conrad
"Araby" by James Joyce
Vocabulary Builder

Using the Root *-vinc-*

A. DIRECTIONS: *In each sentence, cross out the italicized word or phrase and replace it with one of the following words:* convince, evince, invincibility.

1. I have doubts about this alarm system's *unconquerable quality*.
2. What can you do to *conquer the doubt in* me?
3. If you *show* clear, overwhelming evidence of the system's performance, perhaps I'll buy it.

Using the Word List

> conflagration   derided   garrulous   imperturbable   invincible   propitiate

B. DIRECTIONS: *For each related pair of words in CAPITAL LETTERS, choose the lettered pair that best expresses a similar relationship. Circle the letter of your choice.*

1. INVINCIBLE : VICTORY ::
   A. strong : muscula   B. confident : success   C. fear : doubt
2. PROPITIATE : VICTORY ::
   A. welcome : greet   B. confident : success   C. hasten : hurry
3. CONFLAGRATION : SPARK ::
   A. flood : droplet   B. burn : destroy   C. thunder : lightning
4. IMPERTURBABLE : DISRUPT ::
   A. anger : hatred   B. wealthy : inherit   C. contented : dismay
5. GARRULOUS : TALKATIVE ::
   A. sickly : healthy   B. yawning : tired   C. energetic : lively
6. DERIDED : TEASE ::
   A. ran : sprint   B. stretched : squeeze   C. grasped : release

C. *Decide whether each statement below is true or false. Explain your answers.*

1. Erin is *invincible* because she was defeated at every match this season.

   _____

2. After the meeting, Jaime complained about the *garrulous* speaker who rambled on for hours.

   _____

3. The boss finally decided to increase his employees' salaries in order to *propitiate* them.

   _____

4. To humor her loving baby, the new mother *derided* him in front of the other family members.

   _____

5. Some private beaches forbid bonfires, for fear they could lead to a *conflagration*.

   _____

6. Due to the nature of Mick's *imperturbable* behavior while walking the tightrope, he was fired.

   _____

"The Lagoon" by Joseph Conrad
"Araby" by James Joyce
Support for Writing

Both Arsat from "The Lagoon" and the narrator from "Araby" have very strong feelings for a female character in their respective stories. Due to the nature of their feelings, both males behave negatively, the degree of which varies. Pretend you are a defense attorney who needs to formulate a closing statement to help your client. Select one of the protagonists to defend, and identify the poor choices he makes in the story because of his strong feelings. Next, identify the repercussions of his respective actions. Finally, formulate a closing argument in which you try to convince a jury that despite his poor choices, the protagonist deserves to be free.

Protagonist:_____

Poor Choices

Repercussions

Closing Argument Points

"The Rocking-Horse Winner" by D. H. Lawrence
"A Shocking Accident" by Graham Greene

Literary Analysis: Theme, Symbol, and Third-Person Point of View

In most short stories, a **theme** conveys a main idea or message about life to the reader. Writers often use **symbols** to enhance their themes. A symbol is a person or object that represents an idea or a connection point for several ideas. Lawrence uses the rocking horse as a symbol with multiple meanings. Greene, in "A Shocking Accident," strengthens his theme by using the pig as a symbol for what is out of place.

Both stories are told from the **third-person point of view**, which means that the narrator does not partake in the action of the story. Notice how the two authors use this technique to reveal the themes.

DIRECTIONS: *Write your answers to the following questions.*

1. In what way does the **third-person point of view** enhance the idea of appearance vs. reality in "The Rocking-Horse Winner"?

   _____

   _____

   _____

2. What other meanings might the rocking horse have in Lawrence's story? In other words, what does the rocking horse symbolize?

   _____

   _____

   _____

3. How does the symbol of the rocking horse help you define the theme of "The Rocking-Horse Winner"?

   _____

   _____

   _____

4. How does the pig serve as a symbol in "A Shocking Accident"?

   _____

   _____

   _____

5. How does the **third-person point of view** contribute to the reader's impression of Jerome's engagement in "A Shocking Accident"?

   _____

   _____

   _____

"The Rocking-Horse Winner" by D. H. Lawrence
"A Shocking Accident" by Graham Greene
Reading Strategy: Make and Confirm Predictions

While you are reading, incorporate your own background knowledge with the story's descriptions, events, and dialogue in order to **make predictions** about what might happen. Continue reading and collecting information that will either confirm your predictions or cause you to reformulate them. Once the actual situation is revealed, if the story has different events than you anticipated, your prediction needs to be revised. For example, predicting that Sally would laugh, like most other people did, when she found out about the cause of Jerome's father's death allowed tension to build. When it was revealed that she reacted differently, worried and somber, the prediction might then focus on the success of Jerome's relationship with Sally.

DIRECTIONS: *Read the following passages from the stories. For each, make a prediction based on the information within the quote. Then discuss how those predictions would have worked out based on the actual events in the story.*

1. The boy saw she did not believe him; or rather, that she paid no attention to his assertion. This angered him somewhere, and made him want to compel her attention.
Prediction: _____
_____

Confirmation: _____
_____

2. "What, fifteen hundred pounds?"
"And twenty! And *forty*, that is, with the twenty he made on the course."
"It's amazing!" said the uncle.
"If Master Paul offers you to be partners, sir, I would, if I were you; if you'll excuse me," said Bassett.
Prediction: _____
_____

Confirmation: _____
_____

3. "I've had a telephone call, Jerome. From your aunt. I'm afraid I have bad news for you."
"Yes, sir?"
"Your father has had an accident."
"Oh."
"Mr. Wordsworth looked at him with some surprise. "A serious accident."
Prediction: _____
_____

Confirmation: _____
_____

Name _____ Date _____

"The Rocking-Horse Winner" by D. H. Lawrence
"A Shocking Accident" by Graham Greene
Vocabulary Builder

Using the Prefix *un-*

A. DIRECTIONS: *Replace the italicized word or words with the word* unfrock, unbind, unflinching, unassuming *or* unrest.

1. Due to the civil *disturbances* there, travelers have been advised to stay away.
2. Would you please *free* me from these shackles and chains?
3. Jesse's reaction to the sudden burst of flames and siren screeches was *bold*.
4. His parents were very *modest* about their son's prodigal abilities on the piano.
5. *Remove* the cover over the new statue to reveal the artist's detailed craftsmanship.

Using the Word List

apprehension   discreet   embarked   intrinsically   obstinately   uncanny

B. DIRECTIONS: *For each numbered word, choose the word or phrase that is the most similar in meaning. Circle the letter of your choice.*

1. discreet
   A. showing good judgment
   B. behaving wildly
   C. showing favor
   D. acting mysteriously
2. obstinately
   A. regretfully
   B. admittedly
   C. stubbornly
   D. happily
3. uncanny
   A. unique
   B. feverish
   C. unfamiliar
   D. eerie
4. apprehension
   A. reluctance
   B. misgiving
   C. refusal
   D. avoidance
5. embarked
   A. made a start
   B. planned a party
   C. left the scene
   D. greeted a host
6. intrinsically
   A. thoroughly
   B. quickly
   C. superficially
   D. innately

Name _____ Date _____

"The Rocking-Horse Winner" by D. H. Lawrence
"A Shocking Accident" by Graham Greene
Support for Writing

Write a new opening scene for either of the stories, with particular focus on the story's symbol. As the director, what other considerations might be taken into account regarding the presentation and placement of the symbol at various points throughout the scene? What other symbols might you, the director, consider to either replace or enhance the existing symbol? Jot notes in the appropriate areas.

Story & Symbol: _____

New Opening Scene: _____

_____

_____

_____

_____

Potential Other Symbols   How they Connect to/Enhance Original Symbol

Use the information you have compiled in the graphic organizer as you plan and write your new opening scene.

Name _____ Date _____

"The Soldier" by Rupert Brooke
"Wirers" by Siegfried Sassoon
"Anthem for Doomed Youth" by Wilfred Owen

Literary Analysis: Tone and Theme

The **tone** of language conveys an attitude toward the audience or the subject. We recognize tone in spoken language quickly. The way in which words are spoken, as well as the speaker's volume and facial expressions help us sort out his or her attitude. Some of these advantages aren't available to the writer, who must create tone with language alone. In literature, tone is transmitted primarily through choice of words and details.

Tone is particularly useful in discovering the **theme,** or central message, of these poems. Words, details, and the speaker's voice, or use of words, serve as clues to the writer's attitude toward the war and his audience. What does the writer think about soldiers dying, the battles they are fighting, and the value of the war that is being waged? Tone helps answer these questions, and in so doing, helps reveal and explain the theme.

DIRECTIONS: *Analyze the tone of each of the following passages. For each one, explain what impression details, word choices, and voice make. Then describe the overall tone of the passage.*

"Wirers"

. . . I heard him carried away, / Moaning at every lurch; no doubt he'll die today. / But *we* can say the front-line wire's been safely mended.

Details:	Word Choice:	Voice:

Tone:

"Anthem for Doomed Youth"

What passing-bells for these who die as cattle? / Only the monstrous anger of the guns. / Only the stuttering rifles' rapid rattle / Can patter out their hasty orisons.

Details:	Word Choice:	Voice:

Tone:

Name _____ Date _____

"The Soldier" by Rupert Brooke
"Wirers" by Siegfried Sassoon
"Anthem for Doomed Youth" by Wilfred Owen

Reading Strategy: Infer Essential Message

An inference is a conclusion drawn by reasoning. We make inferences all the time in daily life. Someone stands in the hall with wet hair and a dripping umbrella, and we conclude that it has been raining outside. If the sprinkler system had gone off in the building ten minutes ago, however, we might make a different inference. In short, we infer based on all available evidence. In daily life, we do this quickly, almost automatically.

When we **infer the essential message** of a piece of writing, we make educated guesses based on clues in the text. Writers engage readers by portraying a world of details or evidence and understand that readers will draw conclusions from clues they read. With these clues, writers lead readers to infer the essential message of their writing.

Much in literature is implied, especially in poetry, so recognizing the message implied by setting, images, language, and tone is a valuable skill for a reader. What do you know about the setting and speaker? How do you know it? What is going on? What clues do you use? What does this information tell you about the essential message of the piece?

Use the following chart to practice making inferences.

DIRECTIONS: *Write down the inference you make about each element of "Wirers." In the Clues column, identify specifically the evidence that you used to make the inference.*

Element	Inference	Clues
Setting (Where?)		
Speaker (Who?)		
Action/Topic (What?)		
Tone (Attitude)		
Essential Message		

"The Soldier" by Rupert Brooke
"Wirers" by Siegfried Sassoon
"Anthem for Doomed Youth" by Wilfred Owen
Vocabulary Builder

Using the Roots -ghast-, -ghost-

The word *ghastly*, which means "extremely horrible or frightening," originates from the Anglo-Saxon root *-ghast-*, which means "to terrify." The same root also appears as *-ghost-*, meaning "the spirit of a dead person," which can terrify the living. Other related words include *aghast*, *ghostly*, and *ghastful*.

A. DIRECTIONS: *Complete the following sentences with one of the words in the preceding paragraph that use the -ghast- or -ghost- root.*

1. Most people would be _____ at the horrible sight of a World War I battlefield.

2. The _____ battlefield was littered with the bodies of dead and wounded soldiers.

3. At midnight, a nervous person might imagine spirits wandering across the _____ fields where a battle was once fought.

Word List

desolate   ghastly   mockeries   pallor   stealthy

B. DIRECTIONS: *Each item consists of a word from the Word List followed by four lettered words. Choose the word most nearly* similar *in meaning to the Word List word. Circle the letter of your choice.*

1. stealthy
   A. furtive
   B. luxurious
   C. pilfered
   D. invisible

2. desolate
   A. absent
   B. disconnected
   C. selected
   D. deserted

3. mockeries
   A. imitations
   B. farces
   C. symbols
   D. vanities

4. pallor
   A. salon
   B. friendship
   C. gloom
   D. paleness

5. ghastly
   A. laughable
   B. significantly
   C. frightening
   D. generous

Name _____ Date _____

"The Soldier" by Rupert Brooke
"Wirers" by Siegfried Sassoon
"Anthem for Doomed Youth" by Wilfred Owen
Support for Writing

Use the chart to gather and organize ideas for your essay in **response to Yeats's criticism of the war poets.** In the left column, jot specific lines from the poems that you believe either support or refute Yeats's statement. In the right column, explain your interpretation or view of each quotation.

Quotations from Brooke, Sassoon, and Owen	Your interpretation

On a separate page, write your essay in response to Yeats's criticism of the war poets. Be sure to support each of your main ideas with quotations and other details from the poems.

Name _____ Date _____

"Wartime Speech" by Sir Winston Churchill
"Government Evacuation Scheme" Memorandum
Primary Sources: Speech and Memorandum

A **speech** is an oral presentation based on an important issue. Speeches are comprised of three different elements:

- **Purpose** – *the reason the speech is being presented*

- **Occasion** – *the inspiration behind the speech's origin*

- **Audience** – *the person or people who either hear or read the speech*

A **government memorandum** summarizes the reasons for a particular course of action, as well as provides instructions on how to carry out the request; it is both brief and official. This type of communication was intended to reach numerous people; therefore they reveal important information about society at various points of history.

DIRECTIONS: *Use the graphic organizer below to compare the various differences between Churchill's "Wartime Speech" and a "Government Evacuation Scheme" memorandum.*

	"Wartime Speech"	"Government Evacuation Scheme" memorandum
1. Purpose		
2. Occasion		
3. Audience		
4. Features		
5. Importance		

6. What similarities do you notice between the two primary source documents?

_____

_____

7. What might our government use these types of communications for today? Explain your response.

_____

_____

_____

"Wartime Speech" by Sir Winston Churchill
"Government Evacuation Scheme" Memorandum
Vocabulary Builder

Using a Thesaurus

A. DIRECTIONS: *Choose the synonym, or closest in meaning, to the vocabulary word.*

1. **intimidated**   a. frightened   b. depressed   c. mesmerized
2. **endurance**   a. freedom   b. stamina   c. wisdom
3. **formidable**   a. challenging   b. anxious   c. fair
4. **invincible**   a. truthful   b. coy   c. unconquerable
5. **retaliate**   a. renew   b. revenge   c. reclaim
6. **humanitarian**   a. petty   b. aged   c. generous
7. **allocation**   a. specification   b. review   c. consideration

B. DIRECTIONS: *Revise each sentence so that the underlined vocabulary word is used logically. Be sure not to change the vocabulary word.*

Example: The club wanted an easy hike, so they chose the precipice.
　　　　　　The club wanted a challenging hike, so they chose the precipice.

1. The strolling couple was <u>intimidated</u> when they passed the flower stand.

   _____

2. Alex's <u>endurance</u> is worsening as his tenure in the track club grows.

   _____

3. The loser in a battle would be described as <u>formidable</u> by the opponent.

   _____

4. Feeling <u>invincible</u> is like believing that you are easily defeated.

   _____

5. When the store owner was complimented, her instant thought was to <u>retaliate</u>.

   _____

6. The selfish and snobby heiress was a famous <u>humanitarian</u>.

   _____

7. A music fund <u>allocation</u> became necessary when the program was dissolved.

   _____

"The Demon Lover" by Elizabeth Bowen
Literary Analysis: The Ghost Story

One of the offshoots of the nineteenth-century Romantic Movement was the development of gothic novels, so named for settings that often included castles or other buildings of gothic architecture. Inevitably, some were written with an emphasis on the supernatural. The **ghost story,** long an oral tradition, became a popular literary form as well.

Part of the appeal of a good ghost story is that it is about normal people who do everyday things. Somehow, though, their normality is disrupted by something that cannot be easily explained or dismissed. One device writers sometimes use to play upon this idea of disrupted normality is **ambiguity,** which is the effect of two or more different possible interpretations. Ambiguity creates uncertainty and tension. **Flashbacks,** scenes that interrupt a narrative to relate events that happened in the past, are also common in ghost stories and contribute to the sense that the past is still somehow alive.

DIRECTIONS: *Use the following chart to record the "normal" elements in "The Demon Lover" as well as the unusual aspects that creep in almost from the very beginning.*

Scene or Detail	What is normal?	What is unusual?
outside Mrs. Drover's house		
inside Mrs. Drover's house		
the letter		
the farewell, 25 years ago		
Mrs. Drover's marriage and family		
catching the taxi		

"The Demon Lover" by Elizabeth Bowen

Reading Strategy: Relate Literary Work to Primary Source Documents

"The Demon Lover," which takes place during the bombardment of London in World War II, provides an opportunity to **relate a literary work to a primary source document.** Primary source documents, such as Churchill's speech, provide a glimpse of events specific to a particular time in history. By examining these sources and drawing conclusions about the time period they describe, you can gain insight into people's lives and what they thought about and felt, and so better understand the audience for which literary pieces of the time were written. Such an examination gives you a better understanding of the literature itself.

DIRECTIONS: *Read each question about the "The Demon Lover" and Churchill's "Wartime Speech" and answer the questions.*

1. How does the atmosphere evoked in "The Demon Lover" compare to that of Churchill's speech?

   _____

   _____

2. What serves as the source of fear in the story and in the speech? How are they related?

   _____

   _____

3. What similar tactics do the enemies described by Bowen and Churchill use? Are they effective?

   _____

   _____

   _____

4. How is the goal of Bowen's story similar to and different from the goal of Churchill's speech?

   _____

   _____

   _____

5. How do the endings of the two selections compare?

   _____

   _____

   _____

Name _____ Date _____

"The Demon Lover" by Elizabeth Bowen
Vocabulary Builder

Using Cognates

Cognates are words derived from the same original form even though they may have entered the language at different times and have different histories. *Spectral*, which means "ghostly," *spectre*, which means "ghost," and *spectrum*, which means "wide range," are cognates. All are derived from the Latin word *spectrum*, which means "appearance."

A. DIRECTIONS: *Complete the following sentences with one of the cognates discussed above.*

1. When the _____ appeared unexpectedly at the top of the stairs, the hair rose on her head and a cold shiver went down her back.

2. The _____ light would appear and disappear in the empty house every night just at midnight.

3. The scientist listed a wide _____ of explanations for the eerie happenings, which every one of those who had witnessed the phenomena immediately dismissed.

Word List

arboreal   aperture   circumscribed   dislocation   spectral

B. DIRECTIONS: *Match each word in the left column with its definition in the right column. Write the letter of the definition on the line next to the word it defines.*

___ 1. spectral   A. a condition of being out of place
___ 2. arboreal   B. ghostly
___ 3. circumscribed   C. limited
___ 4. dislocation   D. opening
___ 5. aperture   E. of, near, or among trees

"The Demon Lover" by Elizabeth Bowen
Support for Writing

Plan your sequel to "The Demon Lover" by completing the following graphic organizer. First reread the last paragraphs of the story and then ask yourself, "What happens next?" What question does "The Demon Lover" leave unanswered? Write the question and the answer in the organizer. Continue asking and answering questions.

Question that needs to be answered:
Action or event that answers the question:

Question that needs to be answered:
Action or event that answers the question:

Question that needs to be answered:
Action or event that answers the question:

Question that needs to be answered:
Action or event that answers the question:

On a separate page, use information from your diagram to organize your ideas as you draft your sequel. Make sure that the events are in a logical order that helps you tell a story.

"Vergissmeinicht" by Keith Douglas
"Postscript: For Gweno" by Alun Lewis
"Naming of Parts" by Henry Reed

Literary Analysis: Universal Theme: Love and War, and Irony

A **theme** is the central idea of a piece of writing. A **universal theme** is a message that is expressed in the literature of many cultures. The intermingling of **love and war** are two universal themes. Sometimes the theme of love and war is presented ironically. **Irony** is a contradiction between the expectation and the outcome of a situation. Love, for example, creates certain expectations that may, ironically, remain unfulfilled in war.

DIRECTIONS: *Read the following lines from the World War II poets. Then explain how the lines address the universal theme of love and war and identify the irony.*

1. Look. Here in the gunpit spoil
   the dishonored picture of his girl
   who has put: *Steffi. Vergissmeinicht*
   in a copybook gothic script. —"Vergissmeinicht"

   _____

   _____

   _____

   _____

2. Beloved . . .
   You always stay.
   And in the mad tormented valley
   Where blood and hunger rally
   And Death the wild beast is uncaught, untamed,
   Our soul withstands the terror
   And has its quiet honor—"Postscript: For Gweno"

   _____

   _____

   _____

   _____

3. . . . We can slide it
   Rapidly backwards and forwards: we call this
   Easing the spring. And rapidly backwards and forwards
   The early bees are assaulting and fumbling the flowers:
   They call it easing the Spring.—"Naming of Parts"

   _____

   _____

   _____

   _____

"Vergissmeinicht" by Keith Douglas
"Postscript: For Gweno" by Alun Lewis
"Naming of Parts" by Henry Reed

Reading Strategy: Author's Purpose

An **author's purpose** is his or her reason for writing. Each of the poets in this group had a particular reason for writing the poem that appears here. The purpose may be determined by looking at the poet's choice of words and images and considering the main idea of the poem.

DIRECTIONS: *As you read the poems, look at how the following images are used. Tell what they describe and what the author's purpose is for each.*

1. We see him almost with content
   abased, and seeming to have paid
   and mocked at by his own equipment
   that's hard and good when he's decayed.—"Vergissmeinicht"

   _____

   _____

2. And in the mad tormented valley
   Where blood and hunger rally
   And Death the wild beast is uncaught, untamed. . . .—"Postscript: For Gweno"

   _____

   _____

3. Today we have naming of parts. Japonica
   Glistens like coral in all of the neighboring gardens. . . .—"Naming of Parts"

   _____

   _____

"Vergissmeinicht" by Keith Douglas
"Postscript: For Gweno" by Alun Lewis
"Naming of Parts" by Henry Reed
Vocabulary Builder

Using the Word List

abide   combatants   eloquent   sprawling

A. DIRECTIONS: *Rewrite each sentence below, replacing the italicized word or phrase with an appropriate word from the Word List.*

1. He promised to *remain* with her forever, even should he die in battle.

   _____

2. The letter was *beautifully expressive.*

   _____

3. The *fighters* met in a field and the battle began.

   _____

4. The soldiers were *spread out* across the forests and fields.

   _____

B. Directions: *Each sentence has a blank space indicating that a word or words have been omitted. Choose the lettered word or words that best complete the meaning of the sentence and write the word or words in the blank.*

1. When the combatants began _____ around him, the brash young soldier suddenly understood the true meaning of war.
   A. celebrating   B. dying   C. laughing   D. studying

2. The young poet's eloquent verses _____ expressed ideas that many felt.
   A. crudely   B. harshly   C. generally   D. beautifully

3. During the _____ fighting, the officer watched his men sprawling in the warm sunshine.
   A. beginning of the   B. most intense   C. lull in the   D. frequency of the

4. If she decides to *abide* by her decision, she will _____ what she told him.
   A. reconsider   B. change   C. stay with   D. forget

"Vergissmeinicht" by Keith Douglas
"Postscript: For Gweno" by Alun Lewis
"Naming of Parts" by Henry Reed
Support for Writing

Use the chart to gather and organize ideas for your **memo** stating criteria for winning the Best War Poem prize. In the left column, list specific criteria you would look for in the poems. In the right column, explain why the criteria are important.

Criteria	Importance

On a separate page, write your memo stating the criteria for winning the prize. Be sure to clearly state each criterion and explain its importance.

"Vergissmeinnicht" by Keith Douglas
"Naming of Parts" by Henry Reed

Literary Analysis: Universal Theme: Love and War, and Irony

A **theme** is the central idea of a piece of writing. A **universal theme** is a message that is expressed in the literature of many cultures. The intermingling of **love and war** are two universal themes. Sometimes the theme of love and war is presented ironically. **Irony** is a contradiction between the expectation and the outcome of a situation. Love, for example, creates certain expectations that may, ironically, remain unfulfilled in war.

DIRECTIONS: *Read the following lines from the World War II poets. Then explain how the lines address the universal theme of love and war and identify the irony.*

1. Look. Here in the gunpit spoil
   the dishonored picture of his girl
   who has put: *Steffi. Vergissmeinicht*
   in a copybook gothic script. —"Vergissmeinnicht"

   _____

   _____

   _____

   _____

2. For here the lover and killer are mingled
   who had one body and one heart.
   And death who had the soldier singled
   has done the lover mortal hurt.

   _____

   _____

   _____

   _____

3. . . . We can slide it
   Rapidly backwards and forwards: we call this
   Easing the spring. And rapidly backwards and forwards
   The early bees are assaulting and fumbling the flowers:
   They call it easing the Spring.—"Naming of Parts"

   _____

   _____

   _____

   _____

All-in-One Workbook
312

Name _____ Date _____

"Shooting an Elephant" by George Orwell
"No Witchcraft for Sale" by Doris Lessing
Reading Strategy: Analyze and Evaluate Similar Themes

A theme is the central idea or message of a piece of writing. Both the nonfiction work "Shooting an Elephant" and the short story "No Witchcraft for Sale" involve themes of cultural conflict. To understand these two pieces and how they relate, **analyze and evaluate the similar themes.**

DIRECTIONS: *As you read "Shooting an Elephant" and "No Witchcraft for Sale," answer the following questions to analyze and evaluate the similar themes.*

1. What is the principal cultural conflict in "Shooting an Elephant"?

   _____

   _____

2. What is the principal cultural conflict in "No Witchcraft for Sale"?

   _____

   _____

3. How does the cultural conflict influence Orwell's actions in "Shooting an Elephant"?

   _____

   _____

4. How does the cultural conflict influence Gideon's actions in "No Witchcraft for Sale"?

   _____

   _____

5. How do the Farquars react to the cultural conflict with Gideon?

   _____

   _____

6. In your opinion, which character from the two selections responds most effectively to cultural conflict? Explain your answer.

   _____

   _____

   _____

   _____

"**Shooting an Elephant**" by George Orwell
"**No Witchcraft for Sale**" by Doris Lessing
Vocabulary Builder

Using the Etymology of Political Science and History Terms

Words relating to political science and history sometimes originate as a result of social and political events of the past. Examples include *colonialism, democracy,* and *communism.*

A. DIRECTIONS: *Complete the following sentences with one of the political science and history terms in the preceding paragraph.*

1. The United States fought World War II in order to preserve _____ so that Americans would continue to have the right to self-rule.

2. Because of its policy of _____, Great Britain's empire stretched to continents around the world.

3. During the twentieth century, many people supported _____ as a political goal because they believed that the community as a whole rather than individuals should own all property.

Word List

> despotic   dominion   imperialism   incredulously   reverently   skeptical

B. DIRECTIONS: *Match each word in the left column with its definition in the right column. Write the letter of the definition on the line next to the word it defines.*

___ 1. reverently   A. respectfully
___ 2. imperialism   B. with doubt or disbelief
___ 3. despotic   C. doubting
___ 4. incredulously   D. rule or power to rule
___ 5. dominion   E. tyrannical
___ 6. skeptical   F. policy and practice of maintaining an empire through the conquest of other countries

"Vergissmeinnicht" by Keith Douglas
"Naming of Parts" by Henry Reed
Support for Writing

Use the chart to gather and organize ideas for your **memo** stating criteria for winning the Best War Poem prize. In the left column, list specific criteria you would look for in the poems. In the right column, explain why the criteria are important.

Criteria	Importance

On a separate page, write your memo stating the criteria for winning the prize. Be sure to clearly state each criterion and explain its importance.

"Vergissmeinnicht" by Keith Douglas
"Naming of Parts" by Henry Reed
Enrichment: Love and War

The universal theme of love and war that appears in these World War II poems can be found in many other art forms, such as novels, folk tales, mythology, music, and films. Examples include George Lucas's *Star Wars* films, Ernest Hemingway's novel *A Farewell to Arms*, and the legend of King Arthur as told in Sir Thomas Malory's *Le Morte d'Arthur*. In all of these, love and war are intermingled to engage their audience's compassion, horror, and despair.

DIRECTIONS: *Choose an example of a work of art that you know well that involves this theme of love and war. Respond to the following questions to explore how the theme is developed in your selection.*

1. Who are the central characters?

   _____

   _____

2. What is the war and how is it connected to the love between the central characters?

   _____

   _____

   _____

3. Describe the relationship of those who are in love.

   _____

   _____

   _____

4. How does war affect the people who are in love?

   _____

   _____

   _____

5. What is the outcome for the central characters?

   _____

   _____

   _____

6. What is the message of the story?

   _____

   _____

   _____

Name _____ Date _____

"The Train from Rhodesia" by Nadine Gordimer
"B. Wordsworth" by V.S. Naipaul
Literary Analysis: Historical Period—The Colonial Era

The **setting** of a literary work includes its place, culture, politics, and historical period. The stories "The Train from Rhodesia" and "B. Wordsworth" are set in different places but both reflect the effects of the historical period—the colonial era. The **colonial era** refers to the span of history in which Britain became and remained an empire. The British, and other European countries, overtook smaller countries, colonizing them. They placed the British government in control of their newly won subjects and attempted to "civilize" the indigenous peoples of these countries. Many African countries, India, and the islands of the Caribbean were colonized.

The effects of colonization run deep within the indigenous cultures as well as in the cultures of the colonizers. Many post-colonial writers explore these effects in their literary works. They use the setting of the colonial era to establish the place, the time, the conflict, and the characters. As you might imagine, tensions ran high between the colonized and the colonizers. Much of the tension of the period had its roots in ethnic and cultural differences.

As you read literature both from and about the colonial era, take into consideration the way the historical period influences the ideas and the events the writer portrays.

DIRECTIONS: *Answer the following questions about the selections in order to better understand the effects of colonialism.*

1. What perspective do you get of the historical period based on the setting of Gordimer's story?

   _____

   _____

2. What is one of the main external conflicts in Gordimer's story? How does it reflect the effects of colonization?

   _____

   _____

3. How does Naipaul's aligning B. Wordsworth with W. Wordsworth reflect the effects of colonialism?

   _____

   _____

4. What does the lack of evidence of B. Wordsworth's existence say about the effects of colonialism?

   _____

   _____

"The Train from Rhodesia" by Nadine Gordimer
"B. Wordsworth" by V.S. Naipaul
Reading Strategy: Apply Knowledge of Historical Background

To analyze a text, especially one written to express and examine the effects of a particular era, you need to have an understanding of the historical background and be able to apply that understanding to the text. Both "The Train from Rhodesia" and "B. Wordsworth" express and examine the effects of colonialism. Until the mid–1900s, many countries were colonies of Britain. Though the indigenous population was much larger than the British, these people were ruled by a British government. British culture was also forced upon them in many instances.

DIRECTIONS: *Read the following excerpt from "The Train from Rhodesia." Apply your knowledge of the historical background to answer the questions that follow.*

All up and down the length of the train in the dust the artists sprang, walking bent, like performing animals, the better to exhibit the fantasy held toward the faces on the train. Buck, startled and stiff, staring with round black and white eyes. More lions, standing erect, grappling with strange, thin, elongated warriors who clutched spears and showed no fear in their slits of eyes. How much, they asked from the train, how much?

1. How does the description of the Africans in the first sentence reflect the results of colonization?

    _____

    _____

2. What "fantasy" does the narrator refer to in the first sentence?

    _____

    _____

3. What is implied by the Africans selling their fearlessness, in the content of the warrior statues, to the colonizers?

    _____

    _____

All-in-One Workbook
318

"The Train from Rhodesia" by Nadine Gordimer
"B. Wordsworth" by V. S. Naipaul
Vocabulary Builder

Word List

atrophy   distill   impressionistic   keenly   patronize   segmented

A. DIRECTIONS: *Match each word in the left column with its definition in the right column. Write the letter of the definition on the line next to the word it defines.*

___ 1. keenly   A. to be a customer of a store
___ 2. patronize   B. to obtain the essential part
___ 3. distill   C. sharply or intensely
___ 4. impressionistic   D. conveying a quick, overall picture
___ 5. segmented   E. separated into parts
___ 6. atrophy   F. to waste away

B. WORD STUDY: *The Word Bank word* patronize *is a form of the word* patron, *which means "customer, supporter, or benefactor." Write the form of the word* patron *that best completes each of the following sentences. Use context clues and your knowledge of the word* patron *to choose the correct word.*

patronize   patronizing   patronage   patroness

1. The wealthy _____ entered the gallery dressed in jewels and a lavish gown.
2. Unfortunately, the shopkeeper's _____ manner turned away many customers.
3. The wisest shopkeepers appreciate the _____ of each and every customer.
4. We decided to _____ the new Italian restaurant in our neighborhood.

"**B. Wordsworth**" by V. S. Naipaul
Support for Writing

Use the diagram to collect details for your account of a remarkable person. Write the person's name in the center circle. In the surrounding boxes, write words and phrases to describe the person's remarkable qualities. Also, imagine the person in the scene you will describe. Jot notes about the person's reactions, words, and actions.

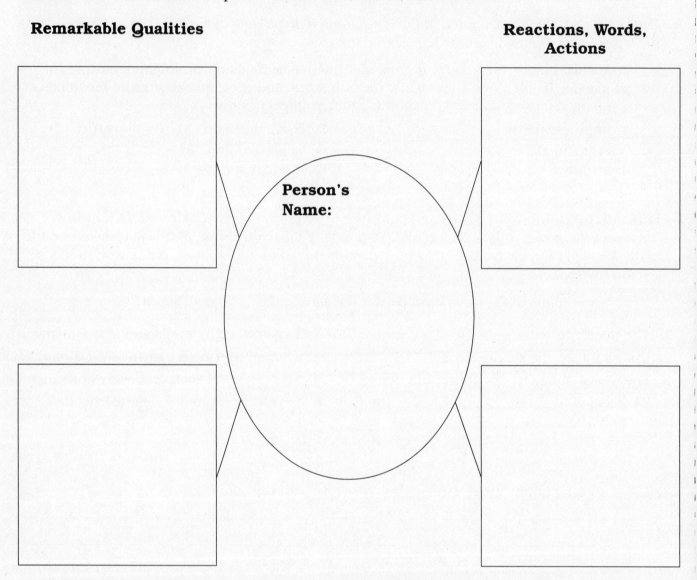

Remarkable Qualities

Reactions, Words, Actions

Person's Name:

As you write your first-person account of a remarkable person on a separate page, draw on ideas from your diagram. Use the details to help your readers see and understand the character and the situation.

from **Midsummer, XXIII** and **Omeros** by Derek Walcott
Literary Analysis: Political Critique of Art and Allusion

Many works of art, including literary works, have serious political implications. A **political critique of art** is an examination of these political implications. In order to critique art in this way, you must first determine the message the author is expressing through a work's content. Then you can examine the literary techniques the author uses to present content and theme.

One of the key techniques author's of political texts use is allusion. An **allusion** is a reference to another literary work, a person, or an event. An allusion implies that the writer and reader share or "own" a common culture.

To conduct a political critique, you must identify the elements of the common culture the author alludes to. Think about the origins, the outcomes, and the implications and meanings of the events, persons, or works, as you conduct your political critique.

DIRECTIONS: *Answer the following questions to examine the political implications of the excerpt from* Midsummer XXIII.

1. What does Walcott allude to in lines 6–8?

   _____

   _____

   _____

2. What does he imply by comparing the riots to this event?

   _____

   _____

   _____

3. What does Walcott allude to in the last three lines of the poem?

   _____

   _____

   _____

4. What does he imply about contemporary Britain with this allusion?

   _____

   _____

   _____

from Midsummer, XXIII and **from Omeros from Chapter XXVIII** by Derek Walcott
Reading Strategy: Repair Comprehension by Understanding Allusion

An **allusion** is a brief reference to a literary work, a person, or an event. Allusions can be direct references, and they can also be emulations of traditional works. In order to understand the implications of an allusion, you must know something about the work, person, or event the author alludes to within his or her own work. You can enhance your comprehension of the work you are reading by building an understanding of the allusions the writer includes. To build this understanding, you should consult background information, the footnotes, and even reference materials.

DIRECTIONS: *Read each allusion. Identify the work, person, or event the author alludes to. Check the background information and footnotes to repair your comprehension of the allusion. Then, record the implications and meanings of the allusion based on your knowledge. The first allusion has been analyzed for you.*

Allusion	Work, person, or event	Background or footnote	Implications and meanings
The leaf stems tug at their chains, the branches bending / like Boer cattle under Tory whips that drag every wagon / nearer apartheid. —*Midsummer*	The writer alludes to the Dutch colonization of South Africa and the effects of that colonization, namely apartheid.	Footnote—The Boers are the Dutch who colonized South Africa in the 1600s. The Tories (a political party) held power in Britain when Britain won control over the colony.	The rioters in England are compared to the colonized blacks in South Africa during apartheid. They are being oppressed and rebelling like their African counterparts.
[W]hen the riot police and the skinheads exchanged quips / you could trace to the Sonnets, or the Moor's eclipse. —*Midsummer*			
Then, when the dead / palms were heaved overside, the ribbed corpses / floated, riding, to the white sand they remem-bered, —*Omeros*			

from Midsummer, XXIII and from Omeros from Chapter XXVIII by Derek Walcott
Vocabulary Builder

Using the Root *-duc-*

The Word Bank word *inducted* contains the Latin root *-duc-*, which means "to lead." Many other words, such as *education* or *ductwork,* that connote "leading" or "bringing something toward" also share this origin.

A. DIRECTIONS: *Match each word with the -duc- word root in the left column with its meaning in the right column. Write the letter of the definition on the line next to the word it defines.*

___ 1. ductile

___ 2. ducat

___ 3. deduce

___ 4. abduct

___ 5. reduction

A. to lead or take away

B. to trace a course of thought

C. a cutting back in number or amount

D. easily drawn or shaped, as metal

E. a coin bearing the image of a duke

Using the Word List

antic   eclipse   inducted   rancor

B. DIRECTIONS: *Each item consists of a related pair of words in CAPITAL LETTERS, followed by four lettered pairs of words. Choose the pair that best expresses a relationship similar to that expressed in the pair in capital letters. Circle the letter of your choice.*

1. ANTIC : DIGNIFIED ::
   A. comic : funny
   B. rushed : sedate
   C. crazy : oddity
   D. frantic : nervous

2. RANCOR : ANIMOSITY ::
   A. malice : generosity
   B. spite : jealousy
   C. kindness : courtesy
   D. revenge : charity

3. INDUCTED : MEMBER ::
   A. honored : hero
   B. called : answer
   C. gave : donor
   D. rejected : quality

4. ECLIPSE : LIGHT ::
   A. darken : darkness
   B. dim : bright
   C. orbit : planet
   D. shade : sun

Name _____ Date _____

from Midsummer, XXIII and from Omeros from Chapter XXVIII by Derek Walcott
Support for Writing

Use the graphic organizer below to collect and organize ideas for your multimedia presentation of either Walcott poem. First, write the poem you have chosen. List the theme and main images in the boxes on the left. Then, list ideas for photographs, artwork, music, video clips, and sound effects that may illustrate the poem.

Poem: _____   **Audiovisual Aids**

Theme:

Image:

Image:

Image:

Draw on details from your graphic organizer as you draft your script on a separate page. Show the line-by-line relationship between the text and the aids you will use.

"Follower" and **"Two Lorries"** by Seamus Heaney
"Outside History" by Eavan Boland
Literary Analysis: Diction and Style, Sestina

Style refers to these poetic elements: **diction,** or word choice; imagery; rhythms; poetic form; and theme. How each poet *uses* these elements is that poet's style. The basis of a poet's style lies in the form the poet chooses to express his or her ideas. Heaney, in "Two Lorries," chooses to use the traditional form of the **sestina** in which six words are recycled to end each line. Boland, on the other hand, uses a freer, contemporary form to express her ideas. The style of a poem adds meaning to the poem and affects how a reader responds to that poem. Though generalizations can be made, a poet's style varies from poem to poem.

Following is the first stanza of "Follower." Read it and then refer to the table for an explanation of Heaney's style.

My father worked with a horse plow,
His shoulders globed like a full sail strung
Between the shafts and the furrow.
The horses strained at his clicking tongue.

Elements of Style	Explanation
Diction—Is the poet's word choice formal or informal, conversational or stilted, concrete or abstract?	Diction is informal and easy to read, just as if a boy were talking to the reader. Poet uses many concrete words.
Imagery—Is the imagery easily perceived by the senses? Or does it create unusual or abstract pictures? Do the images tell a story, or do they just stand next to each other?	The imagery appeals to the senses of sight and hearing. Poet creates a vivid image of the father's strong shoulders.
Rhythm—Does the poet use rhyme? Does the poet use rhythm? How much? Are they conventional or irregular?	Poet uses a traditional *abab* rhyme scheme.
Form—Are there stanzas? Are they regular or irregular? Does the poet write in free verse?	Poet uses regular, four-line stanzas.

DIRECTIONS: *Using the table on this page as a model, examine the first stanza of "Two Lorries" for style. Write your evaluation of each element of style in the space provided.*

Diction: _____

_____

Imagery: _____

_____

Rhythm: _____

_____

Form: _____

_____

"Follower" and "Two Lorries" by Seamus Heaney
"Outside History" by Eavan Boland
Reading Strategy: Summarize to Determine Main Idea

A **main idea** is a key point expressed by a writer. To make sure you understand the main idea of a poem, you can summarize it in your own words. A **summary** is a restatement of main ideas in a condensed form. It makes you think critically about material you read, identifying main ideas and excluding unimportant details or examples.

For poetry, it may be helpful to note the main ideas of each stanza and then build a complete summary from there. Here is a portion of "Outside History" (lines 7–12), accompanied by notes about the main ideas of these two stanzas.

They keep their distance. Under them remains   discovery of humanness—being alive
a place where you found
you were human, and

a landscape in which you know you are mortal.   discovery of mortality; must choose
And a time to choose between them.
I have chosen:

DIRECTIONS: *Use the space on this page to note the main idea of each stanza of "Two Lorries" as you read. Then use your notes to summarize the essence of the whole poem.*

"Two Lorries"

Stanza 1: _____

Stanza 2: _____

Stanza 3: _____

Stanza 4: _____

Stanza 5: _____

Stanza 6: _____

Stanza 7: _____

Summary of "Two Lorries":

_____

_____

_____

_____

_____

"**Follower**" and "**Two Lorries**" by Seamus Heaney
"**Outside History**" by Eavan Boland
Vocabulary Builder

Using the Root -*mort*-

A. DIRECTIONS: *Each of the following words contains the root -mort-, meaning "dead" or "death." Match each word with its definition. Write the letter of the definition on the line next to the word it defines.*

___ 1. mortify

___ 2. mortally

___ 3. postmortem

A. in a deadly or fatal manner

B. to subject to severe embarrassment

C. after death

Using the Word List

furrow   inklings   mortal   nuisance   ordeal

B. DIRECTIONS: *Choose the lettered word or phrase that is most similar in meaning to the numbered word. Circle the letter of your choice.*

1. furrow
   A. groove
   B. mold
   C. measurement
   D. ditch

2. inklings
   A. notes
   B. blotches
   C. suggestions
   D. ideas

3. mortal
   A. impermanent
   B. prone to error
   C. inexact
   D. everlasting

4. nuisance
   A. boredom
   B. excitement
   C. distress
   D. annoyance

5. ordeal
   A. comedy club
   B. severe test
   C. new freeway
   D. light supper

"The Follower" and **"Two Lorries"** by Seamus Heaney
"Outside History" by Eavan Boland
Support for Writing: Travel Directions

Use the following chart to organize the information you will use in your travel directions. Identify at least three sites to see along the way. Include a description of each.

Directions from Belfast to Antrim Coast
Site:
Site:
Site:

On a separate sheet of paper, write your travel directions and include descriptions of the sites you suggest touring on the way.

Come and Go by Samuel Beckett
That's All by Harold Pinter
Literary Analysis: Drama of the Absurd

Unlike its ancient predecessors that expressed elevated emotions through high tragedy, **drama of the absurd** takes a microscope to our everyday life. It works through common situations to express the ridiculousness, and even pointlessness, of life.

In this genre of drama, characters are often interchangeable or indistinguishable. They lack individuality and emotion. In Pinter's That's All, for example, the characters do not even have real names. They are Mrs. A and Mrs. B.

The situations characters are placed in seem pointless or futile. The conflicts are miniscule and often clouded by their abstract presentation. Situations and conversations are repeated seemingly endlessly, illuminating the so-called progress of society. The truth, if such a thing exists, is intangible. Much of the meaning of the plays in this genre lies in the lack of information the playwrights give.

When you analyze drama of the absurd, you must make extra-textual inferences to arrive at the meaning of the work. The playwrights provide a social commentary through their dramatic situations.

DIRECTIONS: *Use the following questions to analyze the elements of drama of the absurd in Come and Go and That's All.*

1. Describe the characters Flo, Vi, and Ru in Come and Go. What does the author imply by the construction of these characters?

   _____

   _____

   _____

2. What happens in Come and Go? What meaning lies within the events or the nature of the events?

   _____

   _____

   _____

3. What is the main conflict in That's All? How would you describe the nature of the conflict?

   _____

   _____

   _____

4. What comment do you think these playwrights make about society and humanity? Explain.

   _____

   _____

   _____

Name _____   Date _____

"**Come and Go**" by Samuel Beckett
"**That's All**" by Harold Pinter

Reading Strategy: Compare and Contrast Literary Elements

When you **compare and contrast literary elements,** you look at how elements are alike and different. You can compare and contrast within a text. For example, you might analyze the similarities and differences between two characters within a work. You can also compare and contrast across texts, analyzing elements such as character, situation, dialogue, and theme.

DIRECTIONS: *Complete the following chart to compare and contrast character, situation, dialogue, and theme of Come and Go and That's All. Describe each element, and then comment on their similarities, differences, and implications. The first item has been completed for you.*

Element	Come and Go	That's All	Similarities, Differences, Implications
Character	The characters Flo, Ru, and Vi are indistinguishable from one another. They lack overall individuality with their indeterminate ages and dress.	Mrs. A and Mrs. B lack individuality, as noted by their generic and interchangeable names. They are mundane characters.	The characters in both plays lack individuality and personality. This lack reflects the playwrights' belief that society has stripped us of individuality.
Situation			
Dialogue			
Theme			

"**Come and Go**" by Samuel Beckett
"**That's All**" by Harold Pinter
Vocabulary Builder

Word List

appalled   clasped   resumed   undeterminable

A. DIRECTIONS: *Choose the letter of the word that is closest in meaning to the numbered item.*

1. **appalled**
   A. thrilled
   B. shocked
   C. uninvited
   D. delivered

2. **clasped**
   A. loosened
   B. tied
   C. intertwined
   D. opened

3. **resumed**
   A. continued
   B. carried
   C. started
   D. denied

4. **undeterminable**
   A. unknown
   B. unlikely
   C. opportune
   D. inept

B. DIRECTIONS: *Complete each sentence with the word from the Word List that makes most sense.*

1. The girls' tightly _____ hands gave them strength in the face of their fears.

2. Though the puppy's breed was _____, we knew he would be big from the size of his paws.

3. After the intermission, the play _____ for the final acts.

4. My mother was _____ when she saw the price of the market's fresh fruit.

"Come and Go" by Samuel Beckett
"That's All" by Harold Pinter
Support for Writing: Scene from an Absurd Drama

Use the following idea web to record your ideas for your dramatic scene.

Characters:

Setting:

Theme:

Situation:

Dialogue:

On a separate sheet of paper, write your scene from an absurd drama. Use the information you recorded in your idea web as a basis for the scene.

"Do Not Go Gentle into That Good Night" and **"Fern Hill"** by Dylan Thomas
"The Horses" by Ted Hughes
Literary Analysis: Style and Theme, Villanelle

A writer's **style** encompasses his or her way of expressing ideas and emotions. To describe a writer's style, you must look at diction, syntax, form, as well as other literary techniques the writer uses, such as figurative language, sound devices, and imagery. Often writers use style to support their expression of theme.

The **theme** of a selection is its central idea or message. When you analyze a work, look at its content, descriptions, and events, as well as style, to determine the central point the author is making.

Poets have the choice of a multitude of forms to express their themes. Some poets choose to write free verse, in which the rhythm, rhyme, and meter follow no specific pattern. Others choose to call upon traditional form in order to express their ideas. Thomas chooses the villanelle form for "Do Not Go Gentle into That Good Night." A **villanelle** is a nineteen-line poem that repeats lines 1 and 3 throughout. The rhyme scheme is set.

DIRECTIONS: *Answer the following questions about Thomas's and Hughes's poems.*

1. How would you describe Thomas's style in "Do Not Go Gentle into That Good Night"? Give reasons for your evaluation.

_____

_____

_____

2. How does Thomas's style in "Fern Hill" compare to that in his other poem?

_____

_____

_____

3. How would you describe Hughes's style in relation to Thomas's two poems?

_____

_____

_____

4. What common theme do these three poems address?

_____

_____

_____

"Do Not Go Gentle into That Good Night" and **"Fern Hill"** by Dylan Thomas
"The Horses" by Ted Hughes

Reading Strategy: Evaluate the Expression of Theme

The **theme** of a selection is its central idea. Authors can state themes directly, but often they are implied by the content and style of a work. To **evaluate the expression of theme**, you must first identify the theme you believe the author is conveying. Then, you must look at the text to analyze how the author supports the expression of the theme. Consider the author's use of literary techniques, word choice, and style. Think about how these add to or detract from the central idea of the text. For example, the form of the villanelle and the repetition of the line "Rage, rage against the dying of the light" supports the expression of the theme of inevitable death.

DIRECTIONS: *Complete the charts to evaluate the expression of theme in "Fern Hill" and "The Horses."*

Fern Hill	
Theme: The inevitable loss of innocence as tied to nature	
Style	
Word Choice	
Imagery	
Form	
Other Techniques	
Evaluation:	

The Horses	
Theme:	
Style	
Word Choice	
Imagery	
Form	
Other Techniques	
Evaluation:	

"Do Not Go Gentle into That Good Night" and "Fern Hill" by Dylan Thomas
"The Horses" by Ted Hughes
Vocabulary Builder

Word List

dregs   grieved   spellbound   tortuous

A. DIRECTIONS: *Each numbered word is followed by four lettered words or phrases. Choose the word or phrase that is most* similar *in meaning to the numbered word, and circle the letter of your choice.*

1. dregs
   A. small pieces
   B. remaining parts
   C. shimmering rays
   D. dark colors

2. grieved
   A. sighed
   B. mourned
   C. hailed
   D. resented

3. spellbound
   A. multicolored
   B. tired
   C. mesmerized
   D. unhealthy

4. tortuous
   A. winding
   B. deceitful
   C. twisted
   D. complex

B. DIRECTIONS: *Complete each sentence with the word from the Word List that makes most sense.*

1. I nearly gave up trying to follow the _____ directions for assembling my new desk.

2. Janelle _____ the loss of her best friend when he moved to another state.

3. Even though the crocus were in bloom, Amanda could not ignore the _____ of winter that lingered in the landscape.

4. Zoey and Ezra were _____ as they lay on the beach watching the meteor shower light up the sky.

Name _____ Date _____

"Do Not Go Gentle into That Good Night" and **"Fern Hill"** by Dylan Thomas
"The Horses" by Ted Hughes

Support for Writing

Use the following diagram to develop ideas for your parody of Thomas's or Hughes's style. In the center circle, write your ridiculous subject. In each of the surrounding circles, write a detail about your subject that you can develop in your parody.

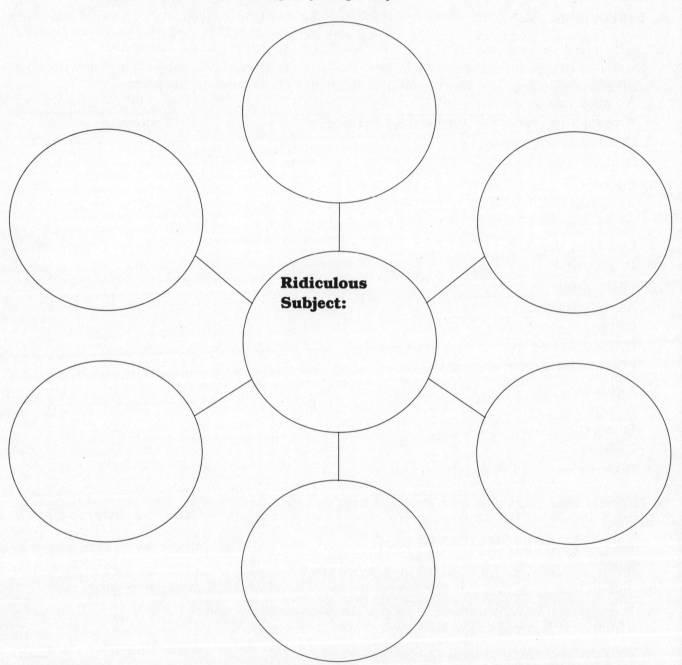

Ridiculous Subject:

On a separate page, use details that you have developed about your subject, as well as the poet's forms, rhythms, and words to help you write a parody. Use vivid language to exaggerate characteristics of the style of the poet you have chosen.

"An Arundel Tomb" and **"The Explosion"** by Philip Larkin
"On the Patio" by Peter Redgrove
"Not Waving But Drowning" by Stevie Smith

Literary Analysis: Free Verse, Meter, and Dramatic Structure

Whether a poet uses free verse or a conventional form of poetry, the lines of poetry likely have some kind of rhythm, or alternation of strong and weak—or stressed and unstressed— syllables. That rhythm may or may not create a regular pattern, or meter. Whether it does or not, though, the poet probably uses the rhythm to add to the meaning of the poem and create a feeling of tension as the poem builds to its climax, creating a **dramatic structure**.

The meter of a poem is measured in feet. One foot consists of one stressed and any number of unstressed syllables. The chart examines the meter Larkin uses in his poems.

Meter	Pattern of Syllables	Example
iambic tetrameter	four sets of iambs per line (˘ ´)	The earl and countess lie in stone
trochaic tetrameter	four sets of trochees per line (´ ˘)	Shadows pointed towards the pithead:

When poets vary the rhythm of a conventional meter, they add emphasis or give special significance to the line. Free-verse poets vary their rhythms to add or create meaning.

DIRECTIONS: *Examine the rhythm and meter in the poems in this section, as directed by the following questions.*

1. Following is the first line of "An Arundel Tomb." Notice how the stressed and unstressed syllables fall.

   Síde by síde, thĕir facĕs blúrred,

   How is this line different from the others? What is the effect of the difference?

   _____

   _____

2. Scan line 15 of "The Explosion." How many feet does it have? What is its rhythm's effect?

   Scarfed as in a heat-haze, dimmed.

   _____

   _____

3. How does Larkin use rhythm and meter to change his dramatic structure?

   _____

   _____

"An Arundel Tomb" and **"The Explosion"** by Philip Larkin
"On the Patio" by Peter Redgrove
"Not Waving But Drowning" by Stevie Smith

Reading Strategy: Read Poetry in Sentences

The key to reading and understanding poetry is to read the punctuation rather than the line endings. The rhythm or rhyme of a poem may seem to require a reader to pause at the end of each line, but one must think beyond the physical line endings to the sense of the words. If you **read poetry in sentences** and listen to others do the same you will find that sense.

In Philip Larkin's "An Arundel Tomb," each of the first three stanzas is one sentence. Though some lines end with a comma, a dash, or a colon, the unit of thought does not end until the end of the stanza.

A. DIRECTIONS: *Write each sentence in stanzas 4–7 of "An Arundel Tomb." Do not pay attention to line endings; write the sentences in the space provided as if they are in narrative form.*

Sentence 1: _____

_____

Sentence 2: _____

_____

Sentence 3: _____

_____

Sentence 4: _____

_____

Sentence 5: _____

_____

Sentence 6: _____

_____

Sentence 7: _____

_____

Sentence 8: _____

_____

B. DIRECTIONS: *Now review the entire poem. Remember that each of the first three stanzas is one sentence. Practice reading them in sentences. Then continue to stanzas 4–7, which you have written on this page. Mark places to pause and breathe that fit with the meaning of the sentences. Practice several times, and then read the poem aloud to an audience. Listen as your classmates read to hear meaning and appreciate the text structures of the poem.*

"An Arundel Tomb" and "The Explosion" by Philip Larkin
"On the Patio" by Peter Redgrove
"Not Waving But Drowning" by Stevie Smith
Vocabulary Builder

Using the Root -fid-

A. DIRECTIONS: *The root -fid-, meaning "faith," is included in each of the numbered words. Match each numbered word with its definition. Write the letter of the definition next to the word it defines.*

___ 1. confidant

___ 2. confidential

___ 3. perfidious

A. one to whom secrets are entrusted

B. faithless

C. private, secret

Word List

effigy   fidelity   larking   supine

B. DIRECTIONS: *Complete each sentence by writing the appropriate Word List word in the blank.*

1. Without knowing anything about the earl and countess, it is hard to tell whether their _____ was the sculptor's imagination or not.

2. Many tombs of royalty traditionally include a(n) _____ of the noble person, in commemoration of his or her rank and importance.

3. The children were only _____; they hadn't meant to tramp through old Mrs. Wilson's flower garden.

4. When performing CPR, the victim should be lying _____ unless other injuries prevent him or her from being so positioned.

C. DIRECTIONS: *Choose a lettered pair that best expresses a relationship similar to that expressed in the numbered pair. Circle the letter of your choice.*

1. EFFIGY : LIKENESS ::
   A. canvas : easel
   B. water : wet
   C. portrait : painting
   D. horse : animal

2. FIDELITY : TRUST ::
   A. greed : money
   B. hope : future
   C. anger : calm
   D. betrayal : disloyalty

3. LARKING : PLAYFUL ::
   A. working : easy
   B. aiming: target
   C. troubling : avoidance
   D. studying : scholarly

4. SUPINE : ERECT ::
   A. recline : stand
   B. careful : mistake
   C. favorable : false
   D. run : jog

"An Arundel Tomb" and **"The Explosion"** by Philip Larkin
"On the Patio" by Peter Redgrove
"Not Waving But Drowning" by Stevie Smith
Support for Writing

Complete the organizer below to collect information for your reflective essay. Write the everyday sight or event that will be the subject of your essay in the center circle. In the surrounding circles, jot down the ideas, feelings, and comparisons that this event evokes in you.

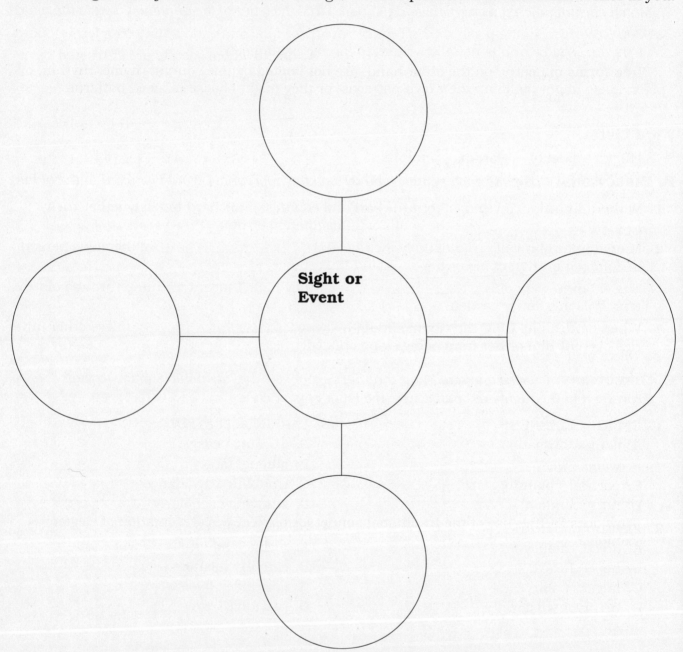

As you write your reflective essay on a separate page, draw on details you have recorded in the organizer. Use them to create deeper meaning about the event or sight you have experienced.

"**In the Kitchen**" by Penelope Shuttle
"**Prayer**" by Carol Ann Duffy

Literary Analysis: Contemporary Elegy, Fixed and Free Forms, Sonnet

The **form** of a poem is the way it is organized. Haiku, villanelle, sestina, and sonnet are all **fixed forms** of poetry. They have a set number of lines and/or stanzas. They also follow a regular pattern of organization, repeating particular lines or incorporating a set rhyme and meter. "Prayer" by Carol Ann Duffy uses the fixed form of the Shakespearean sonnet. The **sonnet** is a fourteen line poem that is broken into three quatrains and a final couplet. It follows a set rhyme scheme and is usually written in iambic pentameter.

Free forms of poetry, on the other hand, are not limited by line counts, rhyme, rhythm, or meter. Poets might make up their own patterns, or they might choose to avoid patterns altogether.

Another way of categorizing poetry is by identifying its topic. An **elegy** is a traditional poetic expression that can have a fixed or free form. The content is the determiner of its categorization. An elegy usually mourns the death of a person. However, the **contemporary elegy** is broader in its acknowledgement of loss. This kind of poem addresses many kinds of loss, from the death of a loved one to the loss of childhood or innocence.

DIRECTIONS: *Answer the following questions about the poems "In the Kitchen" and "Prayer."*

1. Read the following lines from "In the Kitchen." What does this contemporary elegy mourn?

    I am trying to love the world

    back to normal . . .

    I am trying to get the seas back on the maps

    where they belong . . .

    _____

    _____

2. What pattern of her own does Shuttle establish in "In the Kitchen"?

    _____

    _____

3. How does Duffy's use of the traditional sonnet form affect her presentation of elegiac content?

    _____

    _____

    _____

"In the Kitchen" by Penelope Shuttle
"Prayer" by Carol Ann Duffy

Reading Strategy: Read Poetry Aloud to Appreciate Parallel Structure

One element that poets use to emphasize meaning and underscore theme is parallel structure. **Parallel structure** consists of the repetition of a particular syntax. For example, read the following lines from "In the Kitchen."

The ironing-board thanks god

for its two good strong legs and sturdy back

The new fridge hums like a maniac

with helpfulness

The poet uses two lines to address each object in the kitchen. In the first line, she identifies the object and its action. The basic syntax is the same in each couplet.

When you read poetry aloud, group ideas in their parallel structure. For example, in Shuttle's poem, it is appropriate to pause after each couplet.

DIRECTIONS: *Use the following set of marks to indicate pauses and breaks in parallel structure. Then, take turns reading the poem aloud with a partner, following your marked pauses.*

     * Break in parallel structure   ∆ Pause

A jug of water

has its own lustrous turmoil

The ironing-board thanks god

for its two good strong legs and sturdy back

The new fridge hums like a maniac

with helpfulness

I am trying to love the world

back to normal

The chair recites its stand-alone prayer

again and again

The table leaves no stone unturned

The clock votes for the separate burial of hearts

I am trying to love the world

and all its 8000 identifiable languages

"**In the Kitchen**" by Penelope Shuttle
"**Prayer**" by Carol Ann Duffy
Vocabulary Builder

Word List

lustrous   scales   steadfastly   utters

A. DIRECTIONS: *Match each word with its definition.*

___ 1. lustrous   A. speaks
___ 2. scales   B. in a firm manner
___ 3. steadfastly   C. sequences of musical tones
___ 4. utters   D. gleaming, shining

B. DIRECTIONS: *Complete each sentence with the word from the Word List that makes most sense.*

1. Sheila's piano teacher told her to practice _____ every day.

2. Every time Ava sees her little brother making a mess, she _____ her disapproval under her breath.

3. The baby's attention was drawn to the _____ red of the marble apple.

4. Jared stood _____ by his friend Karl, even when Karl was wrong.

C. DIRECTIONS: *Answer each of the following questions about the Vocabulary Words.*

1. What might you commonly describe as *lustrous*?

_____

_____

_____

2. What could somebody *utter*?

_____

_____

_____

3. How does someone behave if they act *steadfastly*?

_____

_____

_____

Name _____ Date _____

"In the Kitchen" by Penelope Shuttle
"Prayer" by Carol Ann Duffy
Support for Writing: Speaker Introduction for a Radio Poetry Spot

Use the following organizer to record ideas for your speaker introduction. Complete an organizer for each of the poems.

Poem:

Author:

Background / Content:

Biographical Info:

Connections Made for Introduction

On a separate sheet of paper, write your speaker introduction using the ideas you recorded in the organizer.

Contemporary Commentary
Anita Desai Introduces "A Devoted Son"

DIRECTIONS: *Use the space provided to answer the questions.*

1. According to Anita Desai, why does writing a short story resemble writing a poem?

   _____

   _____

2. What examples does Desai give of "moments" that serve as inspiration or "seeds" for short stories?

   _____

   _____

   _____

   _____

3. Briefly explain Desai's process of writing a short story. How is this process like "planting seeds"?

   _____

   _____

   _____

   _____

4. According to Desai, what was the "seed" for her story "A Devoted Son"?

   _____

   _____

   _____

   _____

5. Desai claims that art can render complex and mysterious things "utterly pure, clear, and transparent." Do you agree with her claim? Briefly explain your answer, using at least one example from literature, painting, or music to support your opinion.

   _____

   _____

   _____

   _____

   _____

   _____

   _____

   _____

All-in-One Workbook
345

Anita Desai
Listening and Viewing

Segment 1: Meet Anita Desai
- What other languages does Anita Desai speak, and how does she incorporate them into her writing?
- Why do you think knowledge of other languages is important in character development?

_____

_____

_____

_____

Segment 2: The Short Story
- What experience inspired Desai to write "A Devoted Son"?
- What truth about life does the story reveal?
- What experience would you write about that would express a truth about life?

_____

_____

_____

_____

Segment 3: The Writing Process
- According to Anita Desai, why are writing and playing music similar activities?
- Why do you think it is important to practice writing consistently?

_____

_____

_____

_____

Segment 4: The Rewards of Writing
- Why does Anita Desai consider reading her "lifeline"?
- How can entering books add "another dimension" to your life?

_____

_____

_____

_____

"A Devoted Son" by Anita Desai
Literary Analysis: Generational Conflicts; Static and Dynamic Characters

Generational conflicts stem from problems resulting from the clash between generations, as well as cultural, religious, and social belief systems. These overarching conflicts stem from characters but address larger issues that are culturally, if not universally, applicable. To express and examine these generational conflicts, authors sometimes use characters as symbols of ideas or general attitudes. **Static characters,** or those who do not change throughout the course of a selection, work particularly well as symbols: They consistently represent an idea or an attitude. In contrast, **dynamic characters,** or those who do change throughout the course of a selection, work as representatives of the results of the generational attitudes symbolized by the static characters.

Anita Desai, in "A Devoted Son," uses static and dynamic characters to analyze generational conflicts between cultural attitudes, ideals, and traditional roles. She provides a reversal in the story by countering readers' expectations that the young man will be the character who undergoes change. Instead, she examines the change in the father, Varma. To identify the changes in characters, look at their external circumstances and the emotional and physical responses to situations within the plot.

DIRECTIONS: *Answer the following questions to analyze the nature of Rakesh's and Varma's characters, as well as what they symbolize and what message that symbolism expresses. Keep in mind the cultural setting of the story.*

1. How do Rakesh's actions change, if at all, throughout the story?

   _____

   _____

2. Based on Rakesh's experience, accomplishments, and actions, what element of the generational conflict do you think he symbolizes? Explain.

   _____

   _____

3. Describe Varma's perception of Rakesh and how it changes throughout the selection.

   _____

   _____

4. What side of the generational conflict does Varma symbolize? Explain.

   _____

   _____

5. What message do you think Desai presents about this generational conflict?

   _____

   _____

"A Devoted Son" by Anita Desai

Reading Strategy: Identify Causes of Characters' Actions

Characters act for a variety of different reasons, and the motivations for their actions can be read on several different levels. Probably the easiest causes to identify are those associated with the personal level of a character. Perhaps a character chooses to remain quiet in order to avoid offending another character. Or perhaps a character chooses to act in order to gain prestige or money. These causes for action can be interpreted on a "human" level.

When you read deeper into a text, such as "A Devoted Son," you encounter characters who represent something bigger than themselves. For example, Rakesh symbolizes the influence of the West or the new generation of young Indian men. Now you must think about the idea he represents and ask yourself why he acts the way he does and what the author is saying with these actions.

DIRECTIONS: *Read the following passage from "A Devoted Son" and answer the questions that follow.*

Rakesh marched into the room, not with his usual respectful step but with the confident and rather contemptuous stride of the famous doctor, and declared, "No more *halwa* for you, papa. We must be sensible, at your age. If you must have something sweet, Veena will cook you a little *kheer*, that's light, just a little rice and milk. But nothing fried, nothing rich. We can't have this happening again." . . . He opened his eyes—rather, they fell open with shock—and he stared at his son with disbelief that darkened quickly to reproach. A son who actually refused his father the food he craved?

1. Why does Rakesh make the decision to limit his father's diet?

   _____

   _____

2. How does Varma interpret Rakesh's actions?

   _____

   _____

3. Does Rakesh believe he is being disrespectful? Why or why not?

   _____

   _____

"A Devoted Son" by Anita Desai
Vocabulary Builder

Using the Root -fil-

The Latin word *filius* means "son," and *filia* means "daughter." The Word Bank word *filial* comes from these roots, literally meaning "of or befitting a son or daughter." Words formed from the root -*fil*- imply obligation and association.

A. DIRECTIONS: *Match each word derived from the -fil- word root in the left column with its definition in the right column. Write the letter of the definition on the line by the word it defines.*

___ 1. affiliate (verb)   A. relationship between parent and child
___ 2. filiation   B. voluntary connection
___ 3. affiliate (noun)   C. to join or associate
___ 4. affiliation   D. a member or colleague

Using the Word List

    complaisant   encomiums   exemplary   fathom   filial

B. DIRECTIONS: *Each item consists of a word from the Word List followed by four lettered words. Choose the word most nearly* similar *in meaning to the Word List word. Circle the letter of your choice.*

1. exemplary
   A. model
   B. necessary
   C. released
   D. principal

2. filial
   A. equine
   B. teeming
   C. belated
   D. respectful

3. encomiums
   A. campgrounds
   B. tributes
   C. environments
   D. savings

4. complaisant
   A. protesting
   B. supplement
   C. agreeable
   D. courtesy

5. fathom
   A. assist
   B. comprehend
   C. deny
   D. create

"A Devoted Son" by Anita Desai
Support for Writing: Response to Literature

Use the following graphic organizer to record details that do and do not conform to Desai's original concept for "A Devoted Son." The quote found in the center of the graphic organizer sums up the author's original plan.

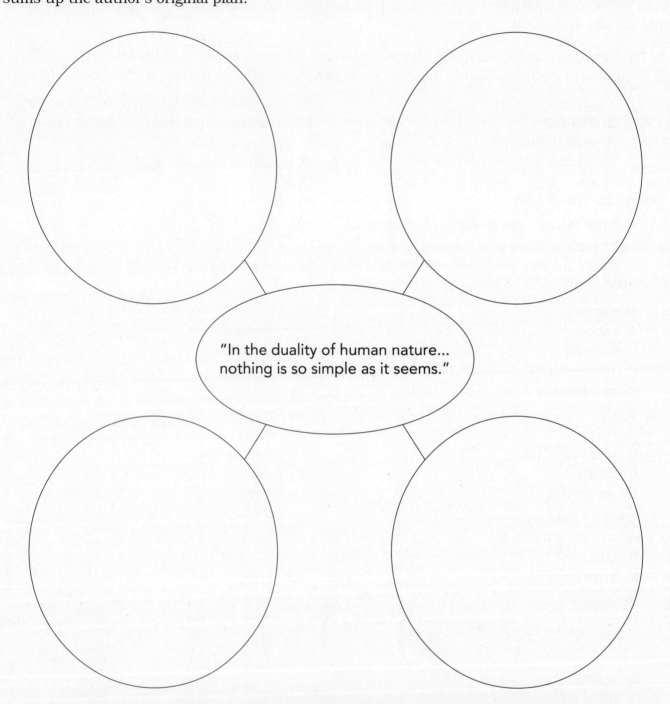

"In the duality of human nature... nothing is so simple as it seems."

On a separate sheet of paper, write a response in which you state whether Desai's story lives up to her original plan. Use your notes from the organizer to guide your writing.

Name _____ Date _____

"Next Term, We'll Mash You" by Penelope Lively
Literary Analysis: Characterization and Dialogue

Characterization refers to the way an author builds a character. It can be **direct,** in which the author describes the character's attributes straightforwardly. *Charlie is a stubborn boy.* Or characterization can be **indirect,** in which the author describes the characters actions, words, thoughts, of other characters' reactions to that character. *Charlie screamed and cried when he didn't get his way.*

One means of characterization is **dialogue,** or the conversations characters have with one another. Through a character's dialogue, readers are able to draw conclusions about the character's personality, beliefs, and thoughts.

DIRECTIONS: *Read the first page of "Next Term, We'll Mash You." Answer the following questions about Lively's characters.*

1. What do you learn about the parents from their dialogue? Think about how they interact with each other, with their son, and what seems important to them.

_____

_____

_____

_____

2. What do you learn about the child from the author's descriptions?

_____

_____

_____

_____

3. Does Lively rely most heavily on direct or indirect characterization? Explain.

_____

_____

_____

_____

4. Based on Lively's overall characterization, write a brief description of the characters.

_____

_____

_____

_____

_____

Name _____ Date _____

Reading Strategy: Evaluate Social Influences of the Period

Every period of history has its own social trends and popular ideas. The period in which a work of literature is set often provides a basis for the cultural beliefs and ideas of the characters. The social influences of the times also contribute to the formulation of the plot and conflict, as well as the characters and their beliefs. When you **evaluate the social influences of the period,** you take into consideration the beliefs and values of a culture and how these are reflected and examined within a story.

"Next Term, We'll Mash You" provides a commentary on contemporary British culture, along with its class system and the beliefs that accompany it. Like American culture, British culture has a class structure. However, the British class structure is more defined because it is closely linked with a person's speech. The accents of the people tell not only their place of origin, but also clearly exhibit their social classes. Much emphasis is put upon speaking the proper "Queen's English" in order to gain a higher class standing. One way of attaining such a higher standing is through education at a high-class school.

DIRECTIONS: *Write a paragraph examining the effects of contemporary British societal views on the characters, setting, and plot of the story. Explain how you think Lively perceives the effects of such social influences.*

_____

_____

_____

_____

_____

_____

_____

_____

_____

_____

_____

_____

_____

_____

Name _____ Date _____

"Next Term, We'll Mash You" by Penelope Lively
Vocabulary Builder

Word List

assessing   condescension   dappled   haggard   homespun   subdued

A. DIRECTIONS: *Complete each sentence based on your knowledge of the italicized word.*

1. If you are *assessing* something, you _____.

2. If someone speaks to you with *condescension*, he or she likely _____.

3. A *dappled* horse is _____.

4. You might look *haggard* if you are _____.

5. A *homespun* person is _____.

6. When you are *subdued*, you _____.

B. DIRECTIONS: *Choose the letter of the word that has the closest meaning to the Word List word.*

____ 1. assessing
    A. evaluating
    B. deciding
    C. questioning
    D. enjoying

____ 2. homespun
    A. unfortunate
    B. plain
    C. quiet
    D. open-minded

____ 3. dappled
    A. questioned
    B. tried
    C. shaded
    D. spotted

____ 4. subdued
    A. excited
    B. upset
    C. quiet
    D. lonely

____ 5. haggard
    A. exhausted
    B. weepy
    C. attractive
    D. delighted

"Next Term, We'll Mash You" by Penelope Lively
Support for Writing: Advertisement

Use the following graphic organizer to record ideas for your print advertisement for St. Edward's Preparatory School. Record ideas from the story, as well as ideas for visuals to accompany each element of your advertisement.

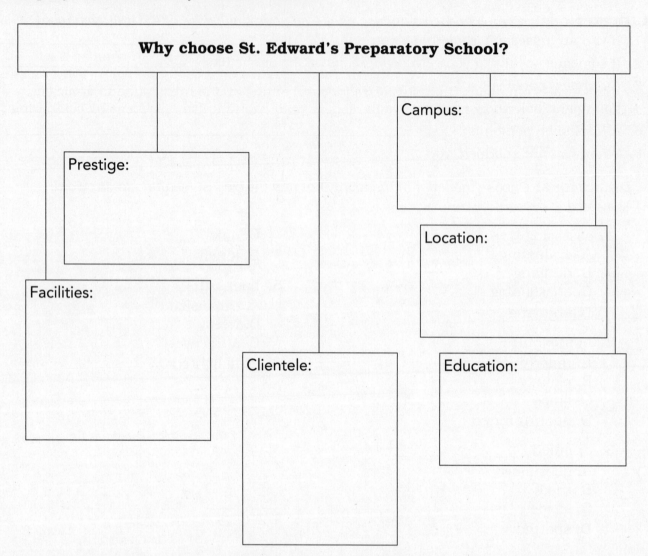

On a separate sheet, create an advertisement for St. Edward's Preparatory School using the ideas you recorded in the graphic organizers.

Name _____ Date _____

from "We'll Never Conquer Space" by Arthur C. Clarke
Literary Analysis: Argumentative Essay and Analogies

An **argumentative essay** makes a case for something. In this instance, Clarke argues that humans will never *conquer* space. He clearly explains the differences between conquering and exploring and provides reasons that we will never conquer. Like other forms of essays, argumentative essays are built around a thesis, or main argument. Details are used to support the writer's opinions, as are facts, statistics, anecdotes, and other ideas.

Authors of argumentative essays must draw on the art of persuasion to enhance their arguments. They frequently call upon traditional rhetorical devices to express their arguments, including loaded language, rhetorical questions, repetition and parallelism, and analogies. Clarke frequently uses **analogies** to help readers understand unfamiliar ideas by comparing them to familiar ideas.

DIRECTIONS: *Answer the following questions to identify the parts of Clarke's argumentative essay and the devices he uses to persuade his audience.*

1. What is the thesis of this argumentative essay?

   _____

   _____

   _____

2. What are two details or ideas that support this thesis?

   _____

   _____

   _____

3. Describe an analogy Clarke uses to support his argument. Do you think the analogy is effective? Why or why not?

   _____

   _____

   _____

Name _____ Date _____

from **We'll Never Conquer Space** by Arthur C. Clarke
Reading Strategy: Expository Critique

When you critique an expository text, you analyze the author's use of literary techniques and rhetorical devices, as well as the structure and soundness of the argument, to evaluate the work.

DIRECTIONS: *Answer the following questions to form a basis for your expository critique.*

1. What does Clarke argue? Does he state his argument clearly?

   _____

   _____

2. What details does Clarke include to support his argument? Does he include facts? Does he support his opinions?

   _____

   _____

3. How does Clarke organize his argument? Is the organization effective?

   _____

   _____

4. What rhetorical devices does Clarke use: appeals to logic, appeals to emotion, rhetorical questions, repetition, loaded language, analogies, etc.? Is his use of these effective?

   _____

   _____

5. Does Clarke ultimately present a convincing argument? Why or why not?

   _____

   _____

WRITING APLICATION: *Write a brief expository critique of Clarke's argumentative essay, using your answers to the questions to help you shape your critique.*

_____

_____

_____

_____

_____

_____

from **"We'll Never Conquer Space"** by Arthur C. Clarke
Vocabulary Builder

Using the Word List

enigma   inevitable   instantaneous   irrevocable   ludicrous

A. DIRECTIONS: *Each item consists of a Word List word followed by four lettered words or phrases. Choose the lettered word or phrase that is most nearly* opposite *in meaning to the Word List word, and circle the letter of your choice.*

1. enigma
   A. query
   B. widely known
   C. negative image
   D. solution

2. inevitable
   A. sure
   B. unlikely
   C. satisfied
   D. unsafe

3. instantaneous
   A. delayed
   B. lacking attention
   C. rough-skinned
   D. precise

4. irrevocable
   A. without words
   B. changeable
   C. finely tuned
   D. permanent

5. ludicrous
   A. boring
   B. serious
   C. miserable
   D. not playful

B. WORD STUDY: *Many words in the English language contain the suffixes -ible or -able, meaning "able to," "having qualities of," or "worthy of." Match the following words with their definitions. Write the letter of the definition next to the word it defines.*

___ 1. applicable

___ 2. commendable

___ 3. negligible

___ 4. negotiable

A. capable of being traversed or dealt with

B. able to be disregarded

C. capable of being brought into action

D. worthy of praise

from "We'll Never Conquer Space" by Arthur C. Clarke
Support for Writing

Use the chart below to gather factual information from Clarke's essay. List facts in the first column. Using reliable print and online sources, **verify and clarify** times, distances, and other facts. In the second column, list evidence that supports or contradicts these facts. Cite your sources in parentheses.

Factual Information	Verification of Facts and Explanations

Use information from the chart as you draft your analysis on a separate page. Then, explain whether any technological breakthroughs or anticipated breakthroughs have undermined Clarke's main points.

Name _____   Date _____

from **Songbook: "I'm Like a Bird"** by Nick Hornby
Literary Analysis: Personal Essay

A **personal essay** is a piece of nonfiction writing that allows the author to share his or her personal views on a particular subject. Authors of personal essays usually use an informal tone to share opinions about and comments on life. Through the expression of their ideas and opinions, authors reveal aspects of their personalities. They share anecdotes and stories from their lives that show the reasons for their opinions and opportunities for the revelations they experienced about the subject. In this excerpt from *Songbook*, Nick Hornby shares his feelings about and experiences with pop music. He works through the essay to persuade readers of the importance of pop music—an importance that lies in the essence of pop, not in evaluating it by criteria that doesn't pertain to the genre.

DIRECTIONS: *Answer these questions to identify and analyze Hornby's opinions and experiences of pop music.*

1. How does Hornby address the argument that pop music is "trashy" among other negative attributes?

   _____

   _____

   _____

   _____

2. What does Hornby mean when he says that pop music's "disposability" marks its "maturity"?

   _____

   _____

   _____

   _____

3. What human connection results from listening to pop music for Hornby?

   _____

   _____

   _____

   _____

4. What positive qualities of pop music would Hornby list?

   _____

   _____

   _____

   _____

Name _____ Date _____

from **Songbook: "I'm Like a Bird"** by Nick Hornby
Reading Strategy: Outlining Arguments and Strategies

To help you better understand the structure of an essay, you can **outline arguments and strategies** the author poses and uses. When authors write persuasively, they use techniques, such as anticipating objections, appeals to emotion, appeals to reason, anecdotes, and a multitude of other strategies to convince an audience.

When you outline arguments and strategies, your first step is to identify the main argument of a text. Then you can look at the strategies the author uses to forward his or her argument.

DIRECTIONS: *Use the outline below to analyze Hornby's argument and the strategies he uses to support his opinions. An example of a strategy has been provided.*

Argument: Pop music has intrinsic value.

    Supporting idea: _____

    _____

    Supporting idea: _____

    _____

    Supporting idea: _____

    _____

Argument: Pop music has intrinsic value.

    Strategy: Anticipating objections

        Example: Oh, of course I can understand people dismissing pop music . . .

    Strategy: _____

        Example: _____

    _____

    Strategy: _____

        Example: _____

    _____

Name _____ Date _____

from **Songbook: "I'm Like a Bird"** by Nick Hornby
Vocabulary Builder

Word List

anemic   cynically   disposable   inane   incessant   languor

A. DIRECTIONS: *Complete each sentence with a the word from the Word List that makes most sense.*

1. The _____ barking of the neighbor's dog kept me awake last night.

2. The book's _____ storyline did not hold my interest.

3. Her _____ after a day spent in the sun was infectious.

4. My father argued that today everything is _____ because things aren't built to last the way they used to be.

5. The politician's _____ promises left the crowd feeling hopeless.

6. Jen responded _____ to the job offer after having had several bad experiences with that company.

B. DIRECTIONS: *Match each word with its antonym.*

___ 1. anemic   A. nervousness
___ 2. cynically   B. hopefully
___ 3. disposable   C. strong
___ 4. inane   D. finite
___ 5. incessant   E. important
___ 6. languor   F. reusable

Name _____ Date _____

from **Songbook: "I'm Like a Bird"** by Nick Hornby
Support for Writing: Liner Notes

Use the following organizer to record your ideas for liner notes for your favorite song. Jot down ideas about each of the following categories to include in your notes.

Artist Information	Background
Lyrics	Music

Song

On a separate sheet, write your liner notes for your favorite song. If possible, include a copy of the lyrics to accompany your notes.

Essential Questions Workshop—Unit 6

In their poems, stories, and nonfiction works, the writers in Unit Six express ideas that relate to the three Essential Questions framing this book. Review the literature in the unit. Then, for each Essential Question, choose an author and at least one passage from the author's writing that expresses an idea related to the Essential Question. Use this chart to complete your work.

Essential Question	Author/Selection	Literary Passage
What is the relationship between place and literature?		
How does literature shape or reflect society?		
What is the relationship of the writer to tradition?		

Name _____ Date _____

Screening Test

Directions: Read the following passages. Then answer the questions. On the answer sheet, fill in the bubble for the answer that you think is correct.

He was walking swiftly through the dark tunnel of foliage that in day-time was a road. The dogs were invisibly <u>ranging</u> the lower travelways of the bush, and he heard them panting. Sometimes he felt a cold muzzle on his leg before they were off again, scouting for a trail to follow. They were not trained, but free-running companions of the hunt, who often tired of the long stalk before the final shots, and went off on their own pleasure. Soon he could see them, small and wild-looking in a wild strange light, now that the bush stood trembling on the <u>verge</u> of color, waiting for the sun to paint earth and grass afresh.

Doris Lessing, "A Sunrise on the Veld"

---

1 On the basis of context clues in the passage, how would you define <u>ranging</u>?
A destroying
B ignoring
C eating
D roaming

2 On the basis of context clues in the passage, how would you define <u>verge</u>?
F end
G brink
H start
J condition

A wave of yet more tender joy escaped from his heart and went <u>coursing</u> in warm flood along his arteries. Like the tender fires of stars moments of their life together, that no one knew of or would ever know of, broke upon and <u>illumined</u> his memory. He longed to recall to her those moments, to make her forget the years of their dull existence together and remember only their months of ecstasy. For the years, he felt, had not quenched his soul or hers. Their children, his writing, her household cares had not quenched all their souls' tender fire. In one letter he had written to her then he had said: *Why is it that words like these seem so dull and cold? Is it because there is no word tender enough to be your name?*

James Joyce, "The Dead"

---

3 On the basis of context clues in the passage, which of the following is the denotation of <u>coursing</u>?
A stopping
B leaking slowly
C running or passing rapidly
D bubbling vigorously

4 Which of the following connotations are suggested by the word <u>illumined</u>?
F insight and warmth
G anguish and fear
H inflammation and pain
J doubt and hesitation

All-in-One Workbook: Standardized Test Practice

> Home is where the heart is. There's no place like it. I love my home with a ferocity totally out of proportion to its appearance or location. I love dumb things about it: the hot-water heater, the plastic rack you drain dishes in, the roof over my head, which occasionally leaks. And yet it is precisely those dumb things that make it what it is—a place of certainty, stability, predictability, privacy, for me and for my family. It is where I live. What more can you say about a place than that? That is everything.
>
> Anna Quindlen, "Homeless"

5 Which of the following sentences gives the main idea of the passage?
A the first sentence
B the fourth sentence
C the sixth sentence
D the last sentence

6 Which of the following is *not* a detail that supports the main idea?
F Home is a place of stability.
G Home is a place of privacy.
H Home is a place of certainty.
J Home is a place of misery.

> The square finger, moving here and there, lighted suddenly on Bitzer, perhaps because he chanced to sit in the same ray of sunlight which, darting in at one of the bare windows of the intensely whitewashed room, irradiated Sissy. For, the boys and girls sat on the face of the inclined plane in two compact bodies, divided up the center by a narrow interval; and Sissy, being at the corner of a row on the sunny side, came in for the beginning of a sunbeam, of which Bitzer, being at the corner of a row on the other side, a few rows in advance, caught the end.
>
> Charles Dickens, *Hard Times*

7 From the description in the passage, you can infer that the boys and girls are *probably* —
A in a schoolroom
B on a trip to the country
C at a playground
D in a school bus

8 What conclusion can you draw about Bitzer?
F He is enamored of Sissy.
G He dislikes Sissy.
H He dislikes school.
J He wants Sissy to block the sunbeam.

9 Which of the following statements is the *best* paraphrase of the first sentence?
A The square finger, moving here and there, lighted suddenly on Bitzer.
B Bitzer points at Sissy because she is sitting in the sun.
C Sissy points at Bitzer because he is sitting in the sun.
D Bitzer is called upon, because, in his perception, he has ventured to sit in the same sunbeam in which Sissy sits.

My loving people, we have been persuaded by some, that are careful of our safety, to take heed how we commit ourselves to armed multitudes, for fear of treachery; but I assure you, I do not desire to live to distrust my faithful and loving people. Let tyrants fear; I have always so behaved myself that, under God, I have placed my chiefest strength and safeguard in the loyal hearts and good will of my subjects. And therefore I am come amongst you at this time, not as for my recreation or sport, but being resolved, in the midst and heat of the battle, to live or die amongst you all; to lay down, for my God, and for my kingdom, and for my people, my honor and my blood, even the dust.

Queen Elizabeth I, "Speech Before Defeating the Spanish Armada"

10 **Two contrasts that Queen Elizabeth makes in this passage are —**
  F between herself and her advisors and between herself and tyrants
  G between herself and tyrants and between herself and the people
  H between the Spanish and the English and between London and the countryside
  J between the courtiers and the common people and between Spain and England

11 **Which of the following is the *best* paraphrase of the second sentence in the passage?**
  A I do not wish to be seen as a tyrant.
  B Some people have called me a tyrant, but I am fearless.
  C Tyrants treat the people badly, so it is natural that they fear them.
  D Tyrants may fear the people, but I place my trust in them.

1   Oak, his features smudged, grimy, and undiscoverable from the smoke and heat, his smoke-frock burnt into holes and dripping with water, the ash-stem of his sheep-crook charred six inches shorter, advanced with the humility stern adversity had thrust upon him up to the slight female form in the saddle. He lifted his hat with respect, and not without gallantry: stepping close to her hanging feet he said in a hesitating voice,—

2   "Do you happen to want a shepherd, ma'am?"

3   She lifted the wool veil tied round her face, and looked all astonishment. Gabriel and his cold-hearted darling, Bathsheba Everdene, were face to face.

Thomas Hardy, *Far From the Madding Crowd*

12 **Which of the following contrasts is *most* important?**
  F Gabriel is poor; Bathsheba is rich.
  G Gabriel is warm and respectful; Bathsheba is cold-hearted.
  H Gabriel is on the ground; Bathsheba is on a horse.
  J Gabriel is practical; Bathsheba is imaginative.

13 **From the description of Gabriel, you can conclude that he —**
  A does not pay enough attention to the way he dresses.
  B has just been fighting a fire.
  C does not know how to herd sheep properly.
  D has overslept that morning.

Name _____ Date _____

Directions: Use the chart below to answer the questions that follow. On the answer sheet, fill in the bubble for the answer that you think is correct.

Geologic Era	Geologic Developments	Life Forms
Triassic: 230–195 million years ago	Climate warming; semiarid to arid; tectonic plates begin to break into continents	First dinosaurs; possible evolution of first mammals
Jurassic: 195–140 million years ago	North America and Africa separate; ocean basins open	Reptiles dominant; first bird appears
Cretaceous: 140–65 million years ago	South America and Africa separate; chalk deposits	Snakes, lizards, flowering plants

14 What are the dates of the Jurassic Era?
F 280–230 million years ago
G 230–195 million years ago
H 195–140 million years ago
J 140–65 million years ago

15 All of the following are associated with the Triassic Era EXCEPT —
A warm climate and arid conditions
B the first dinosaurs
C the possible evolution of the first mammals
D the separation of South America from Africa

16 According to the chart, which of the following events occurred first?
F North America and Africa separated.
G The first bird appeared.
H South America and Africa separated.
J The tectonic plates began to break into continents.

17 Which of the following statements *best* summarizes the purpose of the chart?
A It shows how dinosaurs evolved.
B It explains how reptiles became dominant.
C It shows geologic eras and their characteristics.
D It describes the change in climate from semiarid to arid.

18 According to the chart, the evolution of first mammals happened —
F after dinosaurs became extinct
G before the first bird appeared
H after the climate warmed
J before dinosaurs appeared

19 What *most* likely caused the ocean basins to open?
A the evolution of mammals
B the domination of reptiles
C the appearance of chalk deposits
D the movement of tectonic plates

Name _____ Date _____

Directions: Read the following passages. Then answer the questions. On the answer sheet, fill in the bubble for the answer that you think is correct.

> All mankind is of one author and is one volume; when one man dies, one chapter is not torn out of the book, but translated into a better language; and every chapter must be so translated. God employs several translators; some pieces are translated by age, some by sickness, some by war, some by justice; but God's hand is in every translation, and his hand shall bind up all our scattered leaves again for that library where every book shall lie open to one another.
>
> John Donne, "Meditation 17"

20 What aspects of the human condition does the author of this passage use figurative language to discuss?
F sickness and health
G youth and marriage
H life and death
J success and failure

21 Donne employs which of the following types of figurative language in this passage?
A simile
B metaphor
C hyperbole
D personification

22 The author's purpose in this passage is *most* likely —
F to entertain
G to inform
H to describe
J to persuade

23 Which of the following summarizes the roles described in the passage?
A Mankind is the volume; God is the author; each individual is a chapter.
B God is the volume; Mankind is the author; each individual is a chapter.
C Each individual is a volume; God is the author; Mankind is a chapter.
D Mankind is the volume; each individual is an author; God is a chapter.

> More completely than most writers, perhaps, Dickens can be explained in terms of his social origin, though actually his family history is not quite what one would infer from his novels. His father was a clerk in government service, and through his mother's family he had connections with both the army and the navy. But from the age of nine onwards he was brought up in London in commercial surroundings, and generally in a atmosphere of struggling poverty. . . . If one wants a modern equivalent, the nearest would be H. G. Wells, who has had a rather similar history and who obviously owes something to Dickens as a novelist.
>
> George Orwell, "Charles Dickens"

Name _____ **Date** _____

24 The statement that Dickens's mother had connections with the army and the navy is a(n) —

F opinion
G fact
H exaggeration
J insult

25 Which of the following statements is an *opinion* presented in the selection?

A Dickens's father was a clerk in government service.
B Dickens was brought up in London from the age of nine onwards.
C Dickens can be explained in terms of his social origin.
D The novels of Dickens have remained popular.

26 What causes Orwell to compare Dickens to H. G. Wells?

F Orwell wants to provide a modern equivalent to which more readers can relate.
G Orwell likes the work of H. G. Wells more than the work of Dickens.
H Orwell wants to show how drastically different the two authors are.
J none of the above

27 This excerpt suggests that the writer's overall purpose in writing the selection is —

A to entertain
B to persuade
C to criticize
D to analyze

Directions: Each question below consists of a related pair of words or phrases, followed by four pairs of words or phrases. Select the pair that best expresses a relationship similar to that expressed in the original pair, and then mark that choice on the bubble sheet.

28 ADMINISTER : CURE ::

F bequeath : gift
G banter : discussion
H deliver : promise
J cancel : appointment

29 LEAF : TREE ::

A twig : bark
B coin : money
C paw : foot
D hand : body

Directions: Read the following sentences. Look for mistakes in grammar or usage. For each item on the answer sheet, fill in the bubble for the answer that was the mistake. If there is no mistake, fill in the last answer choice.

30 F "Now, rise your hands slow
  G toward the ceiling,"
  H hissed the robber.
  J *(No mistakes)*

31 A I hate to say this, but I'm certain
  B that your statements will have been
  C misinterpreted in the future.
  D *(No mistakes)*

Practice Test 1

Suppose that you have been assigned to make a five- to ten-minute oral presentation that will attempt to persuade an audience of restaurant owners to ban smoking in their establishments. Answer the following questions.

1. What is the goal of the presentation?
   A. Give the audience a series of statistics about smokers' health problems.
   B. Share a list of characters from literature and movies who smoke a lot.
   C. Persuade listeners to work harder to keep young people from smoking.
   D. Influence the audience's views about smoking in public.

2. What should you do after you state your main idea?
   A. Share anecdotes about your experiences with smokers in restaurants.
   B. Offer detailed examples to support it.
   C. Take questions from the audience.
   D. List objections that people will likely have.

3. What will be the effect of comparing exposure to secondhand smoke to being a passenger in a car driven by an aggressive driver?
   A. It will remind your audience of the dangers of driving on today's highways.
   B. It will address your audience's love of driving.
   C. It will show that many aggressive drivers are also smokers.
   D. It will help illustrate that nonsmokers are put in danger because of the actions of others.

4. Which of the following technological aids will be **least** effective in helping your audience follow your argument?
   A. tables that show illnesses related to secondhand smoke
   B. slides that list your main idea and most important details
   C. photographs of restaurants where smoking is not allowed
   D. pie charts that show the percentage of people who would support a ban on smoking in public places

5. Which of the following words describes the type of language that would be **most** appropriate in your speech?
   A. convincing
   B. jovial
   C. informal
   D. imaginative

6. An effective presentation would persuade this particular audience to do what?
   A. Quit smoking.
   B. Help friends and family members quit smoking.
   C. Visit your school to talk about what it is like to run a restaurant.
   D. Develop a timetable for banning smoking in each restaurant.

7. In order for your speech to be effective, what will you need to do?
   A. Sound as if you know a lot about running a restaurant.
   B. Address the concern that some smokers will not visit restaurants that have banned smoking.
   C. Give examples of the dangers of smoking at an early age.
   D. Tell a few jokes during your speech.

Read the following passages. Then answer the questions that follow.

from *Treasure Island* by Robert Louis Stevenson

In one way, indeed, he bade fair to ruin us, for he kept on staying week after week, and at last month after month, so that all the money had been long exhausted, and still my father never plucked up the heart to insist on having more. If ever he mentioned it, the captain blew through his nose so loudly that you might say he roared, and stared my poor father out of the room. I have seen him wringing his hands after such a rebuff, and I am sure the annoyance and the terror he lived in must have greatly hastened his early and unhappy death.

8. From which of the following is the passage *most* likely drawn?
   A. a play   C. an editorial
   B. a speech   D. a novel

from "Dover Beach" by Matthew Arnold

     The sea is calm tonight.
     The tide is full, the moon lies fair
     Upon the straits;[1] on the French coast the light
     Gleams and is gone; the cliffs of England stand,
5   Glimmering and vast, out in the tranquil bay.
     Come to the window, sweet is the night air!

     Only, from the long line of spray
     Where the sea meets the moon-blanched land,
     Listen! you hear the grating roar
10   Of pebbles which the waves draw back, and fling,
     At their return, up the high strand,[2]
     Begin, and cease, and then again begin,
     With tremulous cadence slow, and bring
     Their eternal note of sadness in.

     [1] **straits** Straits of Dover, between England and France.
     [2] **strand** shore.

Name _____ Date _____

9. Which of the following Romantic themes are found in the excerpt from "Dover Beach"?
   A. interest in antiquity
   B. the power of nature
   C. expression through art
   D. all of the above

10. Which word **best** describes the tone created by the lines "the cliffs of England stand,/Glimmering and vast, out in the tranquil bay"?
   A. cheerful
   B. calm
   C. passionate
   D. dejected

11. In lines 9–11 of the poem, which words does Arnold use to evoke the sense of sound?
   A. grating roar
   B. of pebbles
   C. which the waves
   D. draw back

12. The lines "With tremulous cadence slow, and bring/Their eternal note of sadness in" evoke which of the following emotions?
   A. jealousy
   B. melancholy
   C. rage
   D. pride

from "Song of Myself" by Walt Whitman

I celebrate myself, and sing myself,
And what I assume you shall assume,
For every atom belonging to me as good belongs to you.

I loaf and invite my soul,
I lean and loaf at my ease observing a spear of summer grass.

My tongue, every atom of my blood, formed from this soil, this air,
Born here of parents born here from parents the same, and their
      Parents the same,
I, now thirty-seven years old in perfect health begin,
Hoping to cease not till death.

Creeds and schools in abeyance,
Retiring back a while sufficed at what they are, but never forgotten,
I harbor for good or bad, I permit to speak at every hazard,
Nature without check with original energy.

13. Which word **best** describes the tone set by the first two stanzas of the poem?
   A. solemnity
   B. weariness
   C. bitterness
   D. joy

14. In what way are the poems by Arnold and Whitman are similar?
   A. Both address the past.
   B. Both use the same rhyme scheme.
   C. Both feature dialogue.
   D. Both use images of nature.

15. How does the imagery in "Dover Beach" compare to the imagery in "Song of Myself"?
   A. The imagery in "Dover Beach" is more concrete.
   B. The imagery in "Dover Beach" is more abstract.
   C. The imagery in "Dover Beach" is more complex.
   D. The imagery in these two poems is virtually the same.

from "Reflections on Gandhi" by George Orwell

Saints should always be judged guilty until they are proven innocent, but the tests that have to be applied to them are not, of course, the same in all cases. In Gandhi's case the questions one feels inclined to ask are: to what extent was Gandhi moved by vanity—by the consciousness of himself as a humble, naked old man, sitting on a prayer mat and shaking empires by sheer spiritual power—and to what extent did he compromise his own principles by entering politics, which of their nature are insepa-rable from coercion and fraud? To give a definite answer one would have to study Gandhi's acts and writ-ing in immense detail, for his whole life was a sort of pilgrimage in which every act was significant.

16. Why do you think Orwell is critical of Gandhi's political motivation?
   A. It was fashionable to criticize Gandhi after his death.
   B. Orwell was inclined to criticize anyone involved in politics.
   C. Gandhi didn't like Orwell's books.
   D. Gandhi had defeated Orwell in a bid to become Prime Minister of Great Britain.

Answer the following questions.

17. Suppose you are conducting Internet research. At the bottom of a Web page, you see the word "Home." What will be the result of clicking on this word?
   A. You will see the page that opens every time you launch your Web browser.
   B. You will see the name and e-mail address of the person who wrote the information you found.
   C. You will see the main page for the organization that created the page.
   D. You will see the search engine you used to find the page.

18. You will ***most*** likely encounter words like *trajectory, inertia,* and *kinetic* in a book about what subject?
   A. astrology
   B. archaeology
   C. physics
   D. Latin

Read the following passages. Then answer the questions that follow.

Limited Two-Year Warranty

If your new CityCrawler Mp3 player breaks, it will be repaired or replaced during the first two years of ownership at no cost to you.

This warranty covers only defects in parts or in construction, as revealed through ordinary use. If malfunction occurs as a result of the product being dropped, exposed to moisture, or otherwise abused, CityCrawler will not replace your player. You may choose to have CityCrawler repair your player. Contact us for estimated repair costs.

Your warranty will become null and void if the back panel of your player has been pried open or otherwise damaged.

19. Based on the passage above, what can you conclude is the purpose of CityCrawler Mp3 player's warranty?
    A. to help people who are careless with their possessions
    B. to protect customers against defective merchandise
    C. to explain how the product works
    D. to give information about where to buy other CityCrawler products

How to Operate the Hard Press Sandwich Maker

1. Plug the Hard Press Sandwich Maker into an electrical outlet. The red light will turn on, indicating that the grill is heating.

2. When the light turns off, open the lid and place your sandwich on the grill.

3. Close the lid gently.

4. Remove the sandwich from the Hard Press.

5. To clean up, wipe the grill clean with a damp cloth.

20. What is missing from these instructions?
    A. how to clean the sandwich maker
    B. what the red light on the sandwich maker means
    C. how hard to close the sandwich maker's lid
    D. how long to leave the sandwich in the sandwich maker

from Hard Times by Charles Dickens

"Now, what I want is, Facts. Teach these boys and girls nothing but Facts. Facts alone are wanted in life. . . . [N]othing else will ever be of any service to them. This is the principle on which I bring up my own children, and this is the principle on which I bring up these children. Stick to the Facts, sir!"

The scene was a plain, bare, monotonous vault of a schoolroom, and the speaker's square forefinger emphasized his observations. . . .

from Jane Eyre by Charlotte Brontë

"I hold another creed; which no one ever taught me, . . . and to which I cling: for it extends hope to all: it makes Eternity a rest—a mighty home, not a terror and abyss. Besides, with this creed . . . revenge never worries my heart, degradation never too deeply disgusts me, injustice never crushes me too low: I live in calm, looking to the end."

Helen's head, always drooping, sank a little lower as she finished this sentence.

21. From which point of view are each of the two passages above told?
    A. The first passage is told from the first person, and the second is told from the third person.
    B. Both are told from the first person.
    C. The first is told from the first person, and the second is told from the second person.
    D. Both are told from the third person.

22. How are the two characters alike?
    A. Both seem mentally unbalanced.
    B. Both are well loved.
    C. Both have strong sets of principles.
    D. Both have positions of authority.

23. How do the two characters differ?
    A. One is cheerful, and the other is despairing.
    B. One is obsessive, and the other has a generous spirit.
    C. One is young, and the other is aged.
    D. One is evil, and the other is good.

24. Which of the following **best** describes the tone of the passages?
    A. The first is dry, and the second is dramatic.
    B. Both are sorrowful.
    C. The first is solemn, and the second is earnest.
    D. The first is amusing, and the second is poignant.

25. Which of the following best describes the meaning of the word **monotonous**, as it is used in the Brontë passage?
    A. tediously unvarying
    B. oddly quiet
    C. depressingly dark
    D. unusually diverse

All-in-One Workbook: Standardized Test Practice
375

Practice Test 2

Read the following passages. Then answer the questions that follow.

from *The Tragical History of Doctor Faustus* by Christopher Marlowe

ACT I. SCENE III. IN A GROVE

Enter FAUSTUS...

Enter MEPHISTOPHILIS (like a Franciscan friar).

MEPHISTOPHILIS: Now, Faustus, what wouldst thou have me do?

FAUSTUS: I charge thee wait upon me whilst I live,

To do whatever Faustus shall command,

Be it to make the moon drop from her sphere,

Or the Ocean to overwhelm the world.

MEPHISTOPHILIS: I am a servant to great Lucifer,

And may not follow thee without his leave;

No more that he commands must we perform.

FAUSTUS: Did he not charge thee to appear to me?

MEPHISTOPHILIS: No, I came hither of mine own accord.

1. Which of the following is the **best** summary of the passage's plot?
   A. Faustus is bossy, but Mephistophilis is agreeable.
   B. The scene takes place in a grove. The characters have just met.
   C. Mephistophilis appears to Faustus, who asks Mephistophilis to follow his orders; however, it is not clear that this will happen.
   D. Lucifer did not tell Mephistophilis to appear to Faustus, but Mephistophilis did it anyway.

2. What is the conflict presented in this passage?
   A. Faustus conjured Mephistophilis, but Faustus does not want anything to do with Lucifer.
   B. Faustus wants to flood the world, but there is a drought.
   C. Mephistophilis cannot take Faust's orders until Lucifer grants approval.
   D. Faustus and Mephistophilis are not allowed in the grove, so they trespass.

3. What do Faustus's first lines of dialogue reveal about his character?
   A. He is arrogant and imaginative.
   B. He is not experienced in giving orders.
   C. He is in a great hurry.
   D. He thinks Mephistophilis is not very smart.

4. Which of the following is the **least** likely inference that can be made by a reader considering the scene's setting in a grove?
   A. There is no furniture on the stage.
   B. Mephistophilis and Faust have just met for the first time.
   C. There is an aura of mystery in this scene.
   D. The action may be related to the concept of "original sin."

5. In this passage, how does Marlowe makes Mephistophilis seem like a realistic character?
   A. by giving the audience the name of his boss
   B. by having him speak in the same manner as Faustus
   C. by describing what he looks like
   D. by having him enter the scene after Faustus

from Act I of *The Crucible* by Arthur Miller

A small upper bedroom in the home of REVEREND SAMUEL PARRIS, *Salem, Massachusetts, in the spring of the year 1692…*

…As the curtain rises, REVEREND PARRIS *is discovered kneeling beside the bed, evidently in prayer. His daughter* BETTY PARRIS, *aged ten, is lying on the bed, inert.*

TITUBA, *already taking a step backward:* My Betty be healthy soon?

PARRIS: Out of here!

TITUBA, *backing to the door:* My Betty not goin' die…

PARRIS, *scrambling to his feet in a fury:* Out of my sight! She is gone. Out of my—*He is overcome with sobs. He clamps his teeth against them and closes the door and leans against it, exhausted.* Oh, my God! God help me! *Quaking with fear, mumbling to himself through his sobs, he goes to the bed and gently takes* BETTY'S *hand.* Betty. Child. Dear child. Will you wake, will you open up your eyes! Betty, little one…

6. The passage by Miller is different from the passage by Marlowe in which of the following ways?
   A. It offers detailed stage directions.
   B. Its characters are highly emotional.
   C. Its dialogue is closer to the way people speak today.
   D. all of the above

7. How are the two passages similar?
   A. In both, the action takes place in a grove.
   B. In both, characters are developed through dialogue.
   C. In both, one of the characters is the devil.
   D. In both, prayer is important.

Suppose that you must write a research essay about Mary Shelley's Frankenstein. Answer the following questions.

8. Which of the following is **least** useful for you to do before you begin writing?
   A. Draft an outline.
   B. Look in the novel for passages that demonstrate your main idea.
   C. Read nonfiction sources you may wish to quote.
   D. Draft your Works Cited page.

9. Which of the following should you assume your audience needs in order to understand your researched essay?
   A. a detailed summary of the whole plot of *Frankenstein*
   B. no quotations from *Frankenstein*
   C. brief quotations from *Frankenstein*
   D. no summary of *Frankenstein*

10. Given that you have been asked to analyze the novel, which of the following is the **best** choice for your main idea?
    A. Mary Shelley is a Romantic writer.
    B. The story is a warning about the dangers of playing God.
    C. Percy Shelley, Mary's husband, is a better writer than she is.
    D. No film version of the novel is completely faithful to the book.

11. Which of the following statements is worded **most** clearly?
    A. Victor Frankenstein cannot control his creation that frightens him and makes him feel ashamed.
    B. Because he cannot control his creation, Victor Frankenstein feels frightened and ashamed.
    C. Frightened and ashamed, Victor Frankenstein cannot make his creature control him.
    D. Victor Frankenstein's creature is frightening, and he cannot control him although he makes him feel ashamed.

12. Which of the following sources would be the **most** helpful in writing your essay?
    A. a book about Mary Shelley's life
    B. an article about major themes in *Frankenstein*
    C. an online schedule for the annual Mary Shelley conference in London
    D. a cartoon video featuring Frankenstein

13. Which is the correct way to use MLA style to cite a source parenthetically?
    A. "Shelley only briefly describes what the creature looks like so that he remains a mystery." (Cole, 56).
    B. "Shelley only briefly describes what the creature looks like so that he remains a mystery" (Cole, 56).
    C. "Shelley only briefly describes what the creature looks like so that he remains a mystery" (Cole 56).
    D. "Shelley only briefly describes what the creature looks like so that he remains a mystery (Cole 56)."

The sentence below contains a problem in grammar, sentence construction, word choice, or punctuation. Part or all of the sentence is underlined. Select the letter that contains the best version of the underlined section.

14. Charles Dickens's *Hard Times* and Charlotte Brontë's *Jane Eyre* are representative of the growing popularity of the novel <u>while in</u> the nineteenth century.

    A. before   **C.** at

    B. during   **D.** around

Answer the following questions.

15. What should you do when you find good research for your essay?

    A. Present it before your own ideas.

    B. Use it to make sure your ideas are right.

    C. Place it in footnotes at the bottom of pages where you discuss similar ideas.

    D. Use it to support, extend, or challenge your own ideas after you present them.

16. Where is the ***best*** place to state your main idea?

    A. in the body

    B. in the introduction

    C. after presenting your research

    D. in every paragraph

17. Choose the ***correct*** version of the sentence below.

    A. Art, though often a wonderful endeavor, has been known to lead artists to bouts of frustration and self-doubt.

    B. Art, though often a wonderful endeavor has been known to lead artists to bouts of frustration and self-doubt.

    C. Art though often a wonderful endeavor has been known to lead artists to bouts of frustration and self-doubt.

    D. Art, though often a wonderful endeavor has been known to lead artists, to bouts of frustration and self-doubt.

18. Choose the sentence that needs to be ***revised***.

    A. Literature can help us understand life; we see ourselves in the characters we meet in books.

    B. Literature can help us understand life, because we see ourselves in the characters we meet in books.

    C. Literature can help us understand life. We see ourselves in the characters we meet in books.

    D. Literature can help us understand life but we see ourselves in the characters we meet in books.

19. Choose the sentence that is grammatically **correct**.
    A. Tara collects personal journals written by settlers in the early days of the New England colonies.
    B. Tara collects Personal Journals written by settlers in the early days of the New England colonies.
    C. Tara collects personal journals written by Settlers in the early days of the New England Colonies.
    D. Tara collects personal journals written by settlers in the early days of the new England colonies.

20. Which of the following is the **least** appropriate reason to proofread your essay?
    A. to catch and correct any misspellings
    B. to prove that you really did write the essay
    C. to ensure that all pages have printed correctly
    D. to find and revise any awkward sentences

21. If proofreading reveals two punctuation errors in your word-processed essay, what should you do?
    A. Use black pen to make the corrections.
    B. Use red pen to make the corrections.
    C. Make the changes to the computer file and print the pages again.
    D. Let it go because teachers allow a certain number of mistakes.

Read the passage below. Then answer the questions that follow.

from *Wartime Speech* by Winston Churchill

(1) We must not allow ourselves to be intimidated by the presence of these armored vehicles in unexpected places behind our lines. If they are behind our Front, the French are also at many points fighting actively (2) behind theirs. . . . (3) And if the French Army, and our own Army, are well handled, as I believe they will be; if the French retain that genius for recovery and counter-attack for which they have so long been famous; and if the British Army shows the dogged endurance and solid fighting power of which there have been so many examples in the past—then a sudden transformation of the scene might spring into being. . . .

22. The paragraph is arranged in what kind of order?
    A. spatial
    B. chronological
    C. cause and effect
    D. order of importance

23. Which section in the paragraph contains parallel structure?
    A. section 1
    B. section 2
    C. section 3
    D. all of the above

24. According to the organization of the paragraph, choose the **best** place to insert this sentence: *Both sides are therefore in an extremely dangerous position.*
    A. between sections 2 and 3
    B. after section 3
    C. between sections 1 and 2
    D. before section 1

25. In section 3, Churchill lists which of the following?
    A. first effect, then causes
    B. first causes, then effect
    C. only factual details
    D. irrefutable evidence

26. Which of the following statements is **least** appropriate in a summary of Churchill's key points?
    A. Armored vehicles are behind British lines.
    B. The British Army has a history of solid fighting power.
    C. The French Army is also probably fighting behind their own lines.
    D. The locations of armored vehicles surprised the British Army.

Writing Prompt 1

What is the most important thing about people in your age group that you would like older people to know? Write an essay in which you identify and describe for older readers some important quality of people your age. Be sure to tell why it is the most important characteristic, and give examples and reasons to support your idea. Include ideas that allow the reader to understand how young people fit into the social fabric of our world. Use language and a tone that is appropriate to your audience.

Writing Prompt 2

Choose a favorite piece of writing that you and your classmates studied this year. It could be a poem, a play, a short story, or a piece of nonfiction prose. Reflect on how the author's subject and use of language allowed you to relate the text to your own life. How did your appreciation of the text differ from your peers' responses, if at all? What aspects of your own experience influenced the way you read and understood this text? Write an essay in which you identify the text, explain its meaning and literary characteristics, and describe the ways in which the work influenced your own ideas, feelings, and approach to writing.

SAT/ACT PRACTICE TEST

CRITICAL READING
Section 1: Sentence Completion

Each sentence below has one or two blanks, each blank indicating that something has been omitted. Beneath the sentence are five words or sets of words labeled A through E. Choose the word or set of words that, when inserted in the sentence, best fits the meaning of the sentence as a whole. Mark the letter of your choice on your answer sheet.

Example:

The horror movie depicted many bloodcurdling, ---- scenes.

(A) temperate

(B) lurid

(C) jocular

(D) peaceful

(E) blithe

1. **Even with the microphone in front of her, the little girl was ---- .**

   (A) grating

   (B) inaudible

   (C) brilliant

   (D) clamorous

   (E) harsh

2. **The union employees hired an attorney to ---- on their behalf.**

   (A) intercede

   (B) bellow

   (C) clamor

   (D) scribe

   (E) exhort

3. **Her message was ---- ; she had hoped to teach me a ---- lesson.**

   (A) instructional..useless

   (B) enlightening..fruitless

   (C) didactic..valuable

   (D) in vain..worthless

   (E) educational..tedious

4. **The architect ordered the crew to ---- its work because the boathouse's ---- was not secure.**

   (A) cease..buttress

   (B) admire..foundation

   (C) destroy..future

   (D) redouble..piazza

   (E) enjoy..owner

5. After three years of intense practice, Rinaldo became very ---- at gymnastics.

(A) indigent

(B) inferior

(C) gawky

(D) mediocre

(E) adept

6. In addition to working as a respected news reporter, she is a(n) ---- professor at a(n) ---- university.

(A) adjunct..prestigious

(B) extra..established

(C) auxiliary..questionable

(D) supplementary..controversial

(E) full-time..unreliable

7. He is a master at his work and a model citizen, so you should try to ---- his ideas.

(A) enmesh

(B) enforce

(C) reject

(D) decline

(E) espouse

8. My sister is ---- living in Montana; she longs for the warm Florida sunshine.

(A) blithe

(B) contented

(C) discontented

(D) irate

(E) incensed

9. During the last kilometer of the 10K race, Alyssa was ---- and barely able to walk.

(A) enervated

(B) exuberant

(C) gliding

(D) soaring

(E) blissful

10. My brother and my mother will ---- over any ---- thing, such as whether the laundry is folded correctly.

(A) bicker..important

(B) wrangle..momentous

(C) squabble..significant

(D) quibble..inconsequential

(E) chatter..senseless

11. Debbie would rather date some ---- athlete with a(n) ---- physique than a kind, caring person with whom she has a lot in common.

(A) supercilious..svelte

(B) compassionate..muscular

(C) submissive..hefty

(D) insolent..thin

(E) clement..obese

12. The famous poet Emily Dickinson was a(n) ----; she was afraid of people she did not know.

(A) masochist

(B) manic-depressive

(C) xenophobe

(D) extrovert

(E) claustrophobe

"The Diamond Necklace" by Guy de Maupassant

"The Diamond Necklace" Excerpt from the short story by Guy de Maupassant

(1) The girl was one of those pretty and charming young creatures who sometimes are born, as if by a slip of fate, into a family of clerks. She had no dowry, no expectations, no way of being known, understood, loved, married by any rich and distinguished man; so she let herself be married to a little clerk of the Ministry of Public Instruction.

She dressed plainly because she could not dress well, but she was unhappy as if she had really fallen from a higher station.

(2) Mathilde suffered ceaselessly, feeling herself born to enjoy all delicacies and all luxuries. She was distressed at the poverty of her dwelling, at the bareness of the walls, at the shabby chairs, the ugliness of the curtains. All those things, of which another woman of her rank would never even have been conscious, tortured her and made her angry. The sight of the little Breton peasant who did her humble housework aroused in her despairing regrets and bewildering dreams. She thought of long reception halls hung with ancient silk, of the dainty cabinets containing priceless curiosities and of the little coquettish perfumed reception rooms made for chatting at five o'clock with intimate friends, with men famous and sought after, whom all women envy and whose attention they all desire.

(3) When she sat down to dinner, before the round table covered with a tablecloth in use three days, opposite her husband, who uncovered the soup tureen and declared with a delighted air, "Ah, the good soup! I don't know anything better than that," she thought of dainty dinners, of shining silverware, of tapestry that peopled the walls with ancient personages and with strange birds flying in the midst of a fairy forest; and she thought of delicious dishes served on marvellous plates and of the whispered gallantries to which you listen with a sphinxlike smile while you are eating the pink meat of a trout or the wings of a quail.

(4) She had no gowns, no jewels, nothing. And she loved nothing but that. She felt made for that. She would have liked so much to please, to be envied, to be charming, to be sought after.

She had a friend, a former schoolmate at the convent, who was rich, and whom she did not like to go to see any more because she felt so sad when she came home.

(5) But one evening her husband reached home with a triumphant air and holding a large envelope in his hand.
"There," said he, "there is something for you."
She tore the paper quickly and drew out a printed card which bore these words:

The Minister of Public Instruction and Madame Georges Ramponneau request the honor of M. and Madame Loisel's company at the palace of the Ministry on Monday evening, January 18th.

(6) Instead of being delighted, as her husband had hoped, she threw the invitation on the table crossly, muttering:
"What do you wish me to do with that?"
"Why, my dear, I thought you would be glad. You never go out, and this is such a fine opportunity. I had great trouble to get it. Every one wants to go; it is very select, and they are not giving many invitations to clerks. The whole official world will be there."
She looked at him with an irritated glance and said impatiently:
"And what do you wish me to put on my back?"
He had not thought of that. He stammered:
"Why, the gown you go to the theatre in. It looks very well to me."

(7) He stopped, distracted, seeing that his wife was weeping. Two great tears ran slowly from the corners of her eyes toward the corners of her mouth.
"What's the matter? What's the matter?" he answered.
By a violent effort she conquered her grief and replied in a calm voice, while she wiped her wet cheeks:

"Nothing. Only I have no gown, and, therefore, I can't go to this ball. Give your card to some colleague whose wife is better equipped than I am."

(8) He was in despair. He resumed:
"Come, let us see, Mathilde. How much would it cost, a suitable gown, which you could use on other occasions—something very simple?"

(9) She reflected several seconds, making her calculations and wondering also what sum she could ask without drawing on herself an immediate refusal and a frightened exclamation from the economical clerk.
Finally she replied hesitating:
"I don't know exactly, but I think I could manage it with four hundred francs."

(10) He grew a little pale, because he was laying aside just that amount to buy a gun and treat himself to a little shooting next summer on the plain of Nanterre, with several friends who went to shoot larks there of a Sunday. But he said:
"Very well. I will give you four hundred francs. And try to have a pretty gown."

(11) The day of the ball drew near and Madame Loisel seemed sad, uneasy, anxious. Her frock was ready, however. Her husband said to her one evening:
"What is the matter? Come, you have seemed very queer these last three days."

(12) And she answered:
"It annoys me not to have a single piece of jewelry, not a single ornament, nothing to put on. I shall look poverty-stricken. I would almost rather not go at all."

(13) "You might wear natural flowers," said her husband. "They're very stylish at this time of year. For ten francs you can get two or three magnificent roses."
She was not convinced.
"No; there's nothing more humiliating than to look poor among other women who are rich."

(14) "How stupid you are!" her husband cried. "Go look up your friend, Madame Forestier, and ask her to lend you some jewels. You're intimate enough with her to do that."
She uttered a cry of joy:
"True! I never thought of it."

(15) The next day she went to her friend and told her of her distress.
Madame Forestier went to a wardrobe with a mirror, took out a large jewel box, brought it back, opened it and said to Madame Loisel:
"Choose, my dear."

She saw first some bracelets, then a pearl necklace, then a Venetian gold cross set with precious stones, of admirable workmanship. She tried on the ornaments before the mirror, hesitated and could not make up her mind to part with them, to give them back. She kept asking:
"Haven't you any more?"

13. **Based on the context of paragraph 2, what is the meaning of the phrase "another woman of her rank"?**
   A. a woman with her education
   B. a woman the rank of a Breton peasant
   C. a woman of the working class such as a family of clerks
   D. a woman of the upper class
   E. a woman wed to a rich man

14. **Why *most likely* does Mathilde's husband try to get the invitation to the palace of the Ministry?**
   A. He thinks it would make Mathilde happy.
   B. He wants to impress Mathilde.
   C. He wants to get ahead in his job.
   D. Mathilde grew up in a rich and distinguished family.
   E. All of the clerks received invitations.

15. **Based on the context of this passage, what is Mathilde's greatest desire?**
    A. to go to the palace with her husband
    B. to have a new dress
    C. to be a good wife
    D. to redecorate their home
    E. to be a great lady who others look up to

16. **Why *most likely* did Mathilde's husband give her money for a new dress?**
    A. He does not like the dress she usually wore to the theater.
    B. He had been saving money for her to use to buy a dress.
    C. He wants Mathilde to impress the Minister of Instruction.
    D. He wants her to be happy.
    E. He wants to buy a very fancy dress.

17. **Why *most likely* does Mathilde no longer visit her friend and former schoolmate as often as before?**
    A. Her friend is unkind to Mathilde when she visits.
    B. Mathilde's husband does not want her to visit.
    C. Her friend looks down on Mathilde because Mathilde married a clerk.
    D. Mathilde does not have a dress suitable to wear when visiting her wealthy friend.
    E. Mathilde is jealous of her friend's wealth.

18. **What *most likely* does the word *distress* mean in the last paragraph?**
    A. great difficulty
    B. need for money
    C. great joy
    D. plans
    E. poor conditions

19. **What is the main idea of the selection?**
    A. You should always strive to get more than you have.
    B. Some people are not satisfied with what they have.
    C. You should give someone you love all that you can.
    D. Riches will make you happy.
    E. The life of a clerk is a depressing one.

20. **Based on the context of paragraph 2, what does the word *ceaselessly* mean?**
    A. deeply
    B. greatly
    C. without stopping
    D. without feeling
    E. quietly

21. Which of the following does *not* describe Mathilde?
- A. She is a dreamer.
- B. She is distressed that her home is so plain.
- C. She wants to be rich.
- D. She is materialistic.
- E. She loves her home with its priceless decorations.

22. Based on the context of paragraph 9, what does the word *economical* mean?
- A. careful use of resources
- B. very knowledgeable.
- C. having business sense
- D. greedy
- E. nervous

Questions 23–27 are based on the following passage.

This selection is from The Defense of Poesy *by Sir Philip Sidney.*

There is no art delivered unto mankind that has not the works of Nature for his principal object, without
Line which they could not consist, and on
5 which they so depend, as they become actors and players, as it were, of what Nature will have set forth. So does the astronomer look upon the stars, and, by that he sees set down what order
10 Nature has taken therein. So do the geometrician and arithmetician in their diverse sorts of quantities. . . .

Only the poet, disdaining to be tied to any such subjection, lifted up with
15 the vigor of his own invention, grows in effect into another Nature, in making things either better than Nature brings forth, or, quite anew, forms such as never were in Nature,
20 as the Heroes, Demigods, Cyclops, Chimeras, Furies, and such like: so as he goes hand in hand with Nature, not enclosed within the narrow warrant of her gifts, but freely ranging
25 within the zodiac of his own wit.

Nature never set forth the earth in so rich tapestry as divers poets have done, neither with so pleasant rivers, fruitful trees, sweet-smelling flowers,
30 nor whatsoever else may make the too much loved earth more lovely. Her world is brazen, the poets only deliver a golden. But let those things alone, and go to man (for whom as the other
35 things are, so it seems in him her uttermost cunning is employed), and know whether she have brought forth so true a lover as Theagenes, so constant a friend as Pylades, so
40 valiant a man as Orlando, so right a prince as Xenophon's Cyrus, and so excellent a man every way as Virgil's Aeneas. Neither let this be jestingly conceived because the works of the
45 one be essential, the other in

imitation or fiction, for every understanding knows the skill of each artificer stands in that Idea or foreconceit of the work, and not in the
50 work itself. And that the poet has that Idea is manifest, by delivering them forth in such excellency as he had imagined them. Which delivering forth also is not wholly imaginative, as we
55 are wont to say by them that build castles in the air, but so far substantially it works, not only to make a Cyrus, which had been but a particular excellence, as Nature might
60 have done, but to bestow a Cyrus upon the world to make many Cyruses, if they will learn aright why and how that maker made him. . . .

[Definition] Poesy, therefore, is
65 an art of imitation, for so Aristotle terms it in the word *mimesis*; that is to say, a representing, counterfeiting, or figuring forth—to speak metaphorically, a speaking picture—
70 with this end, to teach and delight. . . .

[W]hen by the balance of experience it was found that the astronomer looking to the stars might fall in a ditch, that the inquiring philosopher
75 might be blind in himself, and the mathematician might draw forth a straight line with a crooked heart, then, lo, did proof, the overruler of opinions, make manifest that all these
80 are but serving sciences, which, as they have a private end in themselves, so yet are they all directed to the highest end of the mistress knowledge, by the Greeks [called] *architektonike*,
85 which stands (as I think) in the knowledge of a man's self, in the ethic and politic consideration, with the end of well doing and not of well knowing only; even as the saddler's next end is
90 to make a good saddle, but his further end to serve a nobler faculty, which is horsemanship; so the horseman's to soldiery, and the soldier not only to have the skill, but to perform the
95 practice of a soldier. So that, the ending end of all earthly learning being

virtuous action, those skills that most serve to bring forth that, have a most just title to be princes over all the rest.
100   Wherein we can show the poet is worthy to have it before any other competitors. . . .

23. What is the main idea of the second paragraph?

(A) Witty poets are the most successful poets.

(B) Nature is restricted only by the minds of poets.

(C) Poets can create things better than Nature creates.

(D) Poets find their most poignant subjects in Nature.

(E) The gifts of Nature far outweigh the gifts of poets.

24. The allusions in lines 38–43 are *mostly* used to

(A) help the audience understand the author's message

(B) persuade the audience to make a change

(C) command the audience's respect

(D) keep the audience's interest in the passage

(E) encourage the audience to read other works of literature

25. You can tell from the context that people who "build castles in the air" (lines 55–56)

(A) have unrealistic hopes or plans

(B) push themselves to do the best that they can

(C) gain the admiration of the people around them

(D) have trouble accepting change

(E) think that they are superior to others

26. On the basis of lines 40, 58–63, you can tell that Sidney assumes that his readers think Cyrus is

(A) controversial

(B) virtuous

(C) mysterious

(D) suspicious

(E) beautiful

27. According to Sidney, the ultimate goal of poetry is to

(A) move and inspire

(B) overrule opinions

(C) record facts and observations

(D) teach and delight

(E) describe the beauty of Nature

Directions: *The two passages given below deal with a related topic. Following the passages are questions about the content of each passage or about the relationship between the two passages. Answer the questions based upon what is <u>stated</u> or <u>implied</u> in the passages and in any introductory material provided. Mark the letter of your choice on your answer sheet.*

Questions 28–33 are based on the two passages that follow.

In 1664, London was struck by a plague that within a year killed 70,000 people in a population of about 460,000. A plague is a usually fatal infectious disease that is spread by fleas from an infected host, such as a black rat. Samuel Pepys's The Diary (Passage 1) touches on the day-to-day details of this time that, hundreds of years later, still fascinates readers. The plague year actually occurred when Daniel Defoe was only four years old. However, his A Journal of the Plague Year (Passage 2) contains a great deal of historical accuracy.

Passage 1

    Sept. 3, 1665. (Lord's Day.) Church being done, my Lord Bruncker, Sir J. Minnes, and I up to the vestry at the
Line desire of the Justices of the Peace, Sir
(5) Theo. Biddulph and Sir W. Boreman and Alderman Hooker, in order to the doing something for the keeping of the plague from growing; but Lord! to consider the madness of the people of
(10) the town, who will (because they are forbid) come in crowds along with the dead corps[es] to see them buried; but we agreed on some orders for the prevention thereof. Among other
(15) stories, one was very passionate, methought of a complaint brought against a man in the town for taking a child from London from an infected house. Alderman Hooker told us it
(20) was the child of a very able citizen in Gracious Street, a saddler, who had buried all the rest of his children of the plague, and himself and wife now being shut up and in despair of

(25) escaping, did desire only to save the life of this little child; and so prevailed to have it received stark-naked into the arms of a friend, who brought it (having put it into new fresh clothes)
(30) to Greenwich; where upon hearing the story, we did agree it should be permitted to be received and kept in the town. Thence with my Lord Bruncker to Captain Cocke's, where
(35) we mighty merry and supped, and very late I by water to Woolwich, in great apprehensions of an ague. . . .

Passage 2

    The face of London was now indeed strangely altered, I mean the whole
(40) mass of buildings, city, liberties,suburbs, Westminster, Southwark, and altogether; for as to the particular part called the city, or within the walls, that was not yet
(45) much infected. But in the whole the face of things, I say, was much altered; sorrow and sadness sat upon every face; and though some parts were not yet overwhelmed, yet all
(50) looked deeply concerned; and as we saw it apparently coming on, so everyone looked on himself and his family as in the utmost danger. Were it possible to represent those times
(55) exactly to those that did not see them, and give the reader due ideas of the horror that everywhere presented itself, it must make just impressions upon their minds and fill them with
60 surprise. London might well be said to be all in tears; the mourners did not go about the streets indeed, for nobody put on black or made a formal dress of mourning for their nearest

(65) windows and doors of their houses,
      where their dearest relations were
      perhaps dying, or just dead, were so
      frequent to be heard as we passed the
      streets, that it was enough to pierce
(70) the stoutest heart in the world to hear
      them. Tears and lamentations were
      seen almost in every house, especially
      in the first part of the visitation; for
      toward the latter end men's hearts
(75) were hardened, and death was so
      always before their eyes, that they did
      not so much concern themselves for
      the loss of their friends, expecting
      that themselves should be summoned
(80) the next hour. . . .

28. You can tell from Passage 1 that the phrase "being shut up" (line 24) *probably* means

(A) locked in one's house

(B) thrown into prison

(C) allowed to roam freely

(D) stricken with the plague

(E) forced to be silent

29. You can tell from Passage 1 that "ague" (line 37) *probably* refers to a(n)

(A) illness

(B) fish

(C) criminal

(D) drowning

(E) antagonist

30. According to Passage 1, people were most likely forbidden to watch their loved ones be buried because

(A) This was common practice in London.

(B) Alderman Hooker said they should not see this.

(C) There were police officers on the streets.

(D) They might contract the plague.

(E) Strict curfews were enforced.

31. You can tell from Passage 2 (line 71) that "lamentations" *probably* refer to expressions of

(A) sorrow

(B) joy

(C) faith

(D) anger

(E) fascination

32. According to Passage 2, people's hearts were hardened because they

(A) cared only about themselves

(B) never despaired of escaping the plague

(C) were so tired and ill

(D) had already lost all of their loved ones

(E) had seen so much death

33. The two passages are alike in that they both discuss

(A) how Londoners kept the plague from spreading

(B) how people who died from the plague were buried

(C) the sorrow in London at the time of the plague

(D) how the plague began and then later spread

(E) how the plague affected the laws

Directions: *The three passages below are followed by questions based on their content. Answer the questions on the basis of what is* <u>stated</u> *or* <u>implied</u> *in the passages.*

During early Norman times, the Church often sponsored plays as part of religious services. In time, these plays moved from the church building to the churchyard and then to the marketplace. The earliest dramas were miracle plays, or mystery plays, that retold stories from the Bible or dealt with aspects of the lives of saints.

During the fifteenth century, the House of York and the House of Lancaster alternately ruled as they fought over the throne in what came to be called the War of the Roses. In these turbulent years, a new kind of drama arose: the morality play. Morality plays depicted the lives of ordinary people and taught moral lessons.

34. According to the passage, how were morality plays different from mystery plays?

(A) Morality plays were supported by the House of York; mystery plays were supported by the House of Lancaster.

(B) Mystery plays were supported by the House of York; morality plays were supported by the House of Lancaster.

(C) Mystery plays used ordinary people as main characters; morality plays used religious characters.

(D) Morality plays used ordinary people as main characters; mystery plays used religious characters.

(E) Morality plays taught morals; mystery plays relied on the audience to help solve mysteries.

35. Morality plays *probably* emerged during the turmoil of the fifteenth century because people

(A) needed to find comfort in the plays' religious characters

(B) wanted to see their own troubles and uncertainties dramatized on the stage

(C) lost interest in seeing mystery plays and needed a change

(D) needed to understand the politics involved in the War of the Roses

(E) found a renewed interest in dramatic plays

For them no more the blazing hearth
    shall burn,
Or busy housewife ply her evening care;
No children run to lisp their sire's
5   return,
Or climb his knees the envied kiss to
    share. . . .

Let not Ambition mock their useful toil,
Their homely joys, and destiny obscure;
10 Nor Grandeur hear with a disdainful
    smile
The short and simple annals of the poor.

The boast of heraldry, the pomp of
    power,
15 And all that beauty, all that wealth
    e'er gave,
Awaits alike the inevitable hour.
The paths of glory lead but to the grave.

—from "Elegy Written in a Country
    Churchyard" by Thomas Gray

Know then thyself, presume not God
    to scan;
The proper study of mankind is man. . . .
With too much knowledge for the
5   skeptic side,
With too much weakness for the
    stoic's pride,
He hangs between; in doubt to act,
    or rest;
10 In doubt to deem himself a god, or beast;
In doubt his mind or body to prefer;
Born but to die, and reasoning but
    to err;. . .
Chaos of thought and passion, all
15   confused;
Still by himself abused, or disabused;
Created half to rise, and half to fall;
Great lord of all things, yet a prey to all;
Sole judge of truth, in endless error
20   hurled:
The glory, jest, and riddle of the world!

—from "An Essay on Man"
    by Alexander Pope

36. The "inevitable hour" that the narrator speaks of in line 17 refers to

(A) death

(B) birth

(C) reincarnation

(D) change

(E) destiny

37. On the basis of the information in the passage, you can *best* infer that the narrator

(A) yearns to be wealthy

(B) is disdainful of the poor

(C) admires people with power

(D) loves children

(E) respects ordinary people

38. According to the passage, what is the result of man being neither skeptic nor stoic?

(A) Man becomes frail and vulnerable.

(B) Man is never certain what to do or think.

(C) Man loses his knowledge of the world.

(D) Man learns to rely on his body.

(E) Man is no better than an animal.

39. The author's main message in this passage is that

(A) humans cannot better themselves

(B) humans take advantage of God's creatures

(C) humans possess both good and bad traits

(D) humans only improve the world

(E) humans rely too much on God's help

WRITING

Directions: *The sentences below contain errors in grammar, usage, word choice, and idiom. Parts of each sentence are underlined and lettered. Decide which underlined part contains the error, and mark its letter on your answer sheet. If the sentence is correct as it stands, mark (E) on your answer sheet. No sentence contains more than one error.*

40. Killed before the age of thirty,

Christopher Marlowe <u>always</u> managed
                 (A)

to <u>achieve</u> <u>renown</u> as a brilliant
    (B)   **(C)**

<u>playwright</u> and poet. <u>No error</u>
(D)   **(E)**

41. He <u>spent</u> his <u>days</u> writing plays and
    (A)   **(B)**

serving <u>at</u> a government <u>agent</u>. <u>No error</u>
    (C)   **(D)**   **(E)**

42. *Tamburlaine*, <u>his</u> first drama, dazzled the
        (A)

public <u>with</u> <u>its</u>' dynamic characterization
     (B) **(C)**

of a <u>tyrant hero</u>. <u>No error</u>
    (D)   **(E)**

43. His tragedy <u>Doctor Faustus</u> <u>is</u>
         (A)   **(B)**

<u>often performed</u> even <u>in this day and age</u>.
   (C)   **(D)**

<u>No error</u>
(E)

44. Marlowe <u>has been described</u> as a
         (A)

<u>scoundrel</u>, a <u>ladie's</u> man, and a <u>hothead</u>.
(B)   **(C)**   **(D)**

<u>No error</u>
(E)

45. <u>Finally</u>, <u>it is clear</u> <u>that</u> he <u>was full</u> of
(A)   **(B)**   **(C)**   **(D)**

personal magnetism. <u>No error</u>
             (E)

46. His numerous friends <u>even his enemies</u>
               (A)

<u>were drawn</u> to him <u>like</u> <u>moths</u> to a flame.
(B)   **(C)** **(D)**

<u>No error</u>
(E)

47. When the council of <u>Queen Elizabeth I</u>
                (A)

wrote a letter <u>implying that</u> Marlowe
         (B)

<u>had performed</u> important government
(C)

services, rumors <u>flew</u> about that he was
         (D)

a spy. <u>No error</u>
     (E)

48. Marlowe was <u>knived</u> <u>to death</u> in a tavern
         (A)   **(B)**

<u>brawl</u> <u>in 1593</u>. <u>No error</u>
(C)   **(D)**   **(E)**

49. <u>To this day</u>, scholars question whether
(A)

his death <u>was really caused by</u> his
        (B)

<u>drunken refusal</u> to pay his bill or
(C)

whether he was murdered <u>despite</u> his
           (D)

undercover activities. <u>No error</u>
          (E)

50. From the outbreak of the <u>French</u>
    (A)
<u>Revolution</u> in 1789 until <u>Napoleon's</u>
    (B)
defeat at the Battle of Waterloo in

<u>1815; Britain</u> focused on <u>foreign affairs</u>
    (C)   **(D)**
at the expense of much-needed domestic

reform. <u>No error</u>
       (E)

51. <u>In fact</u> those demanding reform
    (A)
<u>were often</u> branded <u>as</u> French-inspired
    (B)   **(C)**
<u>revolutionaries</u>. <u>No error</u>
    (D)   **(E)**

52. <u>Even after Waterloo</u>, reform <u>were</u> delayed
    (A)   **(B)**
<u>by</u> a dangerous cycle of <u>protests and</u>
(C)   **(D)**
<u>government crackdowns</u>. <u>No error</u>
                            (E)

53. These protests, <u>sometimes violent</u>, were
                      (A)
caused by <u>postwar</u> depression, high
          (B)
unemployment, and <u>an 1815 Corn Law</u>
                   (C)
protecting <u>landowners'</u> high grain prices.
           (D)
<u>No error</u>
(E)

54. <u>In the Luddite riots from 1811 to 1817</u>,
    (A)
unemployed workers in the industrial

<u>north</u>, <u>claiming</u> as their leader the
(B)   **(C)**
mythical working-class hero General (or

King) Ludd, wrecked factory equipment

that they felt <u>at that time</u> had taken their
              (D)
jobs. <u>No error</u>
     (E)

55. In the <u>Peterloo Massacre</u> of 1819,
          (A)
mockingly named <u>after</u> Waterloo, local
                (B)
officials ordered cavalry to charge a

crowd assembled <u>to hear and listen to</u>
                (C)
reformer Henry Hunt in <u>St. Peter's Field,</u>
                       (D)
Manchester. <u>No error</u>
            (E)

56. Not until <u>it was the 1820s</u> did the
              (A)
<u>reform movement</u> <u>begin</u> to see some
    (B)   **(C)**
<u>successes</u>. <u>No error</u>
    (D)   **(E)**

57. In 1823 Tory <u>Politician</u> Sir Robert Peel
                (A)
<u>reformed</u> <u>Britain's</u> harsh <u>penal code</u>.
    (B)   **(C)**   **(D)**
<u>No error</u>
(E)

58. <u>In 1828 and 1829</u>, Parliament
    (A)
<u>passed</u> laws <u>giving</u> political rights to
(B)   **(C)**
<u>non-Anglicans</u>. <u>No error</u>
    (D)   **(E)**

59. <u>Finally</u>, the Whig party <u>comes</u> to power
    (A)   **(B)**
and, in 1832, passed the Reform Bill,

<u>extending the vote</u> and ending many
    (C)
<u>unfair</u> election practices. <u>No error</u>
    (D)   **(E)**

Name _____ Date _____

60. Charles Dickens's *Hard Times* and Charlotte Brontë's *Jane Eyre* are representative of the growing popularity of the novel **while in** the nineteenth century.

   (A) while in

   (B) before

   (C) during

   (D) at

   (E) around

61. A novel is a long work of fiction with a complicated **plot; many** major and minor characters, a significant theme, and various settings.

   (A) plot; many

   (B) plot—many

   (C) plot: many

   (D) plot, many

   (E) plot. Many

62. In the nineteenth century, the Realists made daily life a subject of literature and **explore** the scope of human experience in the novel.

   (A) explore

   (B) will explore

   (C) explored

   (D) have explored

   (E) explores

63. **There** approach and the growing literacy rate made novels appealing to a large group of people.

   (A) There

   (B) Their

   (C) We're

   (D) Its

   (E) There's

64. For the same reasons, the novel **was also popular** in France, the United States, and Russia.

   (A) was also popular

   (B) were also popular

   (C) also populated

   (D) also gained much popularity

   (E) had popularity

65. Russian novelist Leo Tolstoy was considered the greatest **between** the nineteenth-century Russian writers.

   (A) between

   (B) one of

   (C) in

   (D) of

   (E) to

66. In 1869, *War and Peace,* his masterful historical novel about Napoleon's invasion of Russia **on** 1812, was published.

   (A) on

   (B) on about

   (C) in

   (D) at

   (E) during

Directions: *Questions 67–72 are based on a passage that might be an early draft of a student's essay. Some sentences in this draft need to be revised or rewritten to make them both clear and correct. Read the passage carefully; then answer the questions that follow it. Some questions require decisions about diction, usage, tone, or sentence structure in particular sentences or parts of sentences. Other questions require decisions about organization, development, or appropriateness of language in the essay as a whole. For each question, choose the answer that makes the intended meaning clearer and more precise and that follows the conventions of standard written English.*

(1) The poetry of Samuel Taylor Coleridge stands at the place where real life slips <u>in to</u> dreams, where facts are reborn as fantasies. (2) More than any other Romantic poet, he dared to journey inward—into the world of the imagination. (3) However, in many ways, the imaginary life that fed his poetry was an escape from some very serious problems. (4) These problems included poor health and self-doubt.

(5) Coleridge was born in Ottery St. Mary on the Devon coast of England, the last of ten children, only four of whom survived. (6) When he was nine, his father died, and Coleridge was sent to school in London. (7) Later, Coleridge became a riveting public speaker, mesmerizing audiences with his originality and intelligence.

(8) At Cambridge University, Coleridge was hungry for new ideas, which led him into radical politics. (9) He becamed friends with an idealistic poet named Robert Southney. (10) Together they planned to form a settlement in Pennsylvania based on their utopian political ideas. (11) The plan <u>fell to pieces</u>, however, when Southney's aunt refused to fund their project.

67. Which of the following should be used in place of the underlined words in Sentence 1?

    (A) into

    (B) inside

    (C) onto

    (D) on to

    (E) between

68. Which is the *best* way to combine Sentences 3 and 4?

    (A) However, in many ways, the imaginary life that fed his poetry was an escape from some very serious problems; these problems included poor health and self-doubt.

    (B) However, in many ways, the imaginary life that fed his poetry was an escape from some very serious problems, for example, poor health and self-doubt.

    (C) However, in many ways, the imaginary life that fed his poetry was an escape from some very serious problems, problems such as poor health and self-doubt.

    (D) However, in many ways, the imaginary life that fed his poetry was an escape from some very serious problems, and these problems included poor health and self-doubt.

    (E) However, in many ways, the imaginary life that fed his poetry was an escape from some very serious problems, including poor health and self-doubt.

69. Which of the following, if added between Sentences 5 and 6, is *most* consistent with the writer's purpose and audience?

(A) Coleridge learned to read at a very young age.

(B) At an early age, he developed the habit of retreating into a world of books and fantasy.

(C) I am not surprised that Coleridge became famous—he was a spectacular child who loved reading and had a flair for creativity.

(D) Coleridge believed that literature is a magical blend of thought and emotion.

(E) In Coleridge's works, the unreal (but true) becomes compellingly real.

70. Which of the following uses a nonstandard verb form?

(A) Sentence 2

(B) Sentence 5

(C) Sentence 8

(D) Sentence 9

(E) Sentence 11

71. Which is the *best* revision of Sentence 8?

(A) At Cambridge University, Coleridge was hungry for new ideas and went into radical politics.

(B) At Cambridge University, Coleridge was hungry for new ideas; this led him to join radical politics.

(C) At Cambridge University, Coleridge's hunger for new ideas led him into radical politics.

(D) Coleridge's hunger for new ideas led him into radical politics at Cambridge University.

(E) At Cambridge University, Coleridge hungered for new ideas and this led him into radical politics.

72. Which is the *best* revision of the underlined part of Sentence 11?

(A) fell apart

(B) blew apart

(C) collapsed

(D) destructed

(E) disappeared

Prompt 1

Directions: *Think carefully about the issue presented in the following passage and the assignment below.*

Your school district is considering a proposal that would require each student to take a drug test several times throughout the school year. Tests would not be given without parental consent, and students testing positive would not be expelled; rather, their parents would be notified of the test results and would receive information about drug counseling and treatment centers.

Assignment: What is your position on this issue? Plan and write an essay in which you develop your point of view on this issue. Support your position with reasoning and examples taken from your reading, studies, experience, or observations.

Prompt 2

Directions: *Think carefully about the issue presented in the following passage and the assignment below.*

Because of increased crimes involving teens and traffic in your city, local city council members and many concerned citizens have recently proposed a "cruising law" in which cars driven by teens would be allowed to travel main streets only twice in one evening.

Assignment: Are you in favor of or against the proposed cruising law? Plan and write an essay in which you develop your point of view on this issue. Support your position with reasoning and examples taken from your reading, studies, experience, or observations.

Answer Sheet: Screening Test

1. Ⓐ Ⓑ Ⓒ Ⓓ	17. Ⓐ Ⓑ Ⓒ Ⓓ
2. Ⓕ Ⓖ Ⓗ Ⓙ	18. Ⓕ Ⓖ Ⓗ Ⓙ
3. Ⓐ Ⓑ Ⓒ Ⓓ	19. Ⓐ Ⓑ Ⓒ Ⓓ
4. Ⓕ Ⓖ Ⓗ Ⓙ	20. Ⓕ Ⓖ Ⓗ Ⓙ
5. Ⓐ Ⓑ Ⓒ Ⓓ	21. Ⓐ Ⓑ Ⓒ Ⓓ
6. Ⓕ Ⓖ Ⓗ Ⓙ	22. Ⓕ Ⓖ Ⓗ Ⓙ
7. Ⓐ Ⓑ Ⓒ Ⓓ	23. Ⓐ Ⓑ Ⓒ Ⓓ
8. Ⓕ Ⓖ Ⓗ Ⓙ	24. Ⓕ Ⓖ Ⓗ Ⓙ
9. Ⓐ Ⓑ Ⓒ Ⓓ	25. Ⓐ Ⓑ Ⓒ Ⓓ
10. Ⓕ Ⓖ Ⓗ Ⓙ	26. Ⓕ Ⓖ Ⓗ Ⓙ
11. Ⓐ Ⓑ Ⓒ Ⓓ	27. Ⓐ Ⓑ Ⓒ Ⓓ
12. Ⓕ Ⓖ Ⓗ Ⓙ	28. Ⓕ Ⓖ Ⓗ Ⓙ
13. Ⓐ Ⓑ Ⓒ Ⓓ	29. Ⓐ Ⓑ Ⓒ Ⓓ
14. Ⓕ Ⓖ Ⓗ Ⓙ	30. Ⓕ Ⓖ Ⓗ Ⓙ
15. Ⓐ Ⓑ Ⓒ Ⓓ	31. Ⓐ Ⓑ Ⓒ Ⓓ
16. Ⓕ Ⓖ Ⓗ Ⓙ	

Answer Sheet

Practice Test 1

1. Ⓐ Ⓑ Ⓒ Ⓓ
2. Ⓐ Ⓑ Ⓒ Ⓓ
3. Ⓐ Ⓑ Ⓒ Ⓓ
4. Ⓐ Ⓑ Ⓒ Ⓓ
5. Ⓐ Ⓑ Ⓒ Ⓓ
6. Ⓐ Ⓑ Ⓒ Ⓓ
7. Ⓐ Ⓑ Ⓒ Ⓓ
8. Ⓐ Ⓑ Ⓒ Ⓓ
9. Ⓐ Ⓑ Ⓒ Ⓓ
10. Ⓐ Ⓑ Ⓒ Ⓓ
11. Ⓐ Ⓑ Ⓒ Ⓓ
12. Ⓐ Ⓑ Ⓒ Ⓓ
13. Ⓐ Ⓑ Ⓒ Ⓓ
14. Ⓐ Ⓑ Ⓒ Ⓓ
15. Ⓐ Ⓑ Ⓒ Ⓓ
16. Ⓐ Ⓑ Ⓒ Ⓓ
17. Ⓐ Ⓑ Ⓒ Ⓓ
18. Ⓐ Ⓑ Ⓒ Ⓓ
19. Ⓐ Ⓑ Ⓒ Ⓓ
20. Ⓐ Ⓑ Ⓒ Ⓓ
21. Ⓐ Ⓑ Ⓒ Ⓓ
22. Ⓐ Ⓑ Ⓒ Ⓓ
23. Ⓐ Ⓑ Ⓒ Ⓓ
24. Ⓐ Ⓑ Ⓒ Ⓓ
25. Ⓐ Ⓑ Ⓒ Ⓓ

Practice Test 2

1. Ⓐ Ⓑ Ⓒ Ⓓ
2. Ⓐ Ⓑ Ⓒ Ⓓ
3. Ⓐ Ⓑ Ⓒ Ⓓ
4. Ⓐ Ⓑ Ⓒ Ⓓ
5. Ⓐ Ⓑ Ⓒ Ⓓ
6. Ⓐ Ⓑ Ⓒ Ⓓ
7. Ⓐ Ⓑ Ⓒ Ⓓ
8. Ⓐ Ⓑ Ⓒ Ⓓ
9. Ⓐ Ⓑ Ⓒ Ⓓ
10. Ⓐ Ⓑ Ⓒ Ⓓ
11. Ⓐ Ⓑ Ⓒ Ⓓ
12. Ⓐ Ⓑ Ⓒ Ⓓ
13. Ⓐ Ⓑ Ⓒ Ⓓ
14. Ⓐ Ⓑ Ⓒ Ⓓ
15. Ⓐ Ⓑ Ⓒ Ⓓ
16. Ⓐ Ⓑ Ⓒ Ⓓ
17. Ⓐ Ⓑ Ⓒ Ⓓ
18. Ⓐ Ⓑ Ⓒ Ⓓ
19. Ⓐ Ⓑ Ⓒ Ⓓ
20. Ⓐ Ⓑ Ⓒ Ⓓ
21. Ⓐ Ⓑ Ⓒ Ⓓ
22. Ⓐ Ⓑ Ⓒ Ⓓ
23. Ⓐ Ⓑ Ⓒ Ⓓ
24. Ⓐ Ⓑ Ⓒ Ⓓ
25. Ⓐ Ⓑ Ⓒ Ⓓ
26. Ⓐ Ⓑ Ⓒ Ⓓ

Name _____ Date _____

Answer Sheet for SAT/ACT

1. Ⓐ Ⓑ Ⓒ Ⓓ Ⓔ	16. Ⓐ Ⓑ Ⓒ Ⓓ Ⓔ	31. Ⓐ Ⓑ Ⓒ Ⓓ Ⓔ	46. Ⓐ Ⓑ Ⓒ Ⓓ Ⓔ	61. Ⓐ Ⓑ Ⓒ Ⓓ Ⓔ
2. Ⓐ Ⓑ Ⓒ Ⓓ Ⓔ	17. Ⓐ Ⓑ Ⓒ Ⓓ Ⓔ	32. Ⓐ Ⓑ Ⓒ Ⓓ Ⓔ	47. Ⓐ Ⓑ Ⓒ Ⓓ Ⓔ	62. Ⓐ Ⓑ Ⓒ Ⓓ Ⓔ
3. Ⓐ Ⓑ Ⓒ Ⓓ Ⓔ	18. Ⓐ Ⓑ Ⓒ Ⓓ Ⓔ	33. Ⓐ Ⓑ Ⓒ Ⓓ Ⓔ	48. Ⓐ Ⓑ Ⓒ Ⓓ Ⓔ	63. Ⓐ Ⓑ Ⓒ Ⓓ Ⓔ
4. Ⓐ Ⓑ Ⓒ Ⓓ Ⓔ	19. Ⓐ Ⓑ Ⓒ Ⓓ Ⓔ	34. Ⓐ Ⓑ Ⓒ Ⓓ Ⓔ	49. Ⓐ Ⓑ Ⓒ Ⓓ Ⓔ	64. Ⓐ Ⓑ Ⓒ Ⓓ Ⓔ
5. Ⓐ Ⓑ Ⓒ Ⓓ Ⓔ	20. Ⓐ Ⓑ Ⓒ Ⓓ Ⓔ	35. Ⓐ Ⓑ Ⓒ Ⓓ Ⓔ	50. Ⓐ Ⓑ Ⓒ Ⓓ Ⓔ	65. Ⓐ Ⓑ Ⓒ Ⓓ Ⓔ
6. Ⓐ Ⓑ Ⓒ Ⓓ Ⓔ	21. Ⓐ Ⓑ Ⓒ Ⓓ Ⓔ	36. Ⓐ Ⓑ Ⓒ Ⓓ Ⓔ	51. Ⓐ Ⓑ Ⓒ Ⓓ Ⓔ	66. Ⓐ Ⓑ Ⓒ Ⓓ Ⓔ
7. Ⓐ Ⓑ Ⓒ Ⓓ Ⓔ	22. Ⓐ Ⓑ Ⓒ Ⓓ Ⓔ	37. Ⓐ Ⓑ Ⓒ Ⓓ Ⓔ	52. Ⓐ Ⓑ Ⓒ Ⓓ Ⓔ	67. Ⓐ Ⓑ Ⓒ Ⓓ Ⓔ
8. Ⓐ Ⓑ Ⓒ Ⓓ Ⓔ	23. Ⓐ Ⓑ Ⓒ Ⓓ Ⓔ	38. Ⓐ Ⓑ Ⓒ Ⓓ Ⓔ	53. Ⓐ Ⓑ Ⓒ Ⓓ Ⓔ	68. Ⓐ Ⓑ Ⓒ Ⓓ Ⓔ
9. Ⓐ Ⓑ Ⓒ Ⓓ Ⓔ	24. Ⓐ Ⓑ Ⓒ Ⓓ Ⓔ	39. Ⓐ Ⓑ Ⓒ Ⓓ Ⓔ	54. Ⓐ Ⓑ Ⓒ Ⓓ Ⓔ	69. Ⓐ Ⓑ Ⓒ Ⓓ Ⓔ
10. Ⓐ Ⓑ Ⓒ Ⓓ Ⓔ	25. Ⓐ Ⓑ Ⓒ Ⓓ Ⓔ	40. Ⓐ Ⓑ Ⓒ Ⓓ Ⓔ	55. Ⓐ Ⓑ Ⓒ Ⓓ Ⓔ	70. Ⓐ Ⓑ Ⓒ Ⓓ Ⓔ
11. Ⓐ Ⓑ Ⓒ Ⓓ Ⓔ	26. Ⓐ Ⓑ Ⓒ Ⓓ Ⓔ	41. Ⓐ Ⓑ Ⓒ Ⓓ Ⓔ	56. Ⓐ Ⓑ Ⓒ Ⓓ Ⓔ	71. Ⓐ Ⓑ Ⓒ Ⓓ Ⓔ
12. Ⓐ Ⓑ Ⓒ Ⓓ Ⓔ	27. Ⓐ Ⓑ Ⓒ Ⓓ Ⓔ	42. Ⓐ Ⓑ Ⓒ Ⓓ Ⓔ	57. Ⓐ Ⓑ Ⓒ Ⓓ Ⓔ	72. Ⓐ Ⓑ Ⓒ Ⓓ Ⓔ
13. Ⓐ Ⓑ Ⓒ Ⓓ Ⓔ	28. Ⓐ Ⓑ Ⓒ Ⓓ Ⓔ	43. Ⓐ Ⓑ Ⓒ Ⓓ Ⓔ	58. Ⓐ Ⓑ Ⓒ Ⓓ Ⓔ	
14. Ⓐ Ⓑ Ⓒ Ⓓ Ⓔ	29. Ⓐ Ⓑ Ⓒ Ⓓ Ⓔ	44. Ⓐ Ⓑ Ⓒ Ⓓ Ⓔ	59. Ⓐ Ⓑ Ⓒ Ⓓ Ⓔ	
15. Ⓐ Ⓑ Ⓒ Ⓓ Ⓔ	30. Ⓐ Ⓑ Ⓒ Ⓓ Ⓔ	45. Ⓐ Ⓑ Ⓒ Ⓓ Ⓔ	60. Ⓐ Ⓑ Ⓒ Ⓓ Ⓔ	

Answer Sheet

Short Answer/Essay

_____

_____

_____

_____

_____

_____

_____

_____

_____

_____

_____

_____

_____

_____

_____

_____

_____

_____

_____

_____

_____

_____

_____

_____

_____

_____

_____

_____

Answer Sheet

Short Answer/Essay

_____

_____

_____

_____

_____

_____

_____

_____

_____

_____

_____

_____

_____

_____

_____

_____

_____

_____

_____

_____

_____

_____

_____

_____

All-in-One Workbook: Standardized Test Practice
409